A Normative Theory of
the Information Society

T0386575

Routledge Research in Information Technology and Society

A Normative Theory of the Information Society

Alistair S. Duff

Routledge
Taylor & Francis Group

NEW YORK   LONDON

First published 2012
by Routledge
711 Third Avenue, New York, NY 10017

Simultaneously published in the UK
by Routledge
2 Park Square, Milton Park, Abingdon, Oxon OX14 4RN

*Routledge is an imprint of the Taylor & Francis Group,
an informa business*

© 2012 Taylor & Francis

First issued in paperback 2013

Typeset in Sabon by IBT Global.

Library of Congress Cataloging-in-Publication Data
Duff, Alistair S., 1961-
    A normative theory of the information society / Alistair S. Duff.
        p. cm. — (Routledge research in information technology and society;
13)
    Includes bibliographical references and index.
    1.   Information society. I. Title.
    HM851.D843 2011
    303.48'3301—dc23
    2011029054

ISBN: 978-0-415-95571-3 (hbk)
ISBN: 978-0-415-71963-6 (pbk)

Contents

Acknowledgments

A sequel and companion volume, although freestanding, to my *Information Society Studies* (Routledge 2000), this book was initially drafted during a sabbatical partly spent at the University of Oxford, with generous funding from the Arts and Humanities Research Council. I am grateful to William H. Dutton and company at the Oxford Internet Institute, and to Hazel Hall, Robert Beveridge and other colleagues at Edinburgh Napier University who helped me bear the cross of interdisciplinary work. Going further back, my education benefited from the input of eminent political philosophers such as Peter Winch, G. A. Cohen and Michael Lessnoff and information scientists such as Blaise Cronin and A. J. Meadows. The bibliography registers numerous (some might say, too many) additional influences, not least that of Daniel Bell, whose writings first inspired my interest in the information society thesis. I am thankful to Max Novick, Terry Clague and others at Routledge for having confidence in this project, recklessly ambitious (I can now see) though it was. I wish also here to remember my father, Robert S. Duff (1920–1989), who alongside his achievements as a cardiologist, founded in the late-1970s a small company called The Information Corporation; perhaps he had heard the faint heartbeats of an embryonic society. My main debt, however, must be to Elizabeth, for her indefatigable support of myself and our children, Alexander, Ruaridh and Laura.

Although this monograph comprises original work throughout, early versions of some ideas were published as follows (in chronological order):

Social democracy and information media policy, in B. Rockenbach and T. Mendina (eds) *Ethics and Electronic Information: a Festschrift for Stephen Almagno* (Jefferson, NC: McFarland & Co., 2003), pp. 154-65

Social welfare aspects of information with special reference to news, in *Proceedings of the IADIS (International Association for Development of the Information Society) International Conference on e-Society, vol. 2, Lisbon, Portugal, June 3-6 2003*, pp. 773-6

Ethical messages: R. H. Tawney confronts the information age, *Ethical Space* 1(3) 2004, pp. 17-20 (with R. Melville)

For a new nanny state: the role of national information services in post-industrial societies, in T. Mendina and J. J. Britz (eds) *Information Ethics in the Electronic Age: Current Issues in Africa and the World* (Jefferson, NC: McFarland & Co, 2004), pp. 155-62

The past, present, and future of information policy: towards a normative theory of the information society, *Information, Communication & Society* 7(1) 2004, pp. 69-87

The sickness of an information society: R. H. Tawney and the post-industrial condition, *Information, Communication & Society* 7(3) 2004, pp. 403-22

Social engineering in the information age, *The Information Society* 21(1) 2005, pp. 67-71

'Laying a foundation of fact': Fabianism and the information society thesis, *Information, Communication & Society* 9(4) 2006, pp. 541-62

Neo-Rawlsian co-ordinates: notes on a theory of justice for the information age, *International Review of Information Ethics* 6(12/2006), pp. 17-22 (online)

Documentation and utopia: Fabian anticipations of the information society, in B. Rayward (ed.) *European Modernism and the Information Society* (Ashgate, 2008), pp. 185-99

Information liberation? The relations of freedom and knowledge in social-democratic thought, in N. Stehr (ed.) *Knowledge and Democracy: a 21st Century Perspective* (Transaction Publishers, 2008), pp. 199-215

R. H. Tawney, in W. A. Darity (ed.) *International Encyclopedia of the Social Sciences,* 2nd ed., vol. 8 (Detroit: Macmillan Reference USA, 2008), pp. 271-2

The European information society: scholarly and official perspectives, *Journal of the Japan Society of Information and Communication Research* 26(3) 2008, pp. 29-31

The normative crisis of the information society, *Cyberpsychology: Journal of Psychosocial Research on Cyberspace* 2(1) 2008, article 3 (online)

Rethinking the digital divide: from philanthropy to isonomia, in *Proceedings of the International Conference on New Media and Information: Convergences and Divergences, Panteion University, Athens, 6-9 May 2009* (CD Rom, ISBN 978-960-6746-05-5)

The age of access? Information policy and social progress, in S. Papatha-nassopoulos and R. Negrine (eds) *Communications Policy: Theories and Issues* (Palgrave Macmillan, 2010), pp. 49-64

The information society, in S. Hornig Priest (ed.) *Encyclopedia of Science and Technology Communication* (Sage, 2010), pp. 397-400

The Rawls-Tawney theorem and the digital divide in post-industrial society, *Journal of the American Society for Information Science and Technology* 62(3) 2011, pp. 604-12

1 The Need for a Normative Theory of the Information Society

THE MATRIX OF INFORMATION SOCIETY STUDIES

The existential crisis of the information society is over. The information age is here; or, at the very least, there has been an informatisation of society, what the Japanese, masters at the game (Ito 1981), call *johoka* (pronounced *jouhouka*). There is widespread awareness, not just academically but also at the level of untutored experience, that in profound and complex ways information is implicated in a transformation of the contemporary scene. One of the main premises of this book will be that information and information technology (IT) are not, contrary to popular and official oversimplifications, coterminous. Nevertheless, they overlap sufficiently for a focus on information technology to yield an authentic sense of the social metamorphoses that are underway. IT pervades homes, markets, the mass media and many other matrices of modern being. Pushbutton publishing has been normalised; electronic voting is pressing for acceptance. The virtual *x*—classroom, library, newsroom, imam, whatever—replaces traditional forms of life; *e* is the new language game, with Olympian ambitions. Communication flows proliferate. The quantity of data and entertainment continues to explode; hard information—which I will sharply distinguish from lesser modes—also expands, albeit at a markedly less frenzied rate. Scientific knowledge, which some rank as the only real information in the world, piles up relentlessly. Surveillance fares well too, not least in England (as distinct from Scotland, noticeably less authoritarian since devolution), in some ways, particularly the preponderance of spy cameras, the most 'Orwellian' country in the western world (Royal Academy of Engineering 2007). And Instapundit, Twitter, Wikileaks and innumerable other web actors are surely redefining some of the rules of politics and social accountability. This is just a sample, a snapshot, of the effects of an ongoing multifaceted process that is often called 'information revolution'.

Sociologically, therefore, it might be affirmed with some confidence that the daily grind for many is increasingly, as the world's most erudite futurist foresaw, a game not against nature, nor against fabricated nature, but against, or hopefully with, other persons (Bell 1999: 30; cf. Kim and Nolan 2006; Pruulmann-Vengerfeldt 2006). And not just persons, since cyborgs and other ethically-puzzling entities are clambering onto the horizon. In short, all three realms of society—polity, economy and culture—in this conceptual framework, as in much else below, I follow the late Daniel Bell (1919–2011)—are, if not revolutionised, then at least exposed to major principles of innovation (Bell 1996c; cf. Waters 1996: 27–49). Thus the proposition 'The "information society" is a concept with no objective co-relative in the real world' (Garnham 2000a: 151) is false, at least now in the second decade of the new millennium. Moreover, there is today also genuine purchase on the higher order category 'global information society'. This does not mean that every nation enjoys a similar level of johoka. Absolutely not: but it does imply that the information infrastructure encompasses a ubiquitous circuit of networked systems accompanied by sporadically evolving regional and international institutions (cf. Braman 2004). The information society, as a global socio-technical formation with radically uneven resource-distribution, has arrived. There has been a switch-over to a 'mode of information' (Poster 1990), an 'informatization of the worldview' (De Mul 1999). Post-industrial citizens are even privy to a new social *essentialism*, an insight into the informational ingredients that combust at the epicentre of late-modern societies. It is becoming absurd to suggest otherwise.

Perhaps all of this sounds too assured. The information society concept has admittedly been the victim of more than its fair share of technologically-deterministic and commercial hyperbole, not to mention those vulgar forms of futurology Bell (1995b: 7) lampooned as 'star-trek sociology'. Nevertheless, the case for the information society, what became known as the information society thesis (Lyon 1988; Dearnley and Feather 2001; Mackay *et al.* 2001), is now fairly robust by average social-scientific standards, so long as the thesis is interpreted correctly, that is, abstaining from the grandiose pretensions which poorly-equipped fellow travellers have naively added to its propositional core. Anyway, that core must be assumed here. Those who remain sceptical will just have to be referred back to the major authors. In 1962, the distinguished American economist Fritz Machlup, in his *Production and Distribution of Knowledge in the United States*, initially highlighted the large and increasing role of the 'knowledge industries' in an advanced economy. Subsequently, Marc Porat (1977) took forward the concept of the information economy in the first research monograph of that title, demonstrating, albeit in a work that librarians would grade as 'grey literature', that its activities should by 1980 account for half of the US gross national product. Then in *The Coming of Post-Industrial Society* (1999) and seminal essays such as 'The Social Framework of the Information Society' (1980b; cf. Esping-Andersen 1999; Smart 2010), Bell wove these data into a convincing sociological story, featuring the mutation of industrial societies into post-industrial ones driven not by the manufacture of goods, but by services, technology and information. 'The intellectual task', he explained, 'is how to "order" these changes in comprehensible ways, rather than just describing the multitude of changes, and thus to provide some basis of analysis rooted in sociological theory'—a task Bell himself performed consummately (1989: 167; cf. Duff 1998).

These were the principal writers in the English language, although there were contemporaneous movements elsewhere, notably Japan. In *Information Society Studies* (2000), I brought together the various schools of thought, the *versions* of the information society thesis, and attempted to assess them, both individually and in a synthetic form. That volume concluded that the thesis was now proven, although solely in its more modest, 'evolutionary' form. The present book, therefore, will not revisit the methodological and existential debates. It assumes not a total Kuhnian 'paradigm shift', but the validity of formulae about the partial informatisation of the three realms of advanced societies, and the knock-on effects on developing countries. While we need to accept that continuities with the past are as visible as discontinuities, I think that it is still logically open to us to assert, *pace* Peter Golding (2000: 166), that we are 'on the cusp of a new sociality'. Building upon such foundations, the book intends to address some of the big questions regarding the social-ethical and policy implications of informatisation.

There is undoubtedly a need for such treatments. Neo-Luddites excepted, most people seem to see informatisation as just a fact of life, merely part of the march of progress, and no great cause for alarm. If anything, folk say, it is to be welcomed, insofar as one might want to make a value judgement at all. Many commentators imply that to be against whatever informatisation brings is to be against technology, against historical logic, against the development of one's nation and against any gravitation towards that venerable Enlightenment ideal, a world community enjoying perpetual peace. The basis, or part of the basis, of this attitude is the perception that the information society is essentially a technical concept, hence that the information society thesis is as value-free as any sociological thesis can be. I think, however, that such complacency is badly mistaken. The contention here, on the contrary, is that underneath all the technological advances there is serious confusion about the social norms shaping the new political form, misunderstandings that could have baleful implications for the quality of human experience in the first half of this century and beyond. I begin, therefore, where *Democracy's Discontent* (Sandel 1996: 340) ends, with the conviction that 'converting networks of communication and interdependence into a public life worth affirming is a moral and political matter, not a technological one'.

If one probes even a little, it quickly becomes clear that notwithstanding the bloodless, bureaucratic stereotype, the information society has always been a heavily moralised and politicised concept, one that in all sorts of ways impinges on the main ideological controversies between left and right, between collectivism and individualism, between society and citizen. Richard Barbrook (2007) has even suggested interestingly that competing images of the information society, namely the cybernetic communism of

Russia and the post-industrial welfare state of America, were at the heart of the politics of the cold war. They were actually, he proposes, rival utopias, nothing less. Perhaps these utopias had much more in common than 'cold warriors' on either side would have cared to admit, but in any case it has long since become obvious that advanced nations have stumbled into a veritable moral labyrinth, and that guidance is required to help policymakers find their way through to a desirable destination. For the current situation, as has been shrewdly observed, is one where 'information-society related policies tend to be mushy products of an odd mix of futurology, social forces, aspirations, ideology, and interest-group politics, among other things' (Menou and Taylor 2006: 261). And that is clearly unsatisfactory.

Policy inquiries have always accompanied large-scale ventures in social analysis or forecasting. Near the beginning of the last century, Arthur J. Penty (1917: 14), unsung inventor of the post-industrial brand, pleaded for 'recognition of the ugly fact that the industrial system has reached its limit of expansion'. In tomes such as *Old Worlds for New: A Study of the Post-Industrial State* (1917) and *Post-Industrialism* (1922), he advocated a cooperative handicraft economy rather than the competitive high technology scenarios championed by H. G. Wells and other visionaries, and of course his quaint nostrum was in practical terms a non-starter. However, at least Penty demonstrated that, even in the heyday of industrialism, the nature of post-industrial society, for a few thoughtful individuals, could already be a matter of earnest speculation (cf. Lyon 1983).

The early information society theorists proper, such as the thinkers already mentioned, had primarily an explanatory, empirical mission, yet they too recognised that the problematic would shortly be political. The 'coming' of post-industrial society, Bell noted (1999: 487), 'poses new problems of social management', novel questions for the polity. Bell even outlined a rudimentary theory of justice for post-industrial societies, what he called the 'just meritocracy' (1999: 451–55), a not implausible formula that will be evaluated below. And one of Porat's most important contributions to information society studies was the foundation he laid for an understanding of information policy. His final chapter, entitled, perhaps with a faint echo of Hobhouse (1922), 'The Elements of Information Policy' (Porat 1977: 204–49), was the first dedicated discourse on its subject. Some of Porat's specific recommendations for dealing with the challenges caused by the convergence of IT and telecommunications will also be worth picking up later. Yet Porat himself was satisfied that his main role was that of econometrician, not social philosopher. 'Interpreting the implications of an information economy', he mused (Porat 1977: 12), 'is a riddle with many solutions. Our purpose is served if the basic statistical foundation for the idea is sound. Once the "soapbox" is built and can support the weight, we gladly invite others to Hyde Park for the inevitable debates'.

To engage at all with the social problems of informatisation, it will indeed be necessary to re-enter long-standing debates, to participate at

Speakers' Corner, the Oxford Union, or any other venue where people are still actually listening. And if the original texts of the information society thesis grasped the importance of public policy, how much more pressing must the rising slope of informatisation have made such issues today. While some might question 'the elevation of "Information Society policy" to the status of planetary priority for both developing and developed countries' (Ricci 2003: 178), no one can deny the topicality of the themes. In Bell's eve-of-millennium postscript to *Coming of Post-Industrial Society* (1999: ix–x; cf. Tsay 1995), the founder himself went through a list of citations of his post-industrial concept by politicians and other eminent personages. Margaret Thatcher, Bill Clinton, Leon Brittan (a European Commissioner) and even that satanic priest of neo-Luddism, the Unabomber, were on the roster. Of course, the term was often dished thoughtlessly around like a slogan, but behind it and its synonyms lay concrete agendas. For Mrs Thatcher, it was the enhancement of corporate profitability though the reduction of trade union power, a goal which required the dismantling of those primary-sector and secondary-sector industries in which unions enjoyed their main support. For neo-conservatives in her formidable mould on both sides of the Atlantic, post-industrialism was a rhetorical device that proved helpful in the communication strategies accompanying the pursuit of these controversial political ends. For the Unabomber, at the other extreme, post-industrial society simply represented a cultural enemy to be ruthlessly eliminated, a target that he could blame for his own inadequacy and malevolence.

All the recent evidence confirms that, broadly understood, information is now one of the liveliest policy preoccupations. For example, Mueller *et al.* (2004) have shown that communication and information issues take up more Congressional time in the United States than any other comparable category. And all European nations, both old and new, red and blue, have enthusiastically formulated policy agendas under an information society flag. The European Commission itself has been systematically milking the information society concept in its funding dispositions and federalist pursuits. Parallel efforts can be seen in other regions. Most strikingly, though, we have had the World Summit on the Information Society (WSIS), an unprecedented experiment in world discussion and unassailable proof that information policy is no longer the preserve of think tanks and the academy. Thus the nature of what metaphysician Luciano Floridi (2007: 59) calls the 'info sphere', of the whole information environment, is now high politics, both inside nations and from a cosmopolitan perspective. In short, a new field of politics has emerged, namely 'information politics' (Dutton 1999)—or even more succinctly, *infopolitics*.

Yet the Summit is also a revealing vantage-point from which to begin to register just how contentious information policy has become. While it must be regarded as a laudable achievement and a vital statement of the centrality of information in the world today, in terms of tangible policy outcomes the WSIS, like much else that happens at the United Nations, was disappointing. Many feel that it accomplished little for the developing world, that its attempt to inject social morality into the international information order has failed almost as woefully as the New World Information and Communication Order (NWICO) debacle of thirty years ago, despite its lower expectations and its studious avoidance of left-wing rhetoric. As one scholarly participant related, 'an emphasis on the politics of the ICT [information and communication technology] agenda and the need for a critical assessment of priorities was largely absent in the mainstream debates during the WSIS' (Mansell 2006: 902). The inclusion of civil society representatives at the conference, rather than just politicians and business interests, while cheering, ensured that fundamental value differences would prevent consensus about both the diagnosis of the sickness of the information society in its current condition and the policy cures. These cracks did not suddenly appear in Geneva or Tunis, as shallow news reports of the meetings suggested. In numerous quarters of cyberspace, and at many levels of society, there has been, at least since Bell and the Japanese started drafting their ideas in the mid-1960s, a huge and complex argument about the direction in which society should travel with respect to informatisation.

The arguments in this book, to that end, subsist within the scholarly matrix of information society studies. This interdisciplinary specialism, devoted to all angles of the study of the behaviour of information and its technologies in society, is admittedly not yet established in the academy. It is just one hopeful candidate among many for the job of organising the vast, multifarious scholarly terrain that addresses an ever-expanding family of increasingly salient issues (Duff 2000a, 2001; cf. Saulauskas 2005). As such, it overlaps considerably with several other specialisms, such as social informatics (Kling 2001), technopolitics (Armitage 1999), sociology of information (Lyon 2005), and internet studies (Livingstone 2005), not to mention socioeconomics (Hollingsworth *et al.* 2002) and the even more exotic 'info-socionomics', the last invented by someone occasionally described as Japan's Daniel Bell (Kumon 2006). Information society studies is perforce irreducibly interdisciplinary, because, after all, 'social problems respect no discipline' (Kubin 1996: 202). However, the key point in the current context is that information society studies covers normative and moral, as well as empirical and positive, approaches to the social impact of information. The present volume is thus an attempt to explore the ethics of information, not in the sense of dilemmas facing the individual (Smith 2001), but rather as social ethics, as conceptions of social morality with regard to information. And the main focus is not social morality in the abstract, but social morality insofar as it can be translated into feasible imperatives of political and legal action, into institution-reforming and institution-building.

In conclusion, the general theme of this book is *ethical information policy*, not in its usual single-issue sense—What should be done about broadband access? How should we protect privacy? etc—but as an holistic theory that endeavours to weld together the whole range of information issues peculiar to post-industrial societies. I will make bold to recommend major public decisions about the whole *information infrastructure*, that matrix of institutions, networks and systems which facilitate the production of information, which mediate the societal flow of information, and which determine the level and quality of access to information. The arguments should therefore be judged as a thesis in information policy research *qua* the study of 'social, political, legal, economic and technological decisions about the role of information in society' (Maxwell 2003: 2; cf. Hernon and Relyea 1991; Rowlands 1996). Understood in this full-orbed manner, information policy becomes more or less synonymous with the normative theory of the information society (Duff 2004a; cf. Ducatel *et al.* 2000).

THE NORMATIVE CRISIS OF THE INFORMATION SOCIETY

The ending of the existential crisis of the information society is a seminal event and one which, insofar as the concept of crisis has negative connotations, can only be welcomed. Now, unfortunately, it needs to be declared that we are in the midst of a new and even more fateful challenge, namely a multidimensional, three realms-affecting, *normative* crisis of the information society. This normative crisis both succeeds the existential crisis and throws into sharp relief the policy problematics that have been anticipated since the beginnings of the post-industrial age. The partial failure of the WSIS, on this premise, is merely a symptom of that crisis, one manifestation of an underlying malaise. Some straightforward phenomenological reporting in favour of the proposition will shortly be offered, but first there is a need for clarification about how normativity, a notoriously ambiguous term, is going to be understood here. Given that one could argue, without much exaggeration, that entire academic fields occupy themselves with the task of explaining what norms either are or ought to be, this might be thought to be a foolish endeavour. For example, norms were at the heart of the major works of pioneering sociologists such as Emile Durkheim and Talcott Parsons, as Niklas Luhmann (1995: 325)—himself observing 'skeptical abstinence vis-à-vis norm-centered theory'—correctly noted. Thankfully, however, the remit of a normative theory of the information society, while adventurous, does not carry an obligation to revisit the elements of generic social theory. A plausible working definition of norms, rather than a full exposition of the meaning of normativity, is all that can reasonably be required of applied research in the present rendition. And, as becomes normative information society studies, this can be worked up synthetically from a plurality of disciplinary sources.

Following communication theorists Maria Lapinksi and Rajiv Rimal (2005: 129), therefore, I will be referring to norms at the collective, societal level, as those 'prevailing codes of conduct that either prescribe or proscribe behaviors that members of a group can enact'. Such codes 'operate at the level of the social system, which could be a social network or the entire society. They represent a collective social entity's code of conduct' (Lapinski and Rimal 2005: 129). Norms in this classic sense embody at least three ideas: a collective understanding of what ought to be done; a collective expectation of what behaviour will actually be; and the use of sanctions where norms are infringed. Thus by 'norms' I will always be meaning social norms. Now, as the venerable metaphysical axiom has it, everything is what it is and not another thing. Thus, norms are not identical to laws. They can be partially crystallized in law, but in other cases they operate entirely outside of law's empire. They are internalised, shared rules of action which can be sanctioned in non-legal ways, especially by social approval or disapproval. As philosopher Richard Arneson (2007: 145) points out, 'freestanding social norms could, in principle, regulate matters that are unsuited to legal regulation'. The most that one can safely say of norms in terms of legality is that they are constituent elements of 'regimes', the loosely-defined and fuzzily-bounded constellations of practices that determine conduct in a particular geographic or topical area (cf. Braman 2004). Nevertheless, norms frequently become intertwined with laws and they possess the law-like feature of being constraints on the actions of individuals.

Neither, however, are norms co-extensive with values. Sociologists Steven Hitlin and Jane Piliavin explain (2004: 361) that 'norms are situation based; values are trans-situational. Values, like norms, are a group-level phenomenon requiring shared agreement. However, values typically are measured as an individual-level construct. Norms capture an "ought" sense; values capture a personal or cultural ideal. People acting in accordance with values do not feel pushed as they do when acting under normative pressure'. This seems to be the view of information society theorist Scott Lash too. In *Critique of Information* (2002: 41), he argues that 'norms are procedural', in contrast to 'values'; they are 'rules', organisational, institutional and sometimes constitutional, but not 'substantive', nor close to 'virtues'. And norms, Lash claims (2002: 210), precisely because they are not values, but rules to be followed, typically have a much shorter duration than values. However, such may be going a little too far. While norms are not on the same level as values, they should not necessarily be relegated to the procedural level nor cast as just a function of majority opinion. I prefer to interpret norms as being somehow anchored in the cultural realm of morality, religion and ultimate ends—in the communicative rationality of the lifeworld, to use Habermasian terminology. At their best, norms both represent cherished values and, by cross-over into the public sphere, give the polity a viable social morality. In this way, to switch to the argot of educational theory, norms can be criterion-referenced: they can express unchanging values. It is in this substantive sense that we can and do speak of religious toleration and opposition to abuse of prisoners as norms of all civilised nations, indeed as constitutive of civilisation itself.

Thus while norms belong to the right, they originate in the good. This moralistic interpretation pulls away from some other normative approaches to the information society. Claims that post-industrial society should be distinguished by creativity and imaginativeness, or that it should be infused, as in the Mertonian view of science, by universalism, may be correct, but they are outside the parameters of the present discussion. My burden is rather to develop Arnoldian 'moral thoughtfulness' (Stanley 1844: 261; cf. Copley 2002) about the information society, and the construal of norms will therefore be confined to norms only insofar as they advance or impede social morality. To thus demarcate them is no doubt to invite numerous objections, but it at least introduces a working position whose ultimate defence can perhaps be left for others to execute. Although perhaps not: Derek Parfit (2006: 331; cf. Parfit 2011), whom some regard as the cleverest person in Oxford, judges that 'we cannot explain what normativity is, or what normative concepts mean'.

By way of further characterisation, however, it can be said that the normative crisis of the information society is somewhat analogous to the concept of normative crisis in developmental psychology. According to Erik Erikson (1959), adolescents sooner or later undergo an 'identity crisis'—Erikson of course coined that household term—involving, centrally, a 'normative crisis', where some fundamental assumptions of existence and upbringing are called into question. Perhaps rejecting their parents' values, or half-rejecting them, but at any rate reviewing at various levels the moral-metaphysical meaning of their existence, young people strive to find their own identity. The issue for Erikson was psychosocial, occurring at the communal as well as individual level. He even spoke occasionally in political terms, of 'the identity confusion of an industrial democracy' (Erikson 1968: 195). So the postulate in the present argument is that post-industrial democracy is facing its own identity crisis, more particularly a normative crisis. And we should not be surprised that the coming of post-industrial society is attended by such. Like adolescents, the information society, no longer an infant, but not yet mature, is struggling at profound levels of experience—its existence no longer at issue—to achieve an authentic, cohesive and viable identity.

The challenge for today is that while, under industrialism, compelling normative traditions were quickly forged, notably liberalism and socialism in a spectrum of forms—radically individualistic at one end, wholly collectivistic at the other—it is not at all clear that any impressive normative tradition is close to fruition for the information age. The norms of the industrial era are being contested by a precocious information society, as it were, and in many cases they have already been spurned. Yet nothing, at least nothing self-evidently superior, has so far taken their place in the melting pot of hyper- and post-industrialism. There do not seem to be many

post-industrial equivalents of T. H. Green, J. S. Mill or F. D. Maurice—
to name just three of the creative thinkers who provided normatively-rich
intellectual resources from which distinctive progressive positions on the
social problems of industrialisation could be drawn. So the logic here is
simple enough: if there is any validity in the information society thesis,
then there is a corresponding need for a normative theory of the information society. The information society, long an object of methodological,
empirical and technical interrogations, needs to be problematised axiologi-
cally, and thereafter political steps taken to have those problems solved or
ameliorated. The main thrust of the answer to its normative crisis, I will
argue below, is actually to 'reload' a very special normative tradition of the
industrial past—but that is to anticipate.

However, are not claims of crisis usually little more than a gross rhetorical strategy masking the pursuit of some dubious objective—say, the suspension of habeas corpus—so should not such claims, including my own,
be discounted? After all, the WSIS was in some ways no different from
other summits, and if its disagreements are being cited as main proof of a
normative crisis of the information society, then perhaps my crisis-claim is
no more robust or useful than many another? Is there nothing more to be
said in its favour? One response might be to prescribe the reading of Manuel Castells, author of what is currently the most discussed version of the
information society thesis. His work is essentially empirical and social-theoretical, but it has major normative assumptions and implications. And it
would seem that Castells too has crisis in mind, if not, indeed, apocalypse.
Phrases extracted from the opening pages of volume 1 of his trilogy *The
Information Age* include: 'technological revolution', 'collapse', 'profound
restructuring', 'general overhauling', 'unleashing of formidable productive
forces', 'fundamental redefinition of relationships', 'engulfed in a structural
crisis', 'uncontrolled, confusing change', 'troubled times', 'delegitimation
of institutions', 'fading away of major social movements', and 'structural
schizophrenia' (Castells 2000: 1–3). He thematises problems of identity in
the face of the emergence of an informational society construed as network
society. Although the terminology is different, and although he wisely dis-
tances himself from the more melodramatic claims, Castells paints, on an
immense canvas, an alarming picture of an information age marked by
what is in all but name a normative crisis. However, rather than argue from
grand soundbites, even lifted from the highest authorities, let us focus on
specific evidence.

Major controversies surrounding privacy are perhaps the clearest manifestation so far of an acute normative crisis. Impending real-life scenarios
are rapidly becoming indistinguishable from dystopian science fiction—or
horror stories. The right of individual privacy, of personal space, established since the Reformation as a defining feature of civilisation, has under
post-industrial conditions encountered the many-headed ogre of surveillance. The function of the statist panopticon has crept from reforming

offenders to catching them, profiling them, pre-empting them. Cameras on all sides, drones and satellites overhead, miniature devices within. We are in mortal danger of total ecaptivity. And the state is only part of the problem, now that surveillance is bread-and-butter for private corporations. Yet despite the unflagging efforts of a few civil society organisations and their scholarly champions in the new specialism of surveillance studies, no one seems to be doing anything very effective about it. Technological determinism is regnant. The populace accepts the new intrusions with a resigned sigh; young people positively embrace them. Perhaps privacy is not such a valuable right, after all? Perhaps security is indeed more important, as the politicians say? Perhaps privacy fundamentalism needs to give way to privacy pragmatism? Nicholas Garnham (2000b: 43) notes that 'contemporary societies and policies are increasingly riven by a shifting range of border disputes between the private and the public and by deep normative confusion about them'. Shifting, elastic, fuzzy borders have indeed developed between the private and the public, as well as between other social categories, such as commodity and resource, news and entertainment, the nation and the world system. But it is more than just deep normative confusion; it is normative crisis.

Copyright, at one level less momentous but far from nugatory, is another domain in which there have long been signs of crisis. The ancient issues of property, plagiarism and piracy have returned with a vengeance in the fresh context of informational goods and services. It is no longer an esoteric matter of library science or legal studies, but an acute, agenda-setting policy issue. The European Commission's trend-setting copyright directive (2001)—the Directive on the Harmonisation of Certain Aspects of Copyright and Related Rights in the Information Society, to give it its telling official title—was said, in another signal of the information society's salience, to have been the 'most lobbied piece of European legislation' to date ('European Directive Compromise' 2001). File-sharing controversies vividly illustrate a clash of norms. At a subtler level, similar battles have been and are being enacted. In official contexts, information is hailed as a public good in the same breath that the rights of copyright are extended for publishing houses and record labels. There used to be clear normative traditions surrounding print media, predicated on conceptions of the limits of legitimate ownership and of the complementary rights of the consumer. Information was viewed by democratic policymakers as a utility, something to be careful about protecting from over-exploitation by market interests. Yet a countervailing and increasingly prevalent movement, whose origins predate the commercial colonisation of cyberspace, promotes the faith that information is the next commodity, the new oil. Christopher May, one of the most perspicacious information society sceptics, observes that the normative foundations of copyright have 'crumbled'; he too speaks of a 'normative crisis' that can only be resolved 'politically' (May 2003a; cf. Elkin-Koren 2001). Other intellectual property rights, such as patents, pose even greater dangers of breakdown—the patenting of human genetic code being the supreme issue ('Patenting Life' 2000; cf. Pogge 2006). Yet my point is that these need to be seen as part of a stronger, larger claim that there is a *general* crisis of normativity regarding the *whole* information society. The social system as a totality is failing to adapt, to integrate, to mature.

The information crisis has of course been greatly aggravated since 11 September 2001 and associated days of infamy, and the establishment responses to those events. There is much that can be said about the deeply un-American (or at any rate unconstitutional) 'Patriot' Act, about the suspension of time-honoured rights, about the erosion of civil liberties, and so on. But for present purposes the vital point is that, since that pivotal day, information has been under continuous and strenuous attack from state authorities and their agents. Freedom of information (FOI) can serve as an example. Prior to 9/11 there was a seemingly unstoppable trend— begun in the US in 1966, unless one counts some impressive Scandinavian precedents, notably a Swedish statute of 1766, and gaining momentum since the late 1990s—towards increasing popular access to official information. Now, however, the deeper trend is in the opposite direction, at least according to professional librarians, a community qualified to judge and hardly known for hyperbole. Their statements on the precariousness of public information must give pause for thought: 'trends towards control over access, secrecy over transparency, national security over civil liberties, and surveillance over anonymity' (Caidi and Ross 2005: 664); 'decreased access to government information' (Sleeman 2004: 491); 'right to know' back to 'need to know' (Shuler 2004: 499); this all being part of the 'post-September 11th balancing act' (Herman 2004). Sandra Braman concludes her magisterial treatise *Change of State* (2006: 321) with the judgement that 'the decades-long trend toward increased access to government information, theoretically made much easier with the use of digital technologies, has been reversed via expansion of the definition of types of information use of which may threaten national security'. Other commentators refer more colourfully to an 'information gulag' (Strickland 2005) and outright 'information war' (Snow 2003; cf. Shane 2006). The US polity, not to mention many others, has in effect retreated from the ideal of government resting on popular information.

To be sure, the worldwide wagon of FOI is still very much in motion, spurred, for example, by political assimilationism among new European Union 'member states' and aspirants. Over ninety countries have passed some kind of information law; even the inscrutable People's Republic of China is taking its first tentative steps. However, the fact remains that there is now also a regressive, and in the final analysis stronger, movement towards greater official secrecy at least as regards the most sensitive information. Overall there is even a sense that these FOI statutes, which in many states, both new and old, co-exist with unashamed authoritarianism, are something of a fig leaf covering a tightly-controlled information and media landscape. The problem is set in relief by the fact that, in stark contrast to the environmental crisis, about which we hear *ad nauseam*, there is little overt public recognition of information's predicament. The people appear apathetic: 'has anybody in Britain actually read *1984*?', asks information rights heroine Heather Brooke exasperatedly (2005). And Castells (2004: 340) lends his authority—'Didn't Big Brother arrive, as Orwell predicted, around 1984?'. How, the moral is, can we speak of an oil crisis, an environmental crisis, a whale crisis, etc, and yet keep silent on the damage to a human resource that ought to be natural in, that is indeed definitive of, our information age?

While, *pace* many pundits, the information society is not co-extensive with the internet, the latter has undoubtedly become the information society's most morally-conflicted dimension (e.g. Consalvo and Ess 2011; Fuchs 2008). It is a frontier where the only widespread codes are technical and where any kind of moral settlement is rare. The problem 'push technology' poses for the 'emergence of norms' (Higgs and Budd 2004) is obvious at the most familiar levels. There are the everyday, yet far from insignificant, breaches of netiquette: the workplace emails that defy the regularisation— a form of norms—of office hours; the veiled threats through copying-in; 'blind' copying as if such deception were somehow normal; and all the rest. Abuses are legion, indeed pandemic. Once virtually an ideal-type of collegial communication, email now seems to be enjoying diplomatic immunity from social morality, although it is certainly a gold mine for litigants and their lawyers. This is, to be sure, a classic mismatch between technology and norms. Nor has any remotely consensual answer been found with regard to content regulation of the web. Perfectly normal people are being criminalised because their curiosity tempts them to press a wrong key, accessing illegal material over which governments preside bovinely. Even in the West, arraignment can await the mere viewing of 'jihadist' websites, a draconian development for any liberal society and one that deletes 500 years of discrimination between thought and deed. Then there are the foolish judicial decisions to focus on where information is downloaded, rather than uploaded, in libel cases and the like, and countless similar anomalies. So the law of retributive justice with respect to cyberspace is an ass, and it is an ass not because internet regulators are uniquely dumb, but because, like the rest of us, they are the subjects of a pervasive normative crisis.

Yet these are just superficial manifestations of the legal and ethico-political challenges confronting the information age. The problem is not only that the internet, as a culmination of diverse species of media and technology, inherits a baggage of discordant normative traditions. It is that cyberspace has brought about an as yet unassimilated differentiation of the social system, an unscripted complexification of social relations. We basically still fail to grasp the import of 'cyberocracy' (Ronfeldt 1992).

Cyberspace has also become a new 'site of distributive justice', to adopt characteristically precise language from analytical political philosophy (Baynes 2006). The issues of privacy, copyright and even to some extent content regulation can themselves be constructed as issues of social inequality, but there is definitely also an additional set of issues that picks up on age-old controversies about hierarchy, debates about 'haves and have-nots' (Wresch 1996) and even 'class warfare' (Perelman 1998). A critical discourse on information gaps has existed for decades. More recently, the term 'digital divide' has been the all-conquering focus of such concerns. The quality of some of the arguments marshalled by critics of the digital divide has been mixed, provoking a reactionary school of thought which questions the very validity of the concept. Yet the case for information, including digital-information, divides is sound, not only internationally but also apropos of relatively affluent nations, suggesting indeed the need for new normatively-loaded negotiations of the capitalism-socialism debate. People are having to assess the whole scheme of justice implicit in the outcomes of the information society. Who are the heroes of the information age? billionaires such as the founders of Microsoft and Facebook—in terms of traditional notions of fairness, political, although certainly not personal, monstrosities? We are a little clearer about the losers: non-informational labour, manual workers, minorities—the usual 'systacts', to adopt sociologist W. G. Runciman's (1989: 20–27) excellent technical term for social groups, or, more bluntly, the usual classes. It is a situation of inequality, indicative of the existence of the 'new axes of social stratification' Bell (1999: 483) linked with the coming of post-industrial society. Yet even among policy actors who genuinely believe in social justice, there is chaos about what fairness in the information age might actually rule in, or even rule out—a rare politico-philosophical predicament.

This opens up other classic debates pertaining to social structure. In the 1980s, Murdock and Golding (1989: 192) put their finger on information inequality's *significance* by asserting that it raises 'broader issues in social and political philosophy', issues of citizenship, power, material deprivation and social rights, and of the role of institutions such as markets, the mass media, public libraries and citizens' advice bureaus. One might add that it invites also metaphysical questions about new forms of estrangement between persons, between individuals and their own bodies, and even between humanity and the transcendent realm. Indeed, there is a case for saying that the information age in general, and cyberspace in particular, have already witnessed a resurgence of alienation and anomie, of the instrumentalisation of persons, of commodity-fetishism, of the violation of the kingdom of ends, of disenchantment, bluntly, of moral and spiritual bankruptcy. 'Will we do on our keyboards what we have notably failed to do face to face?', asks 'strong' democracy theorist Benjamin Barber pointedly (1997: 225). Informatisation has occasioned much of positive value too, of course, and it has probably done far more good than harm on any felicific calculation, but there is clearly a host of insistent social problems at its door. Given all the above, which is no more than a brief foray, is it really too much to say that the information society—that is, modern nations in their informatised aspects—are undergoing a normative crisis? And can there be a more overdue research task, therefore, than to 'elaborate on the normative structure of the information policy problem' (Overman and Cahill 1990: 814)?

POLITICAL/PHILOSOPHICAL REACTIONS: UTOPIAN, CONSERVATIVE AND CRITICAL

Political and politico-philosophical responses to the normative crisis of the information society, and more generally to the social-informatisation process, have taken a variety of rival forms. The earliest, and most inspirational, expressed a mood of political optimism, a rose-tinted perspective on the future polis. Since the dawn of the information age, when 'this amazing machine' (Machlup 1962: 307), the information machine of information machines, began to steal the technological scene, there has been a flourishing of visions of society depicting radical alternatives to the status quo. The chief conflicts of the industrial era, between abundance and scarcity and between capital and labour, would supposedly soon be transcended. The late Yoneji Masuda's work, highly influential to this day in official information policy circles in Japan, remains the best example. Masuda is frequently cited in the western information society literature too, although usually critically, because his formulations, as well as having the distinction of being translated into English, were so lucid, dogmatic and brazenly deterministic. 'The information epoch to be brought about by computer-telecommunications technology', he announced in *The Information Society as Post-Industrial Society*, 'does not simply mean that it will have a big socio-economic impact upon contemporary industrial society; it will demonstrate a force of societal change powerful enough to bring about the transformation of society into a completely new type of human society, which is the information society' (Masuda 1981: 59). The post-industrial order, Masuda proceeded to explain, would overcome the materialism, monotony and poverty of industrial societies; in their place, post-industrialism would be characterised by the positive values of spirituality, creativity, prosperity, equality and harmony. 'The spirit of the information society', he exults elsewhere (Masuda 2004: 20), 'will be the spirit of globalism, a symbiosis in which man and nature can live together in harmony'. In short, the information society is to be all good things for all men. Information society enthusiasts in the same mould wrote lyrically of third waves, new ages, a micro-millennium. It must be conceded too that traces of the same optimism can be sensed in sparkling, contemporaneous essays by Bell, from 'Notes on the Post-Industrial Society' (1967b) to 'Teletext and Technology: New Networks of Knowledge and Information in Postindustrial Society' (1980a)—although Bell was always careful to moderate his predictions with scholarly caveats and qualifications.

The basic problem, of course, with maximalist, Masuda-style, scenarios is that they are utopian—utopian to the extent of Leon Trotsky's fantasy communist order wherein men's brains have grown and their voices become more musical (cited in Bell 1967a: 3). A species of the recurrent delusion of technological utopianism, a *mentalidad* that has succeeded in attaching itself to every new device from the printing press to television, it has long since been refuted by reliable scholars, such as Boris Frankel (1987) and Rob Kling (1994). Nevertheless, as we know, the appearance of the worldwide web gave information-technological utopianism an extraordinary boost. 'Information', the mantra went, 'wants to be free', and as late as the mid-1990s much of the atmosphere of the internet clearly reflected the left-libertarianism of 1960s counter-culture. Unfortunately, information liberation is a far more elusive goal than national liberation, women's liberation and the like. Forgetting the actual origins and funding of the new medium by the military-industrial complex (Smart 2010), the proto-information society pursued anti-establishment norms of sharing, cooperation and total openness. Yet it was self-evidently unfeasible, at least when presented, as it often was, as a generalised social philosophy for the post-industrial order. It was just too easy to say that information, by which was primarily then meant the scientific, technical and medical (STM) variety, ought to be free, if one was a university scientist on a salary or a bohemian with a gift for gadgetry; but impossible for anyone else. So Ronald Day (2001: 58–59), in the sober vein of the earlier realists, is right to remind us that 'a communicational or informational utopia is both a practical and a regulative impossibility'.

There is no need to waste any time adding to the critique of technological utopianism. However, now may be the appropriate juncture at which to disclose that I will later be defending a *realistic* utopianism. This is not to be confused either with the Masuda type or with a full-blown Mannheimian counterpoise to 'ideology' (1936). It will rather be a *modest* utopianism, one of setting out a desirable institutional structure capable of guiding the course of practical political reform. Indeed, utopianism in this credit-worthy sense, alongside social informatics *qua* the humanistic study of information and its manifold technologies, is the underlying theme of the whole book—informatics and utopia, as it were.

That unsustainable idealism, in any case, is now only a marginal presence in cyberspace, an ideology in retreat. By far the most common present-day reaction to the normative crisis of the information society is a form of conservatism embedded in, and indulgent of, power politics and technological determinism. As a result, the information society in its concrete manifestations is largely reproducing the dominant norms of mature industrialism. There is ubiquitous evidence of the impact of the philosophy and practice of economic neo-conservatism, *laissez-faire*, or what is now usually termed, somewhat inappropriately, neo-liberalism. Many academic readings of the information society speak menacingly of 'a Neo-Liberal Consensus that has engulfed the world' (Webster 2004: 2) and bemoan the 'neoliberal axiology that underpins most (if not all) of contemporary technology policy' (Graham 2006: 129). 'The tendency', Robin Mansell (2008: 15) notes, 'to favour the search for a universal model of The information Society by fostering market-led arrangements and values and by privileging technologies over human aspirations and needs, remains very strong especially in the higher echelons of policy making'; although more encouragingly Mansell adds that 'there are some signs that attention to the causes of inequality in society and to how these filter into specific information society initiatives may be growing'. Despite any such green shoots, however, there is undoubtedly still a universal gravitational pull towards privatisation of information policy, towards the deregulation of markets including information markets, towards the commodification of information-media, towards the strengthening of intellectual property rights at the expense of free (at point-of-need) information and knowledge—in short, to the 'economising mode' (Bell 1999: 42–43). Such is the antithesis of idealism.

An important illustration can be found in ongoing political efforts to create a European information society. A maximalist version of the information society thesis has been highly influential for at least two decades in Community, particularly Commission, thinking (the European Parliament is always more circumspect, yet relatively powerless). The Bangemann Report of the mid-1990s was seminal in setting the direction of the Commission's strategic aims, and it was an unashamedly neo-conservative manifesto, frankly demanding 'a market-led passage to the new age' (European Union 1994: 8). Now, with a fully-fledged Information Society and Media directorate-general residing in Brussels, it is safe to say that such thinking has been 'institutionalised' in European Union policy (Miles 2002: 160). In a philosophically rich contribution, Shalini Venturelli (1998: 32) has exposed a crude utilitarianism in the Commission's 'policy design for the information society'. That the main political-economic outcome is neo-liberal, Venturelli continues (1998: 168), is shown by the way 'public-access rights are being targeted as obstructions to the global information society'. Public service broadcasting too, long a centre-piece of a European approach to the informational and cultural realms, is being reduced to 'an anachronistic transition in the ultimate realization of the information society' (Venturelli 1998: 221). Of course, there have been countervailing currents issuing from the social democratic political tradition in Europe, yet the main drift has been ineluctably rightward. And as Anders Henten and Knud Skouby (2002: 331; cf. Stewart *et al.* 2006) observe of official information policy across the globe, while some of the second-generation plans had a social democratic dimension, these never succeeded in overcoming the 'clear neoliberal basis for the visions'. There is thus a great deal to be said for the final conclusion that the information society, in its present cryptonormative manifestation—that is to say, despite its unconvincing self-portrait as a purely technical concept—is 'liberalism's political form in late modernity' (Venturelli 1998: 281). We mean here, neo-liberal. Thus the danger is that the normative crisis of the information society will terminate in Eriksonian 'foreclosure', where an adolescent, in this case a young socio-technical formation, simply adopts the norms upon which it has been reared.

In spite of its near-hegemony in the establishment, the conservative default has not been without a host of fierce critics inside the academy. There exists an extensive and fairly impressive body of left criticism of the information society thesis, much of it Marxian and politically radical. Such theorists have been united in seeing the thesis as a deeply misleading account of social reality. In the early days, its golden phase as the coming of a new, improved, post-industrial society, Bell in particular was singled out for excoriation. His work was dismissed as a 'regression behind the ongoing voices of Hegel and Marx', in that it 'does not retain the dimension of conceptualizing economic inequality and political powerlessness' (Schroyer 1974: 164, 166). He was caricatured by no less than Anthony Giddens (1973: 21), as 'advanced capitalism's most persuasive advertising man' (a charge, ironically, that would later fit much better Giddens's pre-eminent disciple, Tony Blair). More popular and arguably derivative authors, such as Alvin Toffler, would receive much the same treatment (e.g. Young 1987). The information society itself was dismissed as 'a phase in the history of capitalism coping with its contradictions' (Dupuy 1980: 4). All that eulogistic new-society 1980s rhetoric around personal computing was just, in Frank Webster and Kevin Robins's (1986: 31) blunt northern colloquialism, a 'snow job' for mercenary interests. 'Technological scenarios', Lars Qvortrup (1987: 140) agreed, 'are transformed social scenarios, and behind the technical categories, social tendencies and interests hide'. Information technology's real function, he concluded, is to 'reproduce capitalism by increasing its productivity and profitability' (Qvortrup 1987: 142). Many others kept up this ideological struggle in the 1990s. Today there is the profound, and perhaps a little more measured, 'informationcritique' of Lash (2002). More recently, Phil Graham (2006) has offered a thorough-going analysis of the 'hypercapitalism' driving the information economy. And there is also the whole corpus of the political economy of communication school (e.g. Mosco 1996; Schiller 1996; Schiller 2007). These are samples of an active and stubbornly uncompromising intellectual resistance movement.

Much of this critical theory rings true. Even those who would eschew radical perspectives have sometimes had to acknowledge that market economics may not be all-sufficient. 'Even if our best sentiments are in favour of market solutions', wrote Porat (1977: 242) in that pioneering chapter on information policy, 'the stark realities of existing market structure defy a *laissez-faire* approach'. But the reality seems to be that what is transpiring is indeed the coming of a post-industrial society incorporating many of the values and agendas of the most powerful forces—financial, commercial, political, hierarchical, military, surveillant—with a vested interest in driving that development. The only information society that can emerge from a passive political economy of *laissez-faire* will inevitably be to a large extent a reification of the spirit of capitalism. '"Information"', Day judiciously observes (2001: 117), 'is a central term of ideology because it determines and patrols its own meaning over a vast expanse of social and cultural spaces'. And where else can its main marching orders originate except in the headquarters of the military-(post-)industrial establishment? What hope then for the sociologising mode?

However, while critical theory has scored palpable hits, it is seriously inadequate as a response to the normative crisis of the information society. The intermingling of neo-conservative values with recent information society discourse cannot be disputed, not just because their time frames coincided but also because they shared, or gave every appearance of sharing, some right-wing socioeconomic goals. However, as has been stressed already, the information society thesis is not only much broader than information technology, but—so long as it is understood in the moderate manner postulated above—it maps verifiable developments in the economies, polities and cultures of advanced societies. The thesis is certainly far more than just an ideological smokescreen for industrial capitalism. John Stuart Mill sagely insisted that a doctrine is not examined at all until it is examined in its strongest form, and most of the radical critiques, frankly, do not pass such a test. Indeed, this whole school of criticism of the information society thesis has about it something of the antinomian spirit of Ned Ludd, the foolhardy Nottingham machine-breaker who inspired not only a resistance movement against industrialisation but also modern philippics like *Information Technology: A Luddite Analysis* (Webster and Robins 1986). Yet the future will hardly be promoted by the anti-establishment orthodoxy of technophobic negations; normative information society theory needs instead somehow to move beyond—once it has been deepened and chastened by—informationcritique.

So if utopian, conservative and critical responses to the normative crisis of the information society are all in various ways found wanting, where exactly does that leave the main argument? If those well-populated encampments are all dead-ends, are we in fact left with nowhere else to go? The answer, thankfully, need not be negative. Another, far superior, option is to work to develop a positive *and* practicable set of sociopolitical ideas for the information age, one that consciously avoids the pitfalls of utopianism, conservatism and hyper-criticism. At the end of *Information Society Studies*, having validated (at least to its author's satisfaction) the epistemological credentials of the information society thesis, it was suggested that the next step for theory is to move from a *de facto* to a *de jure* information society thesis, from 'is' to 'ought'. For social theory must always eventually hand over to social philosophy. So now that it is clear that many of us inhabit *de facto* information societies, our job is to ensure that such are morally decent in their social structures. The remedy for the sickness of the information society will thus be found in the articulation of a new normativity and a correlative social ideal. Accordingly, the task attempted below is an updated—reloaded—theory of social justice anchored in the work of two of the greatest Anglophone thinkers of the twentieth century. This will involve the construction of a model of an ideal society that can orientate mundane decision-making, that is, one predicated on a satisfactory account of social reality. Values in the shape of worthy norms need to be poured into information society discourse, a process that should be carried out systematically and feasibly, in such a way that they can inform live options, not for avatars, but for real-world offline policymakers. I am arguing, then, for utopianism, but only for a *bounded* utopianism, that is, a utopianism founded on a sensible appraisal of human nature and capabilities, in all our complexities, potentialities and limitations. If the correct value settings are in place, the information age will at least have a reasonable chance of not crashing.

All this may sound quixotic, but I am not alone in thinking that such is the requirement of the hour. 'What is required', agrees Paschal Preston (2002: 237) 'is a theory-building project that is empirically grounded'. Noting that 'there are rich veins of intellectual resources that provide alternatives to prevailing orthodoxies', he asks for 'a robust vision of the "good society"' (Preston 2002: 238). And this vision needs to be produced, Jan Servaes (2003: 6) adds, 'at the level of political philosophy'. Now is definitely the time, as norms are in process of being determined both nationally and globally. This is especially the case for internet policy. 'Only now,' Christopher Marsden (2000: 32) concurs, 'with the growing ubiquity of the Internet for business and particularly consumers, are normative values—beyond a crude cyber-libertarianism—being taken more seriously'. 'If technical standard setting in the Internet environment draws on the law and economics of information,' he proceeds, 'the normative standard setting which is increasingly superimposed on that earlier model reflects an extension of law and economics into the moral and social universe'. And as Jeroen van den Hoven and Emma Rooksby (2008: 377) wisely assert of the socioeconomic problem of the information society, 'normative principles are necessary for the articulation of cogent criticism of the market forces and allocative practices that sustain or exacerbate existing social and economic inequalities, as well as to develop proposals for reform, both nationally and internationally'. There is evidently a cloud of witnesses.

The present book is just such an exercise in normative theory-building, an attempt to work out the principles that can sustain a robust moral vision of an open and reasonably egalitarian information age. However imperfect the effort, it is needful for as many as are able to contribute to the worldwide interdisciplinary conversation about the future shape of post-industrial society, and hopefully to influence, if at all possible, the outcomes of policymaking processes. I am aware that there are rough edges and untangled knots in what follows. However, the ancient Jewish proverb, borrowed respectfully from an eminent contemporary political philosopher, brings comfort: 'you are not required to finish the work, but neither are you at liberty to neglect it' (quoted in Walzer 2004b: 1).

DEFENCE OF THE JOURNALISTIC CONCEPTION OF INFORMATION

The information society is the totality of facts, not of flows. The most important premise of any theory of the information society, empirical or normative, is obviously its definition of information. One might argue that a definition of society should also be provided, but that is asking too much. As declared above, I am content in that respect to trust Bell, behind whom lies the vast social-theoretical hinterland of Marx and Weber, in unique formation (e.g. Bell 1995a, 1999: 49–119). Such must suffice. But it is certainly necessary to specify the bandwidth of the other key word, both to determine the theory's intrinsic capacity and to protect it from challenges founded on mistaken conceptions of what the theory is trying to achieve. As we have already had occasion to observe, struggles over the conceptualisation of information lie at the heart of the normative crisis of the information society, as indeed they did during its existential crisis, therefore semantic clarification is obviously a starting-point of the kinds of policy arguments that this book is hoping to put forward.

It has been pointed out that there is as yet no satisfactory theory of communication or information (e.g. Mansell 1996: 40). However, close inspection appears to reveal two major families of meaning in common usage, or, put another way, it seems that the *concept* of information unpacks into two main competing *conceptions* of information. The first refers to the flow of signals across all channels, regardless of content or quality. I shall call this the computing conception of information. The second is confined to social communications with meaningful content, thus involving a much more qualitative approach. This will be named the journalistic conception of information. These conceptions overlap, but they should be separated out because they are in essence different. The simple postulate in the present section, and a cornerstone of the whole subsequent argument, is that the computing conception has crowded out the journalistic in contemporary discourse, and that a return to a journalistic conception is of pivotal importance for the construction of a robust normative theory of the information society. If the journalistic conception is basically sound, it should be capable of fulfilling the central role that the normative theory of the information society requires of it.

The technical field of information theory has produced an account of information/communication that is not just explanatorily powerful but also widely accepted. The definitive exposition was Claude Shannon and Warren Weaver's *Mathematical Theory of Communication* (1949). This book's explication of the binary digit as the fundamental unit of information has proven to be one of the most fecund contributions not just to computer science but to modern thought as a whole. What Shannon and Weaver demonstrated in essence is that the efficiency of a transmission system can be computed according to the extent to which it avoids loss of the integrity of a signal in its journey from 'source' to 'destination'. Where there is no deterioration, the information quality is perfect and isomorphism between sender and receiver is achieved. In the real world, the book explained, extraneous factors, such as crackle over telephone lines, result in some loss of the original signal, that is, in its sense, of information. With electronic systems, the whole transaction can be measured in bits; as a result, steps can be taken to counteract such 'noise' by repeating the signal or otherwise building 'redundancy' into the system. It is easy to see how the theory doubles as a theory of information and communication, since information on the Shannon/Weaver definition can only be quantified once it has been propelled into some kind of transmission situation. Communication is thus information in motion.

On its own terms, the computing conception is probably irrefutable, but it is too often forgotten that for Shannon and Weaver (1949: 8, 31), 'information must not be confused with meaning' and that 'semiotic aspects of communication are irrelevant to the engineering problem'. Perfectly legitimate within their own context, these propositions are unacceptable as a general account of information. They do not signify the ordinary meaning of the word at all, since that requires, as a minimum, meaningfulness. Such was demonstrated in great depth by Fred Dretske in *Knowledge and the Flow of Information* (1981). By reducing information to mere ones and zeros, the computing conception allows any kind of data flow to count, thereby liquidating the kinds of distinctions upon which human language—and reliable social theory—are built. This is not the fault of the computing conception; the problem lies with those who have imported it into other domains without due care. And information society discourse, both academic and official, has yielded more or less comprehensively. Information flow censuses, a major strand within the johoka research tradition, for example, conform entirely to this purely quantitative approach (Duff 2000b; Japan Ministry of Internal Affairs and Communications 2010). Asked directly, Tetsuro Tomita, an early insider, responded that 'we just measure volume of information. We don't measure information quality' (quoted in Edelstein 1978: 25). The same holds for most western theorists. Thus a well-received monograph on the global information infrastructure defines information as 'things that can be managed in information systems' (Borgman 2000: 79). And a recent multi-volume collection, apparently installing itself as the canon of information society studies, has as its point of departure that the information society denotes 'a particular vision of developments arising from the growing use of information and communication technologies (ICT) in the acquisition, storage and processing of information' (Mansell 2009 vol. 1: xvii).

It is time for this conception to make way for one properly moored in ordinary language. The reasoning is plain. Information has an internal relationship with meaning. Gobbledygook can be acquired, stored, processed and managed by a computer, or transmitted by a telecommunications system, just as well as meaningful propositions, but nonsense is not information. Nonsense has no real social function. This is the fundamental point. Moreover, information is not only meaningful, it is also the subset of the meaningful that is also factual. Theodore Roszak (1994: 3) correctly casts it as the set of responses to the request for 'information, please'. It is what the woman in the Tokyo metro, arguably post-industrialism's equivalent of English jurisprudence's man on the Clapham omnibus, expects to receive when she asks a guard, or perhaps a robot, for directions. In other words, it is about hard facts. Etymological warrant goes as far back as the myth of Vulcan hammering out, or in-forming, shields for Aeneas and thunderbolts for Zeus (Capurro and Bjorland 2003: 351–52). The concept of information needs to be reconnected to these steely roots. Such traits as referentiality and truth, not just computability or communicability, pick out the normal meaning of information, as has been confirmed by up-to-date scholarship on ordinary language philosophy (Dretske 2008). To argue thus is of course in a sense already to adopt a normative theory of the information society; it is to urge a renormalisation of language. It is to lead our key word, our lost *logos*, back from the data wilderness. In the beginning, after all, was the word.

This approach is supported by a number of special categories which, at least in principle, have a high informational content in the required sense. News is one such, at its best a paradigm of pure information. 'The newspaper', writes Lash insightfully (2002: 2), 'gave us the model for the information age'—that is to say, the information society is characterised by a rapid profusion of short, disembodied messages. Yet news, in the authentic newspaperman's sense, is more than the mere relaying of succinct telegrams of information. It involves also a structure of news values, including, over and above cosmetic aspects of narration and style, norms of accuracy, currency, societal relevance, etc. In *Discovering the News*, Michael Schudson (1981: 5) showed how this 'information model' of news came to triumph over the 'story model'. 'Most people', media ethicist Chris Frost explains further (2000: 33), 'buy into information systems because they want high-grade information, not just entertainment'. 'By emphasizing "facts", "news value", and "social responsibility"', Klaus Krippendorff argued in another study (1993: 492), 'journalism links information to some concept of truth and to a professional ethic', as part of an 'hierarchical' paradigm of information involving 'absolutism' and 'universalism'. Krippendorff, however, seems to be sceptical of such lofty values, and sadly even some at the forefront of practice-led journalism research today are beginning to look askance at 'a Thomas Gradgrindian devotion to facts' (Keeble 2005: 56). I wish to maintain contrariwise that such devotion lies at the very core of the conception of information that should be being promoted. The information society, to echo Ludwig Wittgenstein again (1974: 5), is the totality only of facts, not of all flows.

The normative theory of the information society thus needs to break free not only from the conception of information cradled in computing and information science, but also from journalism's spongy penumbra of media and cultural studies (cf. Lewis 1997). Such fields, generally proceeding with very much looser definitions, have increasingly queered information's pitch. They tend to pay too much respect to flows such as soap opera, advertising and infotainment, signaling thereby that the distinction between fact and fiction is unimportant, and sometimes even insinuating that those who strictly defend it are simple-minded, if not, indeed, dogmatic. Their relativism should be stoutly resisted, because while the boundary between information and other modes is of course blurred, it does not at all follow that outside of the overlap there is not a huge domain of pure information, pure fact, pure epistemological gold. It is hardly surprising that in the vicinity of these fashionable fields, journalism proper, with its supposedly antiquated belief in 'straight' reporting, has become something of an anomaly, an inconvenience. Barbie Zelizer (2004: 188) observes that, unlike other forms of cultural argumentation and production, 'journalism remained constrained by its somewhat reified but nonetheless instrumental respect for facts, truth, and reality', resulting in its being criticised for 'remaining a bastion of positivism'. Perhaps then, rather than retreating, we should grasp the nettle fully and rebond with positivism, over-against postmodernism? From that perspective, informatisation is the realisation of the society of facts, a social order based on solid documentation, as envisioned not just by journalists but by the founders of public libraries and other intrepid ambassadors of European modernism (Rayward 2008).

In any case, another paradigm of the normative concept of information is the domain of documents and public information subject to freedom of information legislation. Such statutes define information strictly as presumptively veridical recorded materials residing in public authority files. They typically deal with facts, with what has actually been said or done, with materials that are verifiable, traceable and indexable. To say that government information is a paradigm of information is not to capitulate to propaganda. This is not about lines propagated by spin doctors, but, quite the opposite, about the inner workings of the state apparatus, matters government is not necessarily wanting to disclose, matters indeed that under a good FOI regime, such as Scotland's (Brooke 2007), it might have been forced against its will to divulge. Of course, the information that is sought by an FOI request may turn out to be false, but in that case it is false information, an inference that depends on a prior notion of information as something that is generally not false. Increasingly, modern journalism involves precisely the journalism of information in this substantive sense, the filing of FOI requests and the turning of the results, where newsworthy, into published stories. Even refusals of FOI requests on some of the many grounds of exemption can themselves be newsworthy, since they imply the existence of facts which the authorities wish to suppress.

To summarise, information will be understood henceforth as a social, semantic, factual, verifiable and valuable category, exemplified by paradigms such as hard news and FOI. Some of this swims against the tides of contemporary thought, but it is only by restricting the conception of information to that which is the case, to that which is true and significant, that we can bring order to the information society thesis and rescue it from the reckless parameters with which it has become associated. And there is at least one illustrious precedent in the information society canon. For Bell (1985: 17)—a jobbing journalist before he became a professor of social science—'information is news, facts, statistics, reports, legislation, tax-codes, judicial decisions, resolutions and the like'. So I reject, with him (1999: xxiv), the 'postmodern logorrhea'. Admittedly, Bell himself sometimes departed from verbal discipline, for example when he defined the 'information explosion' in terms which swept in all varieties of media and communications, including magazines, entertainment and the 'vivid pictorial imagery of television' (1980b: 525–26). Yet this only goes to show that the risk of logorrhea is everywhere, that our mission will require unceasing patrols of information's real borders. There is no room for the false or the fake in the logical space bounded by the concept(ion) of information.

The conception that will be developed below is thus the information society as informed society. Armed with such a definition, we are at last in a position to be able to begin to develop the actual content of the normative theory of the information society. This can only be about redeeming the original promise, contained in the very term, namely the creation of a society in which everyone has the information that they need. Or to quote the fine title assigned to the posthumous writings of telecommunications visionary Colin Cherry (1985), the information society is about achieving nothing less than 'the age of access'—and more particularly, the 'Age of Fact' (Mills 1970: 11). It is to the imagination of that sociological ideal that the remainder of this book is dedicated.

2 Reloading Social Democracy
A Rawls-Tawney Synthesis

TWO KEY THINKERS FOR AN AGE OF CRISIS

After rolling out a hopefully well-founded definition of information, a normative theory of the information society must stand or fall with its ability to identify and justify a convincing schedule of norms. This is a very steep challenge, one that begs fundamental questions of social and political philosophy. The present chapter cannot supply complete answers, but it can venture to lay down the main principles, marking, as it were, a few lines in the sand as the norm-busting 'third wave' (Toffler 1981) crashes onto the shores of polity, economy and culture. My argument, which some may initially find counter-intuitive or even reactionary, will be that the normative tradition of *social democracy*, and specifically an ethical, Anglo-American version of such, still provides the sturdiest foundation for the construction of a normative theory of the information society. The claim will not be that this moral-political tradition offers a direct source of off-the-peg prescriptions. Instead, guided by the conviction that it still constitutes a basically serviceable normative matrix, the objective will be to show that a reconstruction in light of what is valid in the information society thesis can yield a range of coordinates within which details of application can then be outworked. It is an experiment, so to speak, in normative information retrieval, in extracting resources for our future from the norms embedded in our past. Its aim is to map out some strategic conceptual hinterland, terrain from which the salient normative problems of the information age may be attacked.

The chapter thus employs a specific 'method' of grounding normativity, namely, the mining of presumptively durable elements of an established normative school. It might be thought that to face backwards in this way is immediately to commit some kind of philosophical error, to be at odds with the spirit of the age. Is not post-industrialism about the coming of a new society, or at least about major technological and social innovations, in which case should we not be trying somehow to discover a *new* normativity? Ought we not to obey Jurgen Habermas's (1984; 1987) precept that modernity must generate a normativity out of itself, as he himself laboured to do on an epic scale in the theory of communicative action? And given that Bell himself (1999: lxxxv) identified future-orientation as the hallmark of post-industrial society, what is presumably required now is futurology rather than historiography. However, these are all *non sequiturs*. I will deal with Habermas in due course, but Bell would have been the last person to marginalise the moral and religious traditions of the past. On the contrary, he maintained adamantly that the survival of the great monotheistic religions falsified secularist philosophies like Marxism, and he similarly rejected the rhetoric of those fashionable futurists who wish to make everything traditional appear obsolete. 'Bombastic phrases', according to his 'Reflections at the End of an Age' (Bell 1996b: xxiv), 'careening about like a Tom-and-Jerry cartoon in overdrive, will not do'. The issues, Bell insists, are still those of normal political theory, requiring 'value and communal judgments'. And, he adds (1996b: xxxviii), 'technology provides no answers, no matter on what wave it rides'.

His juniors concur. 'There is no need', May (2003b: 2; cf. Duff 2008a) argues in *Key Thinkers for the Information Society*, 'to discard all previous analysis and insight, no need to dispense with our previous "ideological baggage"'. Supplying some content, Venturelli's elaborate case (1998: 8–34) for 'the normative grounds of information policy' is safely tethered to the classic texts of liberal western political theory, the works of Locke, Kant and so on. For Kieron O'Hara and David Stevens too (2006: xii), being progressive about the information society 'does not require us to jettison our moral, ethical or political framework, as numerous commentators have suggested, though it might require us to rethink parts of it'. The message is that we may continue to live off at least a proportion of our accumulated normative capital.

Yet even granting the intellectual legitimacy of recovering religious, moral or political schools, social democracy is hardly the most prepossessing such option at the inception of a new millennium. 'Few', asserts the *Encyclopedia of the Future* (Gore 1996 vol. 2: 848), 'doubt that social democratic governments will continue to have a central place in the future of Europe', but they will practice social democracy, so this impressive reference work implies, only in a much diluted form. As regards classical, redder-blooded, social democracy, it is commonplace to hear lamentations about its inevitable demise, alongside radical socialism, on the rocks of globalisation and other harsh economic and political realities. 'Little is left of the traditional left', we are told, with a brutal pun (Pels 2005: 272). Such perceptions partly explain the rise of flash brands of pseudosocial democracy which, whatever their short-term electoral advantages, have more or less abandoned equality and other cardinal values of the tradition. The 'third way' (Giddens 1998), which did so much to reconcile the rank-and-file of the British Labour Party to market economics and its societal corollary, inflationary inequality, is a prime example. 'These days', Sheri Berman observes (2003: 113), 'the term social democracy has been stripped of all concrete referents and transformed into a content-free label'. I prefer to join Berman herself and a small but growing band of commentators (e.g. Callaghan and Tunney 2001; Pierson 2001) in contesting the judgement that social democracy of the original stamp is more or less played out. The trademark syntheses effected by real social democracy, of equality and authority, individualism and collectivism, freedom and fairness, are still, we are suggesting, viable. Thus the following argument will be that while the theory of social democracy requires some recalibration for the information age, it can and must retain its traditional values in a recognisable combination.

So where exactly can the sources of this particular normative school be found? According to another reputable encyclopaedia, 'there is no systematic statement or great text that can be pointed to as a definitive account of social democratic ideals' (Miller 1998: 827). This may be true in the sense that social democracy shuns the kind of binding canon associated with Marxism, its main twentieth-century rival for the allegiance of the underdog and of those one-in-a-hundred *bourgeois* who, gifted with the capacity to see through the mystifications of a class society, sympathise politically with the underdog. However, social democracy certainly has its own informal repository of key texts, and the pair of thinkers whose ideas I wish to retrieve for the information age, R. H. Tawney and John Rawls, furnished the tradition with two of its finest twentieth-century statements. Together they point, it will be argued, to a resolution of the essential tension at the heart of twenty-first century information politics: that the economy, at least in its capitalistic functions, wants to treat information as a private commodity, but that democracy, intrinsically, must still view it as a social utility.

Richard Henry Tawney (1880–1962), a pioneering economic historian based at the London School of Economics and a central figure in the Labour Party in its vitality, has been called the 'crowning figure of ethical socialism in the twentieth century' (Dennis and Halsey 1988: 149; cf. Duff 2008c). Two of his publications, *The Acquisitive Society* (1982) and *Equality* (1964b), became textbooks of the non-Marxian British left for many decades. Michael Walzer (1981: 487), an analytical philosopher not given to hyperbole, readily rates Tawney the 'most important socialist moralist of the twentieth century'. However, while the standing of Tawney in the halls of social democratic thought is easily verified, this does not necessarily justify the coopting of his ideas for a normative theory of the information society. Indeed, at first blush this theorist might seem singularly ill-suited to a post-industrial makeover. There are what appear to be plausible reasons why Tawney's work has rarely been seen in this light, beyond the bald fact that he died the year Machlup's *Production and Distribution of Knowledge in the United States* appeared and long before IT revolution became a popular theme. Tawney seemed to cut a quintessentially manufacturing-era figure. The categories within which his mind operated were deeply industrial, exemplified by his regular references to 'Henry Dubb', a stereotype representing the doughty, card-carrying member of the factory proletariat—the 'civilian' equivalent of the 'PBI' (poor bloody infantry) (Tawney 1981a: 163). Politics were about the 'emancipation' of the 'workers', a task to be facilitated by a vanguard of upper-middle class intellectuals in the Workers' Educational Association or the Fabian Society, such as the Rugby- and Balliol-educated Tawney himself.

Today all this looks patronising, almost Dickensian, and profoundly alien to a new universe of telecommuters, hackers, bloggers, digerati. Moreover, there were gaping holes in Tawney's theoretical system at precisely those points where a nod to the future might without much effort have been achieved. Tawney had nothing to say about the mass media, even though their golden age began and ended during his life-time, or about telephony, or about information technology in any of its embryonic forms. In this respect, his writings compare very badly with those of his contemporary Wells, for whom being politically advanced was a function of a self-conscious futurological imagination and belief in a world order founded on encyclopaedic information (e.g. Wells 1901, 1935). Tawney specifically disowned a line of thought prevalent among his Fabian Society colleagues and regarded by them as the hallmark of a progressive mentality, namely that the acquisition of facts and statistics was the key to the solution of social problems. 'What', he asked impudently (1972: 79), 'is the use of them when they are collected? No amount of conjuring will turn a fact into a principle'. The development of a heightened social morality was what really counted, as we will see.

However, there are several compensatory reasons why Tawney's philosophy cannot be confined within the iron cage of industrialism. To begin with, there is the simple fact that, while Tawney was no futurist, neither was he a socio-technical reactionary. His *Commonplace Book*, the personal diary whose posthumous publication led to the remarkable Walzer tribute quoted above, reveals the young Tawney (1972: 26) explicitly repudiating the Penty-style post-industrialism which wanted advanced nations to 'retreat from the industrial stage' on account of its attendant capitalist evils, and to somehow settle for an idyllic, if poverty-stricken, agrarian communalism. Another primary source, this time from Tawney in his maturity (1952: 3), confirms that he was flexible enough to recognise that 'realities change; fresh experience is acquired; the sciences concerned with society are young and growing'; and that 'unless Socialism is to succumb to dogmatic petrifaction, it must develop with them'. But the main reason why Tawney is not past his sell-by date is that his articulation of social democracy was profoundly ethics-based. It was precisely his presentation of social democracy as an expression of *social morality* that made his political philosophy so powerful and also so durable. In this respect, his position was bound to weather far better than that of many other left-wingers of his day, both Fabian and Marxist, whose approaches were trendier, were more reliant on technical arguments, were vehicles more of contingency than necessity. And I will try to show too that deep within Tawney's ethic of social democracy is a latent ideal of interpersonal communication which is extremely resonant for the politics of post-industrial egalitarianism. That which is most lacking in contemporary social democracy, an ideal of relational justice—of human fellowship—is what Tawney emphasised above all, as his biographer and chief commentator, among others, has noted (Terrill 1973; cf. Duff 2004b; Ormrod 1990).

The American philosopher John Rawls (1921–2002) also produced, in *A Theory of Justice* (1973), a seminal work of social democratic thought, in this case—such would probably not be asserted on behalf of Tawney—as part of a major contribution to the western canon of moral and political philosophy. Amy Gutmann (1989: 338–9) believes that 'among twentieth-century philosophical works Rawls's theory may be our most common possession'. Thomas Nagel (1999: 1; cf. Honderich 2003: 68; Skinner *et al.* 2002: 6–9) confirmed on the eve of the millennium that 'it is now safe to describe [Rawls] as the most important political philosopher of the twentieth century'. While Rawls was not a socialist, his position was avowedly left-liberal, 'closer in spirit to European social democracy than to any mainstream American political movement' (Nagel 2003: 63). Yet much the same initial caveat applies to his post-industrial cooptation. Like Tawney, Rawls never came near to discovering the value of information in the sense that Machlup, Porat and other information society theorists have done. Rawls too toiled inside the iron cage of industrialism, and given his advantageous chronological position, the guilt of his sociological narrowness must exceed Tawney's. One searches his work in vain for 'informatisation', 'cyberspace', 'virtual reality', or any other contemporary key word, and even references to the traditional mass media are rare. The closest that Rawls (e.g. 1973: 101, 106) came to the information society thesis was occasional overtures to the platitude that modern societies are technological societies, or routine warnings about the perils of technocracy. This is disappointing, especially in light of the fact that Bell himself engaged respectfully with Rawls's work in the coda of *Coming of Post-Industrial Society* (1999: 440–46). Rawls failed to respond to Bell's critique, if he ever noticed it, despite their both being senior professors at Harvard University.

Even in his final work, Rawls (2001: 77, italics added) persisted in restricting his role to that of devising principles of justice for 'running an *industrial* economy'. Moreover, in one respect his philosophy appears to be fundamentally anti-information. The theory's famous central construct, a version of the social contract he calls the 'original position', involves precisely an information blackout. This 'veil of ignorance' will be analysed in more detail below, but at first sight it is clearly a device of apriorism, not of empiricism, still less of informationalism; and in its own way it seems to imply, as did Tawney's basic approach, that what does *not* really count, from a moral point of view, is information. Not surprisingly, then, an information perspective never swings fully into view in *Reading Rawls* (Daniels

1975) or any of the subsequent major collections of secondary literature (e.g. Richardson and Weithman 1999).

Nevertheless, Rawls can and must be appropriated for the normative theory of the information society. If Robert Nozick (1974: 183) was correct that 'political philosophers now must either work within Rawls' theory or explain why not', this is the case especially for theories of social democracy, including informatised social democracy. Thankfully, Rawls's philosophy is powerful enough to support such applications. The main reason, again as with Tawney, is that his prescriptive formulae were predicated not on historical or deterministic arguments, but on a chain of moral reasoning that is, in relevant respects, timeless and unfalsifiable—unfalsifiable in the modest sense of not being hostage to science or technology. And while it must be admitted that compared to Habermas or Foucault, say, Rawls has not found a prominent place in the information society debate, his relevance has slowly begun to be appreciated. Venturelli (1998: 8–32) argues with painstaking care that Rawls's work helped to establish the 'normative grounds of information policy'. Richard Collins (2000: 111) also describes Rawls's theory of justice as 'particularly germane' to discussions about the social goals of the 'global information society'. Several other contributions will be quoted below. But even if there were no Rawlsian information society theorists, the appropriation would still have to take place. The simple fact is that, such is his stature in moral-political thought, a reconstruction of Rawls is indispensable for any serious work today bearing at all on questions of social justice.

An undertaking to read Rawls and Tawney together is not original. Some of the most interesting and fruitful political philosophy of recent decades has been engaged in inquiries about social justice that negotiate the territory between Rawls and Tawney, and it is in these tracks that I wish to follow (e.g. Gutmann 1980; Emmet 1985; Kymlicka 2006). My argument will be that Tawney and Rawls represent respectively the left and right wings of social democratic thought, and I hope to be able to demonstrate that a combination of their positions, suitably updated and contextualised, represents a sound basis for a normative theory of the information society. The intention is to appeal to Rawls and Tawney, not in a genuflectory or propagandistic manner, but in order to appropriate their best ideas afresh—from an information perspective. Each, it will be suggested, has weaknesses as well as strengths, but the strengths can be amalgamated and the weaknesses ameliorated in such a way that a compelling synthesis materialises. Thus a Rawls-Tawney synthesis seeks to recover the authentic content of social democracy. If Tawney's socialist moralism can be coupled with Rawls's liberal proceduralism, along with an intelligent grasp of our new informatised socio-technical context, then perhaps we will have a promising programme for dealing with the normative crisis of the information society. For it is in the force-field between the left and right poles of social democratic thought that political wisdom will always be located.

DEONTOLOGICAL FOUNDATIONS OF INFORMATION POLICY

Like any other policy field, information policy needs to filter from not just empirical but also normative sources, including, ultimately, an account of the nature and requirements of social morality. Put another way, the normative theory of the information society involves the application of a doctrine of social ethics to post-industrialism. Perhaps unsurprisingly, such a demanding intellectual summons is rarely met, with the result that much information policy discourse appears strangely disconnected, if not downright superficial, and specific proposals, policies and laws go forth into the world devoid of robust normative underpinning. This does not mean that such policies are value-free, of course; it usually means that they are cryptonormative, that their values are hidden, either unintentionally or otherwise. While here is not the place for casework, inspection of information policy specimens generally exposes prescriptive propositions plucked out of nowhere, riding, we have to presume, on putatively morally-significant descriptive premises. 'Contemporary policy', as Graham (2006: 111) astutely observes, 'relies upon operationalizing what can only be described as an ongoing naturalistic fallacy: a continual movement from "is" to "ought," from fact to exhortation'. It is an ancient philosophical heresy.

This is especially true of much of the argumentation that has been thrust into the political public sphere on behalf of the purportedly 'new' social democracy of Giddens and others. Kanishka Jayasuriya (2000: 282–83) points out that 'third way theory is not a political theory in the conventional sense but an attempt to think through the emerging social complexity of contemporary society'; the problem with this is that 'it is simply a logical error to proceed from a description of social reality to the justification of a set of institutions'. And it is in addressing the fact-value problem, in supplying the path through what he referred to as the 'intermediate region where abstractions and practice meet' (Tawney 1952: 3) that Tawney— and also Rawls—make their first contribution, as it were, to the normative theory of the information society. Both thinkers won their international reputations for staking out that murky borderland between ethics and politics. The present section, accordingly, describes how, in their individual yet congruent ways, Tawney and Rawls explicated social morality and the foundations thereof. The headline finding, to anticipate, is that they both produced a counter-utilitarian, strongly deontological ethic, and one deliberately geared to the political and socioeconomic realms. The Rawls-Tawney synthesis that will be sketched below makes no more than a start, but hopefully it can serve as the base of a plausible trajectory for future normative information society theory. I begin here with Tawney.

Tawney's principal axiom, expressing what today would be called an holistic approach, was that morality is not merely a rulebook for individuals in their pilgrimage through life's innumerable dilemmas, as convention liked to suggest, but also applies directly and wholly to broader spheres, including the political, the cultural and the economic. The failure to project morality onto the communal scene was at the heart of the social problem as Tawney, unlike most of his Edwardian peers, saw it, since such a failure meant that society would be governed by self-interest rather than ideals. As he (Tawney 1972: 9) poignantly put it, 'modern politics are concerned with the manipulation of forces and interest. Modern society is sick through the absence of a moral ideal'. This luminous proposition, penned in his diary in 1914, eventually evolved into a famous pamphlet published by the Fabian Society (although it was not an official Fabian Tract), *The Sickness of an Acquisitive Society* (1920), and shortly thereafter into Tawney's first monograph on social philosophy, *The Acquisitive Society* (1982). There Tawney sought to diagnose the ills of the normless, materialistic, amoral world of industrial capitalism, and to prescribe a different order where every occupation and activity fulfilled a useful 'social function' and contributed to an overarching 'moral purpose'. For many of his generation, suffering economic mayhem shortly after the First World War, Tawney's message offered an attractive— although some thought utopian—ethical-socialist alternative.

The second main plank in Tawney's doctrine of social morality was a belief in the essential equality of human beings, a strong version of what is now termed moral egalitarianism. His other major work of social and political philosophy, *Equality,* still regarded as the bible of unreconstructed British socialism, began by citing cultural critic Matthew Arnold's polemic against the British (more specifically, English) 'religion of inequality' (Tawney 1964b: 33). Tawney identified in his egalitarian precursors a basic humanism, in the sense of a core belief in the value of our shared humanity. The equality which they championed was rooted not in any empirical reality but in an *a priori* judgement that what counts most about people is their relatedness. 'They are concerned', Tawney wrote (1964b: 49), 'not with a biological phenomenon, but with a spiritual relation and the conduct to be based on it. Their view, in short, is that, because men are men, social institutions—property rights, and the organization of industry, and the system of public health and education—should be planned, as far as is possible, to emphasize and strengthen, not the class differences which divide, but the common humanity which unites, them'. The enemy for such idealists then and now is class, caste and other inequitable modes of social division. The English class structure, like any other, was invidious because it was an unnatural, socially constructed, morally arbitrary expression of inequality, hence a form of political oppression. Tawney (1972: 69) also denounced racial inequality, including the virulent form then rampant in the Klan-infested US, while differences grounded in nature rather than nurture, such as those inextricably rooted in gender, rightly escaped his censure. However, the fact remains that we are equal not because we are equally muscular, intelligent or virtuous—or, it should now be added, because we are all information processors—or because of any other physical or psychological contingency, but simply because we are all human.

This unphenomenological equalitarianism issued in strict regulations for social and economic relations. Tawney spoke hauntingly of an objective moral order against which all actions and institutions will be judged, a framework of right for those negotiating the hazardous currents of modern politics. In particular, he derived from his own premises an outright rejection of the consequentialist morality which progressive thinkers, especially in the utilitarian tradition, seemed to share with right-wing apologists for the status quo. 'The rule is clear', Tawney (1972: 65–66) countered, '*no* convenience can justify *any* oppression. . . . One may *not* do evil that good should come'. Morality is not a cost-benefit analysis about possible states of the world, not a calculus of how an end might justify a means. Indeed, morality is not really about information at all. As Tawney put it (1972: 30), 'what is needed for the improvement of society is not so much that men should have profound information as to the possible result of their actions, but that they should realize that the conceptions "right and wrong" apply to all relations of life, including those where their application is most inconvenient, such as those of business, and that they should act on their knowledge'. Thus, what was being expressed was a *social deontology*, an absolutist doctrine of socioeconomic right, designed to place politics on an immovable, incorruptible basis.

Tawney, the high-born patrician who turned against private education and devoted his life to the empowerment of subordinate systacts, can be seen to have been treading in the footsteps of Thomas Arnold, father of Matthew and celebrated reforming headmaster of Rugby School. Dr Arnold had argued (1845: 3, 6), on what he called 'the grounds of right', in favour of Catholic political rights—'even at the hazard of injuring the Protestant Establishment'. The principle he supplied for what at the time was a courageous contribution to a divisive national debate—'all who possess the same human nature should be regarded as fit elements of civil society' (1845: 11)—was identical to the one later proposed by Tawney. Indeed, Tawney's entire philosophy can be viewed as an exercise in Arnoldian moral thoughtfulness and in the concomitant politics of *iustitia fiat et caelum ruat* (let right be done even if the sky falls). All of this can of course be brushed aside as 'cliché-ridden high-mindedness' and 'banal earnestness' (MacIntyre 1971: 39). However, while there may indeed be a rather ingenuous, even dogmatic, feel to Tawney's idealism, it at least seems to capture something of the essence of our profoundest inclinations about social morality; and Rawls's theory of justice, which no one would dare to accuse of being either banal or earnest, is arguably an expression of exactly the same basic intuitions.

Rawls, no less than Tawney, upheld the equality of man and, like Tawney, deduced from it a set of practical political principles. Born into a well-to-do Baltimore family, he described how in the summer holidays he would meet other boys who, for no evident reason, seemed to have far fewer opportunities—what he would later call 'life-chances'—than himself (Pogge 1999:

4). This sense that everyone shared the same basic worth was the seed of the moral egalitarianism to whose exposition he would dedicate his philosophical career. However, asked wherein the equality essentially lay, his answer would be different from Tawney's. Fascinatingly, the recent publication of his Princeton undergraduate dissertation on theology (2009) indicates that the young Rawls shared Tawney's belief in the kinship of all God's children. However, unlike Tawney's, his faith did not survive the experience of world war. So it is not, Rawls eventually concluded, some 'spiritual relation' that gives every human being a right to equal justice; rather, it is a natural or at least semi-natural attribute, what he calls a 'capacity for moral personality', specifically a capacity, or potential capacity, for having both a sense of fairness and a conception of the good life (Rawls 1973: 505). Every class and race has this attribute, and where in the occasional individual it may be lacking, as a result of mental retardation or some other special circumstance, this is easily accommodated as an abnormality. Rawls concedes that moral personality may be held in differing degrees among the normal too, but insists that a minimal capacity is all that is required as a foundation for equality. 'Those', as he expressed it in one of his pithy aphorisms (1973: 510), 'who can give justice are owed justice'.

Rawls's doctrine of equal rights was framed as a professional philosophical response to utilitarianism, the teleological ethical theory that could be used, and was actually being used, to justify not only major improvements in social welfare but also serious infringements of the rights of the individual. Like Tawney's, therefore, Rawls's egalitarianism resulted in an uncompromising deontological ethic. 'Each person', *A Theory of Justice* famously states (Rawls 1973: 3–4), 'possesses an inviolability founded on justice that even the welfare of society as a whole cannot override'. 'For this reason', it proceeds, 'justice denies that the loss of freedom for some is made right by a greater good shared by others. The rights secured by justice are not subject to political bargaining or to the calculus of social interests'. Rawls (1973: 31) soon honed his own social deontology into a concise formula, namely 'the priority of the right over the good'. While this proposition would later be debated by communitarian political philosophers (e.g. Sandel 2005: 152–55, 212ff.; Walzer 2004a) among others, it quickly established itself as the mantra of contemporary moral-political theory in the Kantian tradition. Its political significance hinges on the fact that people can be more easily led to find agreement on principles of justice, on rules of behaviour, on norms, than on what defines their ultimate goal in life (Rawls 1973: 447–48).

In such, Rawls-Tawney, if that phrase can be allowed when the two thinkers converge, has supplied for the post-industrial age a moral legacy of supreme importance. The emerging socio-technical formation must be built on solid grounds of right, on a rejection of the perilous, perennial principle that the end justifies the means. Specifically, the social deontology means that we should resist all attempts, however clever and well-intentioned, to revive a consequentialist justification of information policy (e.g. Fallis 2004a). However, the priority of the right over the good does not entail that the theory of the good can be neglected. It is a moral framework for holding together the differentiated subsystems of modern societies, one that imposes restraints on the excesses of teleological political action, but it is not a trump card for thwarting progressive social engineering. The theory of the good always holds a vital companion role in normative theory, balancing the theory of right by defining the moral purposes of social organisation. Once deontology's 'Thou shalt nots' have been saluted, positive politics must begin; or, as Rawls (1999a: 449) perspicuously rendered the relation, 'justice draws the limit, the good shows the point'.

Granting that egalitarianism and deontology are constitutive of the basic structure of the Rawls-Tawney perspective, there remains the question of their ultimate justification. Here, of course, we enter even more complex and controversial philosophical territory. And it is probable that even contemporary information society theorists comfortable with the methodological principle of drilling into the past for a source of norms for the future, and also enamoured with the traditional ideals of ethical egalitarianism, would—at least some would—want to distance themselves from Tawney's old-fashioned, Arnoldian anchor in Christianity. 'By affirming that all men are the children of God', he wrote in *Acquisitive Society* (1982: 185), the Christian religion 'insists that the rights of all men are equal'. The propositional content of social deontology is even portrayed as a preserve of western peoples, providing an inheritance from which the normative sociologist can derive his policies:

> We know it to be wrong for a man to live as though the effects of his actions upon his neighbours did not concern him. We know it to be wrong for one man to deceive another in order that thereby he may obtain pecuniary advantage. We know it to be wrong for one man to take advantage of the weakness of another in order to wring out of him terms to which he would not submit if he were a free agent. This knowledge is, I would urge, the common property of Christian nations . . . Very well then—what is the task of the sociologist? It is, I submit, to show how these universally accepted principles may be applied to particular sets of social conditions. (Tawney 1972: 30–31)

Moral knowledge is not, however, merely a function of historical or geographical contingency. It is ontologically, that is, necessarily, dependent on a theistic faith. 'The essence of all morality', Tawney continued, 'is this':

> to believe that every human being is of infinite importance, and therefore that no consideration of expediency can justify the oppression of one by another. But to believe this it is necessary to believe in God.

To estimate men simply by their place in a social order is to sanction the sacrifice of man to that order. It is only when we realize that each individual soul is related to a power above other men, that we are able to regard each as an end in itself. In other words the idea of 'humanity' stultifies itself. The social order is judged and condemned by a power transcending it. (Tawney 1972: 67–68)

Startling though such statements may look, they rest unproblematically within a major tradition of British political thought, Christian socialism (e.g. Bryant 1996; Reisman 1996). Of course, that would not prevent their being anathema to some of the thinkers who have set the philosophical-political pace in critical information society theory. Donna Haraway's promethean 'Manifesto for Cyborgs', notably, puts cyborgs rather than God's children at the heart of her 'ironic faith', her 'blasphemy' (2001: 28). For Lash too there is no moral fulcrum outside the information society itself, outside the matrix. He cites Haraway's 'modest witness' as the most that can be attained, one that permits only a form of judgement 'without transcendentals' (2002: 9) and definitely without theological transcendentals. And Castells's hostility to religion is palpable throughout *The Information Age*. At the very start, he reports darkly that 'the informational society, in its global manifestation, is also the world of Aum Shinrikyo, of American Militia, of Islamic/Christian theocratic ambitions, and of Hutu/Tutsi reciprocal genocide' (Castells 2000: 2-3). Later he sees fit to discuss Christianity under the mocking heading 'God Save Me! American Christian Fundamentalism' (Castells 2004: 23). Yet antagonism to religion cannot be found anywhere in the original manifesto of the information age, *The Coming of Post-Industrial Society*. On the contrary, there is only respect. Far from dismissing religious belief as an irrational form of identity, Bell always maintained its continuing value and significance. Indeed, his Hobhouse Memorial Lecture (1977), delivered at the LSE a generation after Tawney's retirement, accurately predicted, without alarm and contrary to then sociological orthodoxy, the flourishing of spirituality in the twenty-first century. Some social philosophers have gone much further, seeing the 'venerable but by no means outdated social values of Christianity' as integral to the computerised future (Lenk 1986: 245). I will return to this nexus shortly.

Rawls, who stands alongside Tawney as a precious source of wisdom for the post-industrial epoch, justified his social morality very differently. Eschewing all appeals to metaphysics, he sought instead to locate in pure practical reason a moral point of view of sufficient weight to serve as an acceptable basis for a modern theory of justice. The task of moral epistemology as Rawls recast it was to work up a manageable intellectual procedure for deducing specific principles. As mentioned above, his solution took the intriguing form of the 'original position', essentially the familiar liberal concept of the state of nature taken to a much higher level of abstraction. His version of the social contract 'signed' in this, as it were, virtual environment had one outstanding peculiarity. The 'veil of ignorance' stipulates that principles of justice must 'be chosen in the absence of certain kinds of particular information' (Rawls 1973: 449). At first sight, this looks paradoxical, even perverse, from an information perspective. However, it was actually only one class of information that was hidden. There needed to be no limitations on *general* information, the kinds of information germane to what I have called the journalistic conception of information. On the contrary, Rawls's contracting agents are apprised of numerous relevant facts about political affairs, economic theory, psychology, and all the sciences that they require to know 'if they are to choose the principles to regulate their social world' (1973: 137–38). It was only personal knowledge that was redacted in this imaginary state of nature, such factors as the contractors' race, gender, social class, occupation, ambitions and even their 'theory of the good', including their conception of the meaning of life. Thus veiled, Rawls plausibly suggests, the argument could be followed wherever it led.

In this way the original position achieves for political principles a large measure of objectivity, to some extent 'proofing' them against the sociology of knowledge:

> They are the principles that we would want everyone (including ourselves) to follow were we to take up together the appropriate general point of view. The original position defines this perspective, and its conditions also embody those of objectivity: its stipulations express the restrictions on arguments that force us to consider the choice of principles unencumbered by the singularities of the circumstances in which we find ourselves. The veil of ignorance prevents us from shaping our moral view to accord with our own particular attachments and interests. We do not look at the social order from our situation but take up a point of view that everyone can adopt on an equal footing. (Rawls 1973: 516)

Rawls did not just devise and elaborate this abstract position; he argued that principles of justice evolving from behind the veil, and indeed from any alternative heuristic device, needed to be tested against ordinary moral sentiments. Moral theory is thus to be understood as an iterative experiment to find a match between general philosophical principles and particular real-world intuitions. 'There is', he wrote, 'a definite if limited class of facts against which conjectured principles can be checked, namely, our considered judgments in reflective equilibrium' (Rawls 1973: 51).

Reflective equilibrium should be greeted as another major Rawlsian contribution to normative thought, including the normative theory of the information society. It is defined as the mental state reached after that

Socratic process of interrogation of principles against intuitions, a plateau, as it were, from which a higher match cannot be seen. It is found 'after a person has weighed various proposed conceptions and he has either revised his judgments to accord with one of them or held fast to his initial convictions (and the corresponding conception)' (Rawls 1973: 48). The essential idea is that innovative normative theories should not be allowed to ride roughshod over strongly-held moral views, because if they do they will lack popular legitimacy and thus have little feasibility as prescriptions for democratic politics. On the other hand, however, people's less confidently-held intuitions should be open to revision in light of well-argued normative theory, otherwise they may be no more than flimsy prejudices. For example, while convictions regarding the wrongness of slavery are fixed—for, as the greatest US president wrote, 'if slavery is not wrong, nothing is wrong' (Lincoln quoted in Rawls 2001: 29)—the vulgar prejudice supporting the existence of a class of idle rich (whether aristocrats or 'celebrities') may be vulnerable to cogent social democratic argumentation. The aim of political reasoning is to pass *via* this methodology to a secure normative position. Such, according to Rawls, is the only reasonably safe way to conceptualise moral-political knowledge.

In thus orienting the theory of justice, Rawls demonstrates that it is not necessary to sign up to what some would find a burdensome metaphysical commitment, in order to ground policymaking in a robust social morality. However, one wonders if more synergy cannot be found in this dimension of Rawls-Tawney. For while Rawls's account is indeed overtly secularist, it could be argued that the differences are to some extent more apparent than real. 'Axiological patterns', Graham registers (2006: 161), 'are achievements of history—a massive accumulation of normative work'. Yet while secular universalism is definitely 'normatively inscribed' in liberal democracy (Venturelli 1998: 10), especially in its doctrine of rights, this is hardly the only fount of our way of life. The widespread intuitions which comprise the raw stock of Rawls's theory of justice, and which he acknowledges to be peculiar to advanced liberal democracies such as the US, can be seen as having been partly moulded by a specifically Christian mentality as well. It is a matter of uncontroversial historical record that the Judeo-Christian tradition has enjoyed a salient position in the social morality of the West, and in this sense Tawney was expressing no more than a platitude in that reference above to 'the common knowledge of Christian nations'. Even his atheistic contemporary George Orwell could pay tribute to 'the liberal-Christian culture' (1962: 48) of Britain. So the claim can be made, by social democratic thinkers sympathetic to *both* Rawls and Tawney, that Rawls's deontology owes more to Christianity than Rawls himself was (after his apostasy) prepared to acknowledge.

This line of reasoning has been deftly developed by theologian Duncan Forrester (1997, 2001; cf. Cort 2003). However, it has also recently been pursued from outside the fold, by no less a philosophical-sociological authority than Habermas. Tawney's ontology is an articulation of the kind of position Habermas used to refer to caustically as a 'religiously sublimated sacred realm . . . rooted in the sacred fusion of facticity and validity' (1996: 26), and presumably therefore an egregious instance of the naturalistic fallacy. 'The idealistic content of normative theories', Habermas eloquently declared (1996: 329), 'has been evaporating under the sun of social science'. But now he seems to be retreating from these grand, and arguably hubristic, claims of 'sociological enlightenment' (1996: 329). The mature Habermas has upset some of his admirers by affirming that religious normativism has to be taken seriously. In *Dialectics of Enlightenment*, a momentous dialogue with Joseph Ratzinger prior to the latter's elevation to the papacy, he argues that 'philosophy must be ready to learn from theology, not only for functional reasons, but also for substantial reasons', and in particular to assimilate the value of 'normative conceptual clusters', namely those encased in religious concepts like 'responsibility', 'emancipation' and 'fellowship' (Habermas 2005: 44). These clusters, he now believes, can still serve to assist in the recovery of 'social solidarity' (2005: 44–45), that vital ingredient which is now so lacking in liberal democracies, and whose defence arguably has been the central thread of the entire Habermasian *oeuvre*. Influencing any conceivable characterisation of the original position, or at any rate western conceptualisation of such, these moral lumps compose a proportion of the pre-political foundations of democratic civilisation. Do unto others as you would have them do to you: such is the substance of the 'overlapping consensus' (Rawls 1999c) out of which the politics of post-industrial nations must be wrought. Thus, even if one rejects the view that it enjoys any transcendent validation, the social deontology as articulated by Rawls-Tawney remains a major cultural resource for the normative theory of the information society—or so I beg to suggest.

PRINCIPLES OF JUSTICE: THE CONVERGENCE OF RAWLS AND TAWNEY

While attempts to underpin information policy with moral and political philosophy are not uncommon, a twinned invocation of Rawls and Tawney in this relatively new department of thought is extremely rare. It is therefore gratifying to come across Anthony Wilhelm's *Digital Nation: Toward an Inclusive Information Society* (2004). The book projects a vision of the good society which is social democratic in more or less the same sense that the present chapter is seeking to develop. Sporting at the beginning a quotation from *A Theory of Justice*, it ends by loudly echoing both Rawls and Tawney. 'Navigating this society', Wilhelm writes (2004:

134), 'will require that people be motivated and empowered to invent their own futures, buoyed by a new social contract in which rampant inequalities sown by the acquisitive spirit are tempered by the tender embrace of liberty, equality, and solidarity'. However, while the treatise is a competent contribution to what I am calling the normative theory of the information society, it does not fully explicate the nature of liberty, equality and solidarity, nor specify in sufficient detail the ways in which such potentially divergent ideals can be made to hang together in the post-industrial era. Thus, building upon the common ground identified in the previous section—albeit terrain ultimately located in alternative world views—this section seeks to further develop a thorough Rawls-Tawney synthesis. Synthesis has just taken place 'upstream', in the philosophy of social morality, but it now needs to be outworked 'downstream', in the form of practical politico-economic principles. The contention here is that Rawls and Tawney can offer a smart, future-proofed blend of the right-wing and left-wing poles of social democratic thought.

Rawls explicitly positions social justice as the superordinate, regulative concept, the umpire, as it were, between liberty, equality and fraternity. 'Justice', proclaims that magisterial first page of *A Theory of Justice*, 'is the first virtue of social institutions, as truth is of systems of thought. A theory however elegant and economical must be rejected or revised if it is untrue; likewise laws and institutions no matter how efficient and well-arranged must be reformed or abolished if they are unjust' (Rawls 1973: 3). Rawls famously propounded two 'principles of justice', as well as articulating, with a precision unequalled in the history of political thought, the relationship between them, and between the social values that they define. Although wedded to basically the same values, Tawney, being a much less organised and systematic thinker, did not supply an account that was anything like as complete or exact. For that reason, and recalling Nozick's gauntlet quoted above, the proper approach from now on must be for Tawney's ideas to be welded onto the Rawlsian framework, rather than the other way round. While chronological considerations suggest the reverse, logic dictates that the synthesis in all its essential phases is Rawls-Tawney.

At the heart of any doctrine of social justice must be some kind of specification of the resources whose scarcity makes considerations of fairness or equity necessary in the first place. Rawls calls such resources 'primary goods' (or more precisely, 'social primary goods', as distinct from natural primary goods such as beauty or intelligence), defining them as 'things every rational man is presumed to want' (Rawls 1973: 62). 'These goods', he continues, 'normally have a use whatever a person's rational plan of life. For simplicity, assume that the chief primary goods at the disposition of society are rights and liberties, powers and opportunities, income and wealth'. The list clearly identifies the priorities of most normal human beings in any era. It may not be exhaustive, but it contains nothing that would not be sought by any adult, barring lunatics, saints and the other usual exceptions. Rawls's next move was to argue that while fairness demands that an equal division of primary goods should act as the initial benchmark, the default, inequalities *may* be sanctioned if every member of society, and in particular its worst off members, benefit materially from them. This far-reaching value judgement is expressed in the following principle, which Rawls calls the General Conception of Justice:

General Conception of Justice

All social primary goods—liberty and opportunity, income and wealth, and the bases of self-respect—are to be distributed equally unless an unequal distribution of any or all of these goods is to the advantage of the least favoured. (Rawls 1973: 302)

According to Rawls, this conception applies only to pre-industrial countries: in such societies, no single good has priority over another. Thus, on such premises, it is conceivably fair even to limit certain basic liberties if doing so can be shown to maximise the production and distribution of economic goods. The operative intuition is that, where life is primitive, or as Bell (1999: 30–31) would put it, 'a game against nature', bread comes before even freedom. Such has, of course, been integral to the ideological rhetoric of most outbreaks of revolutionary egalitarianism in the third world. Its most eloquent philosophical champion was perhaps Ted Honderich in *Violence for Equality* (1980).

In industrial societies, however, and presumably also in post-industrial societies, the primary goods should not be treated uniformly. According to Rawls, now indisputably representing our tradition of social democracy, a particular ranking captures non-negotiable intuitions about justice. Social democracy must be first and foremost a politics of liberty, because it is a variant—many supporters would say, a logical extension—of liberal democracy. Rawls therefore enshrines freedom as his first principle of justice, and gives it absolute (or what with typical exactitude and originality he calls lexicographical, i.e. the kind of priority codified in an alphabetical dictionary) priority over socioeconomic rights. This fundamental bifurcation of justice into two parts, applicable only to societies wherein the achievement of a reasonable level of material security has made possible a preoccupation with liberal freedoms, obviously covers the present case. A normative theory of the information society pertains by definition only to those nations that have already undergone industrialisation, and where the issue of a stark choice between famine and freedom does not arise.

The exact wording of the first principle of justice underwent subtle refinements during Rawls's career, as he responded to his critics. However, the final formulation, to be found in *Justice as Fairness: A Restatement*, reads as follows:

First Principle of Justice

Each person has the same indefeasible claim to a fully adequate scheme of equal basic liberties, which scheme is compatible with the same scheme of liberties for all. (Rawls 2001: 42)

Rawls believed that this paramount right to freedom followed from his bedrock moral egalitarianism. Equality is explicitly built into the principle, in the sense that 'each person' means literally all adult citizens regardless of colour, race or gender. Such, of course, is the very charter of liberal democracy. The particulars of Rawls's 'fully adequate scheme' are also unremarkable from a modern point of view. The scheme consists of a familiar set of legal rights, including freedom of conscience and expression, freedom of religion, freedom of association, freedom from arbitrary arrest and seizure, political liberty in the contemporary liberal democratic sense of the right to vote, and also the right to own private, although not necessarily productive, property. Hence it covers what Rawls elsewhere (1996: 5) called the 'liberty of the ancients'—political autonomy and participation—as well as the 'liberty of the moderns'—individual privacy and choices.

Tawney too insisted on a literal interpretation of political freedom. He made liberty the cornerstone of his politics, and held to it even as many of his peers in politically advanced circles were succumbing enthusiastically to the proverbial totalitarian temptation. By 'socialism', he stated unambiguously, 'we mean freedom' (Tawney 1981b: 82). He compared 'authoritarian collectivisms' unfavourably with 'democratic socialism', and unpacked the latter in unashamedly bourgeois-democratic fashion in terms of non-negotiable accountability to elected assemblies (e.g. Tawney 1964a: 169). His outspoken, unequivocal attack on 'Russian police collectivism' demonstrated his integrity:

The truth is that a conception of Socialism which views it as involving the nationalisation of everything except political power, on which all else depends, is not, to speak with moderation, according to light. The question is not merely whether the State owns and controls the means of production. It is also who owns and controls the State. It is not certain, though it is probable, that Socialism can in England be achieved by the methods proper to democracy. It is certain that it cannot be achieved by any other; nor, even if it could, should the supreme goods of civil and political liberty, in whose absence no Socialism worthy of the name can breathe, be part of the price. (Tawney 1981a: 165–66)

This liberty-first stance is evident also throughout his unpublished materials, for example in a speech to the London Fabian Society where he counselled that as regards foreign policy in a bipolar world the British left had no choice but to side with the US; otherwise, they were contemplating 'the end of social democracy' (Tawney 1952: 17). That is to say, 'he self-consciously remained faithful to the liberal democratic tradition in his vision of a fully socialist society' (Gutmann 1980: 78). Bell expressed the same priority rule with his usual panache, insisting in *The End of Ideology* (1988: 447) that 'democracy and legal rights are an inviolable condition for a decent society and that liberty, necessarily, has to be prior even to socialism'. In Rawlsian terms, Tawney (and Bell) endorsed the lexical priority of liberty over other social values.

It can be said that the liberty principle constitutes the first component in a set of principles produced by a convergence of the political ideals of Rawls and Tawney. It is also the most important generic policy orientation of the normative theory of the information society. Of course, the retrieval of the liberty principle does not in itself solve all, or even any, of the concrete information policy issues of freedom in our epoch. Even within the political solar system of liberal democracy, much of the daily business of public debate revolves around divergent interpretations of particular aspects of the liberty principle, such as freedom of expression or of assembly. Never was this more the case than today (although it is too easy to speak that way), when civil liberties face new, restrictive construals as a result of anti-establishment threats real and imagined, and when corporations overpower individuals by intrusions into privacy and expansions of the dominion of intellectual property rights and libel. The normative theory of the information society is confronted, therefore, with its own full agenda of interpretation and casuistry. It must decide where exactly the liberty principle points on the political questions that distinguish right and left, libertarianism and collectivism, entitlements and responsibilities. Subsequent chapters will make bold to participate in some of those ongoing conversations.

The first principle enjoys supremacy, but once it has been satisfied other claims immediately come into play. The priority rule allows that once a conception of *political* justice has been defended, we are in a position to address *economic* justice, since both are necessary elements of social justice. In its final formulation, Rawls's second principle was drafted as follows:

Second Principle of Justice

Social and economic inequalities are to satisfy two conditions: first, they are to be attached to offices and positions open to all under conditions of fair equality of opportunity; and second, they are to be to the greatest benefit of the least-advantaged members of society (the difference principle). (Rawls 2001: 42–43)

The two conditions can be regarded as ways of *realising* the freedoms guaranteed by the first principle. 'Taking the two principles together', Rawls wrote (1973: 205), 'the basic structure is to be arranged to maximize the worth to the least advantaged of the complete scheme of liberty shared by all. This defines the end of social justice'. This confirms that the conception of freedom which the first principle expresses is indeed the straightforward, dictionary one. It defines social spaces wherein an agent is empowered to act without interference by other agents. Rawls thereby disowns the proposition, advanced by some left-liberals since at least as far back as Green (1986b), that poverty or ignorance reduce one's liberty; rather, Rawls stresses (1973: 204), they reduce the *worth* of liberty. This is a significant clarification, because it instantly rules out Marxism-Leninism and other species of vanguard politics notorious for cracking down on the press, etc, in the name of a putative 'positive' freedom. Social democratically-inclined analytical philosophers since Bertrand Russell (1896, 1920) have made sure to avoid bewitchment by that particular language-game.

The second principle is evidently duplex; one might say that it is two principles, yet they are better treated as sides of a coin because they are both intrinsic elements of socioeconomic justice. The first clause requires equality of opportunity. Now formal equality of opportunity has for many liberals been the alpha and omega of their egalitarianism, but both of my key thinkers convincingly exposed its limitations as a complete social ideal. Thus Rawls (1973: 65) makes a distinction between 'formal equality of opportunity' and 'equality of fair opportunity'. The former captures the classic modern idea of 'les carrières ouvertes aux talents', a situation which obtains when all classes, creeds, and colours have the same rights of access to desirable professions and positions. This is a necessary legal component of social justice, one almost too obvious to mention and of course universally recognised in advanced societies, at least on paper; it is 'the acceptable face of equality, commanding support across the political spectrum' (Swift 2001: 98). However, it does not go nearly far enough. It needs to be filled out by a more substantive socioeconomic conditioning as defined by fair equality of opportunity. 'The thought here', Rawls writes (1973: 73), 'is that positions are to be not only open in a formal sense, but that all should have a fair chance to attain them. Offhand it is not clear what is meant, but we might say that those with similar abilities and skills have similar life-chances'. However, fair equality of opportunity is also inadequate. Even if the state guarantees everyone a roughly equal start in life it does not follow that social arrangements can claim to be civilised. The intuition now is that a society where all start the race together but where there develop serious gaps in the running-rates and at the finishing-post can hardly be a model of social democracy, of the sisterhood of humanity, of the kingdom of ends. What counts as 'serious' is a moot point that will be addressed shortly, but there is no doubt that justice as fairness asks questions of egalitarianism as pure equality of opportunity; the latter can too easily lead, as not just Rawls but many other left-liberals have pointed out, to a callous society, a world of stark contrasts between winners and losers.

For Tawney, too, equality of opportunity was profoundly insufficient. He caricatured it quaintly as the 'Tadpole Philosophy', i.e. the idea that the tadpole community should be reconciled to its predicament because a tiny fraction of its number turns into frogs (Tawney 1964b: 105). His expressive version of the critique of equal opportunities has been influential in political philosophy, reaching other distinguished practitioners in the analytical tradition (e.g. Barry 2005: 40ff.). The lesson is that the concept of equality of opportunity forces upon us the deeper and more politically-contentious issue of equality of outcomes. Once the outpost of political democracy has been secured, just how far into the socioeconomic hinterland do we want to push the principle of democracy? Should the grim sight of an underprivileged neighbourhood evoke British conservative leader Margaret Thatcher's slogan 'get out if you can' or American socialist leader Eugene Debs's 'I don't want to rise above the working class, I want to rise *with* the working class'? Fundamentally incompatible images of the good society are at stake. Hence a second principle, a second clause, must impose itself.

It is an issue whose central importance for the information age was clear to the ever-watchful Bell. 'The post-industrial society', he stated, 'in its initial logic, is a meritocracy. Differential status and differential income are based on technical skills and higher education. Without those achievements one cannot fulfill the requirements of the new social division of labor which is a feature of that society' (Bell 1999: 410). Writing in the late 1960s and early '70s, Bell observed that meritocracy had come under severe attack from egalitarians, for being a form of elitism. Indeed, he goes as far as to say that precisely this struggle between meritocracy as equality of opportunity and a stronger version of egalitarianism demanding equality of outcome is 'the central value problem of the post-industrial society' (Bell 1999: 425). 'The claim for "equality of result"', in the Bellian classification (1999: 433), 'is a socialist ethic (as equality of opportunity is the liberal ethic)'. He notes too that in Marxism, a major inspiration of that era, 'the normative ethic was only implicit; it was never spelled out and justified' (Bell 1999: 433). In Rawls, on the other hand, normative reasoning is central; indeed, in *A Theory of Justice* 'we have the most comprehensive effort in modern philosophy to justify a socialist ethic' (Bell 1999: 444). Incidentally, Bell himself (1999: 451ff.) came down in favour of a 'just meritocracy'. While he endorsed the welfare state as a safety-net for those deficient in the merits demanded by the post-industrial interpersonal game (e.g. Bell 1996d: 266, 281–82), he spurned arguments for a fuller, more radical ('rigid, ideological') egalitarianism (1999: 452). That is why he has been targeted, although the charge is actually absurd, as a neo-conservative (e.g. Steinfels 1979).

In any case, the normative theory of the information society here must part company decisively with the stern father of post-industrialism and embrace a redder version of social democracy. Tawney and Rawls, being each in his own way enthusiastic rather than merely clinical about achieving more fairness in society, were able to appreciate that equality of opportunity needs to be made good by a significant measure of equality of results.

And this was definitely about more than the relief of distress. They were both egalitarians in the true sense; they had made that crucial leap from liberal democracy, the politics of individual freedom, to social democracy, the politics of the common good. Certainly there must first be political and civil liberty. There must also be equal opportunity. Yet those principles have for aeons sat more or less undisturbed across the entire range of mainstream political opinion within democratic states. It is only when a party starts moving further towards social equality that it will run into political flak. Equality of outcome is the Rubicon of European and North American politics, at least, and it is an ideological river that Rawls and Tawney, unlike Bell, crossed. Yet what lies beyond? The land on the other side of the river is far from homogeneous, and it is there, a good distance downstream from the ontological differences that separated them, where more philosophical tensions between Tawney and Rawls surface. How exactly should equality of outcome be understood? What is its extent? Precisely what level of permissible differential are we talking about? Their answers to these politically-loaded questions are far enough apart to make necessary a meticulous analytical and then synthetical operation.

The traditional interpretation of social democracy, what is sometimes called 'arithmetic' egalitarianism, advocates policies to reduce inequalities, leading to more or less identical shares of land, wealth, income, or other base of social status. It is the common-sense meaning of the word 'equality' and it is this goal that has inspired countless movements for social justice, with varying degrees of reflexivity. But Rawls crafted a fresh approach. He did not invent the intuitions on which it rests, but he expressed and presented them with such persuasiveness that he succeeded in opening a new vista for egalitarian thinking, a new paradigm. While acknowledging the moral force of arithmetic equality as a benchmark, he argued that it is possible to justify departures from the benchmark if, and only if, everyone, and particularly the worst off, benefit from them. 'There is no injustice', he writes, 'in the greater benefits earned by a few provided that the situation of persons not so fortunate is thereby improved' (Rawls 1973: 15). This 'difference principle' is widely hailed as Rawls's special contribution to the repertoire of principles of distributive justice in the western tradition. Its genius consists in its holding in creative tension two very powerful moral intuitions: that equal shares are fair, at least as the default; but also that inequalities can be acceptable if the incentives that they allow lead to a greater total cake, thus benefiting everyone, including the worst off. For who really wants an equality of misery? The economic assumption is that the generation of primary goods such as wealth is not a zero-sum game. If the total pie can be increased then everyone can be better off than they would be with an exact share of a smaller pie. It is thus a form of 'geometric' egalitarianism, an egalitarianism with carefully-drawn spaces for individuality and differentiation, and from its perspective arithmetic equality is simplistic, if not, indeed, irrational.

The difference principle, Rawls asserts (1973: 101), 'transforms the aims of the basic structure so that the total scheme of institutions no longer emphasizes social efficiency and technocratic values'. But it also upholds a sober understanding of human nature. Bluntly, Rawls's belief was that even under the best conceivable conditions people would still be interested in bank balances, not just their own but also those of their neighbours. While he accepted that people can act altruistically, he also thought, and codified in what he called 'the circumstances of justice' (1973: 126ff.), that there are unavoidable limits to that side of our motivational structure. It is important to understand that when he argued for limited inequality as the principle that should govern the distribution of socioeconomic goods, this was not because he thought that some deserved more than others. It was because he thought that, given human nature, if one lets the few win, the many will also benefit. It thus involves a less naive idea of political possibilities than that dear to arithmetic egalitarians. A manifestation of the difference between liberal egalitarianism and the utopian bent of much leftism, it implies that Bell was factually mistaken to categorise Rawls's theory of justice as socialist. Instead, the difference principle seems to find a halfway-house between the draconian socialist doctrine that all inequalities are evil, a function of exploitative surplus value, and the complacent neo-conservative conceit that social justice is satisfied by a few resources eventually trickling down from rich to poor. Arguably, the profound, far-reaching value judgement crystallised in Rawls's principle helped social democracy to grow up and join the adult political world. By prompting a paradigm shift to differential equality, it put justice on a feasible electoral trajectory in a post-utopian—in the sense of 'utopian' applicable to Masuda and his ilk, among others—and post-industrial dispensation.

However, while the difference principle should be clasped, it must be handled with caution. As a long tradition of exegesis attests (e.g. Lucas 1980; Martin 2001; van Parijs 2003), it lends itself to both left-wing and right-wing readings. Indeed, the interpretation of the difference principle could be seen as being more or less coterminous with the entire territory of mainstream economic politics in western democracies. Staunch socialists were quick to denounce it as 'profoundly wrong', as amounting to little more than a sophisticated justification of neo-liberalism (Crick 1972; cf. Cohen 2008). A rising economic tide lifts all boats, so does the difference principle not allow great gains for the rich for only small gains for the poor? Rawls himself always denied this, and in later statements (e.g. 1999b: 416) confirmed, albeit belatedly, that he saw European-style social democracy as a concrete instantiation of his principle. We must believe Rawls's own account, surely, bearing in mind that he had always presented the difference principle as a 'maximin' principle, i.e. one that maximised—not just marginally improved—the minimum, the position of the worst off (Rawls 1973: 152). However, there is something important in the objection. If there is a weakness in Rawls's theory, it is an undeveloped and inadequate conception of fraternity. It is not that he entirely forgot it. 'In justice as fairness', he movingly wrote, 'men agree to share one another's fate' (Rawls 1973: 102). However, Rawls's value of fraternity is very thin. Indeed, on his own admission it vanishes entirely into the difference principle: as he put it, 'the difference principle expresses [fraternity's] fundamental meaning from the standpoint of social justice' (1973: 106). There is surely more than that to the brotherhood of man?

So it is here that the Rawlsian framework again needs to be reinforced by the ideas of Tawney. Arithmetic egalitarianism is a school within which Tawney's work has been naturally situated. *Equality*, in particular, tends to be referenced as a statement of egalitarianism in this strict sense (e.g. Barry 2000; Clift and Tomlinson 2002; Radice 1965). Such attributions are entirely warranted. According to the text, social justice prescribes a united moral relationship among social actors, a uniform pattern in civil society's fabric. It demands not only the opening of the social heights to outstanding individuals, as in equality of opportunity, but also collective movements to narrow the space between the submerged systacts in the social valleys and those atop the 'Himalayas' of wealth (Tawney 1964b: 120). To reduce social space, a bold political pincer movement was required. Tawney upbraided egalitarians who shrank from the logical consequences. 'When the press assails them', he wrote (Tawney 1964b: 40; cf. 1972: 52), 'with the sparkling epigram that they desire, not merely to make the poor richer, but to make the rich poorer, instead of replying, as they should, that, being sensible men, they desire both, since the extremes both of riches and poverty are degrading and anti-social, they are apt to take refuge in gestures of deprecation. They make war on destitution, but they sometimes turn, it seems, a blind eye on privilege'. Tawney himself boldly attacked not just poverty but also wealth, because he believed that only a large measure of equality of circumstance, of outcome, could express real social morality. The axiom that every person is, in some deep sense, of equal worth, might not entail identical resources, but it does place a severe cap on the gap between rich and poor, *whatever* the GNP or other indicator of the total social cake.

Tawney was in practice rather evasive about the specifics of differentials, partly because he knew that as a university professor he accepted an income 'five times as large as that of the average working-class family' (1964b: 40). However, it is fairly clear that his conception of social democracy involved top earners taking home only *circa* five or six times, and certainly no more than nine or ten times—thirteen was definitely 'shocking' (Tawney 1952: 7)—the income of the lowest paid. He always argued for progressive taxation, including heavy death-duties, setting the maximum heritable estate at £50,000, at most a modest few million euros in today's terms. Fiscal policy should eventually guarantee that there would be no more haughty rich and their self-centred, insufferable offspring, no long-term viability of the odious social construct 'gentleman', no more of what his contemporary

Thorstein Veblen (1953) memorably called the 'leisure class'. Tawney's overriding concern was that differentials should not be allowed to turn into class divisions, because he saw social classes as anathema, as shallow artifices that militated against an essentially communal moral order. As *Equality* thundered (1964b: 113):

> What is repulsive is not that one man should earn more than others, for where community of environment, and a common education and habit of life, have bred a common tradition of respect and consideration, these details of the counting-house are forgotten or ignored. It is that some classes should be excluded from the heritage of civilization which others enjoy, and that the fact of human fellowship, which is ultimate and profound, should be obscured by economic contrasts, which are trivial and superficial. What is important is not that all men should receive the same pecuniary income. It is that the surplus resources of society should be so husbanded and applied that it is a matter of minor significance whether they receive it or not.

'Men', for Tawney, as for any real leftist, should always *treat* one another as comrades. If fellowship is merely *implicit* in fair institutions, as Rawls held, then much of the meaning of our common humanity remains politically untapped. 'The sage', Tawney elaborated (1964b: 160), 'who defined his Utopia as a society in which any man can say to any other, "Go to hell", but no man wants to say it, and no man need go when it is said, may have been crude in expression, but he was sound in substance'. That is to say, inequalities are allowable if the worst off benefit materially from them, but they must be stopped before they reach the point at which they tip over into interpersonal communicative breakdown, into estrangement—what Robert Fortner (1995) would call 'excommunication'. 'All decent people', Tawney had confided to his diary shortly before the internecine apocalypse of the Great War, 'are at heart conservatives, in the sense of desiring to conserve the human associations, loyalties, affections, pious bonds between man and man which express a man's personality and become at once a sheltering nest for his spirit and a kind of watch-tower from which he may see visions of a more spacious and bountiful land' (Tawney 1972: 14). That marvellous vision of human solidarity, conspicuous by its absence in Rawls's intentionally unencumbered theory of justice, is at the very centre of Tawney's social ideal—which is indeed 'socialism as fellowship' (Terrill 1973). It should be considered the greatest gift to the normative theory of the information society from Tawney, indeed from the whole corpus of Christian socialism that had originated with Maurice a century before (Marsden 2004). That tradition answered Cain's savage question in Genesis, 'Am I my brother's keeper?', with a resounding 'Yes'. And in the Tawney formulation it would have allayed the late G. A. Cohen's misgivings about the difference principle, misgivings which, as he confessed on a number of occasions (e.g.

2001: 1), brought the distinguished Marxian philosopher surprisingly close to Christianity.

Fortified by Tawney's fraternalism, Rawls's second principle rises out of mere liberalism or progressivism, out of the respectable politics of anti-poverty action, and into unmistakable social democratic country. The option for the poor is joined by the much more troublesome option against the rich. Thus what we have arrived at is a basic philosophical fusion of Tawney's and Rawls's positions on socioeconomic equality. This comprises the third module of the Rawls-Tawney synthesis, the first being the major overlap in their accounts of the deontological foundation of policy, and the second the shared ground in their doctrines of the priority and content of political liberty. It offers a new form of what Will Kymlicka (2006: 31) calls 'left-liberal marriage', a convergence of the hard-headed liberal conception of distributive justice and the emotive ideal of social equality and comradeship preached by socialism. Before moving on, however, there is another important dimension of economic justice, quite separate from fair shares in the consumption of resources, namely the politically explosive issue of justice as regards control of the means of production, or, in the vernacular, the question of 'public ownership'. In this matter too, the two key thinkers represent very clearly the left- and right-wing poles of the social democratic tradition, so again a *via media* needs to be found.

Rawls leaned firmly towards a private economy. Formally, he argued that both are *a priori* compatible with his principles. 'The choice between a private-property economy and socialism', he says (1973: 258), 'is left open'. 'Which of these systems', he proceeds (1973: 274), 'and the many intermediate forms most fully answers to the requirements of justice cannot, I think, be determined in advance. There is presumably no general answer to this question, since it depends in large part upon the traditions, institutions, and social forces of each country, and its particular historical circumstances. The theory of justice does not include these matters'. However, in the second part of *A Theory of Justice*, where we are vouchsafed a case study of an institutional setup that would satisfy his principles, we find a free enterprise, private property system. Rawls can plead that this is just by way of example, but it is difficult not to see it as his preference. He appeared to accept social control of the economy only in the textbook macroeconomic sense: government leverage of base lending rate, money supply, taxation, and so on. That is to say, he was a Keynesian, and certainly no Marxist—confirming that Bell was indeed badly mistaken to label Rawls's theory as socialist. Admittedly, Bell elsewhere (1989: 176) proposes that the term 'socialism' be reserved for 'more humane societies' than those put in place by Marxists. 'For me', he said, 'it is a judgment on the priorities of economic policy' (Bell 1996a: xii). However, if the meaning of socialism is confined, as it normally is in the present context, to the narrow issue of ownership of the means of production, Rawls's predisposition can actually be classed as *anti*-socialist.

Economic justice for Tawney, however, was always a central preoccupation, and this emphasis in his thought underlines his distance from Rawls on the left-right spectrum. His socialist stall was set out very forcefully. 'If arbitrary contrasts of circumstance and opportunity are one form of inequality', he wrote, 'they are not the only form. There is an economic, as well as a social, stratification; a hierarchy of industry and labour, as well as of leisure and enjoyment. When the injustices of the second have been softened or abolished, it still remains to eliminate the tyranny of the first' (Tawney 1964b: 158). Tawney's solution was radically 'collectivist', in the standard sense of government *ownership*, not just control, of the means of production. While, as a good Fabian (a school of thought assessed below in Chapter 4), he conceded that collectivisation should be 'gradual' (Tawney 1982: 123), he definitely meant a gradual road to a more or less fully collectivised economy, rather than to a mixed economy. The list of industries Tawney targeted (1964b: 186) for immediate public ownership—whether by a Whitehall takeover, municipalisation or some other political method—was extensive, including banks, transport, power, coal-mining, land and agriculture, arms, alcoholic drinks, and many more. The 'dignity of public ownership' (Tawney 1949: 109) was eventually to be conferred upon the bulk of the economy. In language that symbolised the British labour movement's thinking for most of the twentieth century, the 'strongholds of capitalism' (a.k.a. 'commanding heights') were to be 'nationalized' first and the remaining industries subjected to 'mopping up' later (Tawney 1964b: 205).

While these ideological differences between Rawls and Tawney should not be glossed over, an accommodation can still be found. A Rawls-Tawney synthesis, like any other variant of social democracy, will contend that neither wholesale collectivism nor blanket privatisation is appropriate, hence that policymakers should seek some kind of intermediate route. And it will posit the so-called mixed economy not as a shady compromise between two pure positions, but, much more positively, as a golden mean, a creative combination that transcends the polarisation and extremism of the past. It is easy to say that this is mere wishful thinking, that it harbours philosophical betrayals, or ineradicable tensions, or even logical contradictions, yet economic politics should not be fought out in Manichean mode, or made hostage to Platonic forms and Weberian ideal-types; nor are all socioeconomic compounds necessarily unstable. Social democracy's historical record on this issue, a record of ideological principle blended with open-eyed pragmatism, is successful enough to make optimism about the future perfectly rational.

Specifically, the synthesis maintains, on the one hand, that it is wrong to dictate that the economy cannot allow carefully-circumscribed major spaces for market freedoms. *Pace* Tawney, there is no moral imperative to ban 'acquisitiveness', that is, the pursuit of profit, or to forbid, in Nozick's (1974: 163) mordant phrase, 'capitalist acts between consenting adults'. Social democracy can permit capital accumulation in the development of an energetic economy and it can recognise the value of choices offered by markets, both to consumers and to employees. Yet while there is no intrinsic case, moral, spiritual or political, for nationalisation of the whole economy, there is still an overwhelming argument both for economic activity as a whole to be under firm social control and for a sizable proportion of industry to reside in the public sector. Employee rights, collective bargaining, consumer protection, health and safety at work, monopoly commissions, resale price maintenance, even prices and incomes policies, the entire panoply of politico-economic responsibility, or some variation thereof, is still a requirement of justice. The politics of state 'interference' in the market—that is, state participation, involvement, solicitude, concern—remain obligatory in a civilised society. In addition, a flourishing, although regulated, private economy must be matched by a strong public sector. Many of the traditional candidates, including arms, airports, railway lines, water, gas and other utilities, and much of the health service and of primary, secondary and tertiary education, would still be better off under state ownership. Where these have fallen into private hands under conservative and other administrations, a party subscribing to the Rawls-Tawney synthesis would make a high priority of somehow recollectivising them. Of course, this would put such well to the left of most current outfits parading in social democratic stripes, but where the political spectrum is viewed in proper historical perspective, it clearly denotes a politics of the centre, not far, left.

What has been said above aims to be a cogent, if at times abbreviated, restatement of social democracy. I am hopeful that the Rawls-Tawney synthesis does represent, broadly speaking, the instincts of many who are gifted, or perhaps cursed, with a compulsive social conscience; and, in Rawlsian language, that it coheres with our considered judgements in reflective equilibrium. By bringing together the tradition's left (Tawney) and right (Rawls), it upholds what is most valuable in both strands of social democracy. To borrow from Seyla Benhabib's fabulous treatise *Critique, Norm, and Utopia* (1986: 13), it captures two 'moments', not only the Rawls-type 'vision of a community of rights and entitlements', but also the 'utopian', Tawney-type vision of 'a community of needs and solidarity'. To those who reply that this permutation is either undesirable or impossible, I would ask if they can step forward with anything superior. For the main live options—neo-conservatism or yet another instalment of flexi-Marxism—are at least equally open to challenge, being, arguably, morally repugnant and economically disastrous respectively. The fact is that we need a socio-philosophical position to help to deal with the normative crisis of the information society, one issuing in a feasible model of a just basic structure towards which reforms can be geared. Applying such to contemporary conditions, it *should* be possible to arrive at a conception of informatised social democracy.

THE INFORMATISATION OF ETHICAL SOCIAL DEMOCRACY

Prior to working through the application of these principles, more perhaps needs to be said about the basic legitimacy of the project of imposing a Rawls-Tawney synthesis on the information society thesis. One can retrieve a school of thought or propound a putatively original permutation of familiar ideas, but it does not follow that the resultant construct can assist the normative theory of an unprecedented state of affairs. Does there need to be root-and-branch conceptual modernisation in light of post-industrialism and informatisation? The answer, thankfully, is that social democracy as construed here needs only limited readjustments. The moderate—neither maximalist nor minimalist—understanding of the information society thesis implies that no radical changes are necessary with respect to the empirical aspects of the social democratic conception. Those who think that the information society has totally abrogated industrial society would have to produce a comprehensive revision, but this is not necessary for those of us who approach the information society as 'a study of continuity and change' (Feather 2008).

In addition, the form of social democracy sketched above is not, unlike some alternative traditions, deterministic. It is predicated on an account of social morality, a social deontology, and this means that it does not come with a sell-by date—on the contrary, it has, assuming its cogency, a timeless quality. This was always one of the great strengths of the tradition of ethical social democracy. The main rival approaches, prevalent in the early days especially on the European continent, sought instead to justify social democracy as a necessary stage within a supposed process of social evolution. Such, for example, was the view of the Marxist revisionist Karl Kautsky, but it was also influential—despite its nominal disownership of Karl Marx—in British Fabian thought, evident, indeed, in the latter's signature precept, discussed below, of 'the inevitability of gradualness'. The position adopted in the present study is different. It is not that we *are* moving towards a just society, but that we *should be* moving towards such; it is a normative theory of the information society, not an empirical or scientific one, and as such, it is not hostage to historical contingencies.

By the same token, however, this approach disallows any attempt to claim that social democracy is definitely going to arrive, courtesy of the IT revolution or any other phenomenon. Normative theory has to avoid the tempting route of arguing that informational forces, akin to the deterministic role that productive forces play in classical historical materialism, necessarily bring into being an information society. While it might be pleasant to believe that justice as fairness is the natural form of the post-industrial epoch, such beliefs are founded on mere wishful thinking and its pseudo-scientific idealisations in the academy. Nor can discursive capital be made out of the popular claim that informatisation is inherently corrosive of hierarchy. Given that social democracy's crusade is principally against the 'disease' of social inequality, this is a significant sacrifice. Admittedly, there may be some evidence of a levelling effect of new media, particularly the internet, so it is easy to appreciate why this attribute has at times been seized upon by champions of the disadvantaged (e.g. Jenkins and Om-ra-seti 1997). But there is also ample counter-evidence, and it is simply not safe to say that the internet is automatically conducive to, or possessed of an Innis-style bias towards, democracy and justice. We must instead heed Webster and Robins's (1986: 27) rejection of any technology-based aspiration towards a society similar to that envisaged by socialists—free, equal, communal, peaceful, abundant, etc—without the need for political action. A social democracy for the information age, as for the industrial era, will come about through reliance 'not on the impersonal forces beloved of doctrinaires, but on human minds and wills' (Tawney 1981a: 156).

However, the fact that a total overhaul is unnecessary does not entail that a conception of informatised social democracy is merely a matter of bolting on a few informational and technological concepts to 'standard' social democracy. The fundamental value settings remain as they were— basic liberties first, opportunity and equality second, fraternity/sisterhood third—but the logic of the information society thesis, and of the modest information revolution that it acknowledges, imply some significant modifications in the conceptualisation of social democratic theory. The task is not to find ways, as some have done, to quietly drop the settled principles of the centre left, but rather to effect an accommodation that maintains them under new conditions, during this episode of 'fresh experience'. Social democracy has to be *partially* rethought and, hopefully, as a consequence, reenergised in light of the pervasive changes epitomised in the concept of informatisation. To recapitulate, the ugly neologism unpacks into three sets of phenomena: the development of a post-industrial economy based on services and information; an information technology revolution; and an information explosion. All three will need to be assimilated by the Rawls-Tawney synthesis, or by any other up-to-date version of ethical social democracy. While an absolutely smooth result will not be achieved here, some of the main contours must be drawn.

To begin with post-industrialism: one of the empirical realities that has changed in ways obviously pertinent to social democratic thought is the statistical reduction of the industrial working class as a proportion of the labour force in advanced societies. It might have been possible to walk by on the other side back in 1962 when Machlup first reported that the largest industry in America was knowledge production and distribution, and, fifteen years later, to ignore Porat's painstaking delineation of the information economy; but no longer. The post-industrial services-information economy, now mainstreamed in economics and cognate disciplines as well as outside the academy, brings with it a palpable challenge to any doctrine for which a perspective on the industrial work force has been central. All the recent statistics shout that there has been a migration from blue-collar to white-collar or no-collar, that 'the industrial working class has been shrinking steadily' (Bell 1999: lxvi). For example, a useful abstract from the Bureau of Labor showed agriculture enjoying only 1.4 percent of civilian employment in the US, with industry at 19.8 and services at a mammoth 78.8, dramatically different from the scenario as recently as 1960—8.4, 33.4 and 58.2 percent respectively (United States Bureau of Labor 2008). While the US has led the way, there is now a similar situation in many other developed countries, and projections everywhere point in the same direction. So if by 'working class' is meant manufacturing workers, it must indeed be conceded that they do not offer much of a political or psephological critical mass any more. In that sense, André Gorz (1980) was justified in wishing 'farewell to the working class'.

And on this front, of course, Tawney's preoccupation with the industrial PBI looks particularly vulnerable. Tawney was not a Marxist but he was certainly 'labourist'; as one of his latter-day Labour Party disciples wrote, his 'case for socialism did not depend upon a theory of class formation, but it did assume the existence of a traditional proletariat as indispensable socialist agency' (Wright 1987: 146). However, the Rawls-Tawney synthesis is capable of dealing with this contingency in several ways. For a start, the moderate information society thesis that it wants to embrace does *not* assert that industrialisation has arrived at some kind of vanishing-point. The information sector in advanced societies has indeed eclipsed the industrial and extractive sectors, but it has not achieved a total annihilation thereof. Informatised social democracy can continue to acknowledge what remains of those sectors which, *underneath* the services-information palimpsest, remain partially constitutive of the thicker economic and occupational texture of post-industrial societies. This means, crucially, that informatised social democracy can hold onto its venerable doctrine of the dignity of physical labour. For social democrats, the doctrine has nothing to do with the Marxian labour theory of value, but refers rather to a basic moral-political intuition that honest manual labour is not just a major source of the common wealth but also an inherently noble, sociable and praiseworthy activity. Automation, outsourcing and myriad other aspects of the post-industrial economy may have ended the blue-collar worker's near-monopoly on left-wing attention, but wherever physical labour remains its dignity is undiminished. Indeed, *pro rata* 'the workers' are even more laudable, since never before have so few of them carried so many of the rest of us on their bent backs.

On the other hand, the Rawls-Tawney synthesis must also agree that new forms of post-industrial labour now have greater salience. The stereotype can no longer be council-house renting Henry Dubb toiling in the factory from nine to five, but, to coin another, Katy Dubovksi, a youngish immigrant part-time office-worker struggling with her ageing free-lance journalist 'partner' to pay off their mortgage. Her kind are the new political agency, or a considerable part of it. Of course, some of what currently occurs in the information economy is unattractive from a moral-political point of view. Junk emailers, internet gambling outfits and the less salubrious satellite television channels, to pick on three intrusive, if arbitrary, examples, are no more than parasites on the body politic. Such trades play into the hands of radical critics, much as coal-mine owners and stock-exchange speculators were obvious targets for levellers of the industrial era. However, the vast bulk of the information economy—technicians, post-industrial services in education, health and welfare, as well as numerous types of information producer, processor and distributor—can be reckoned genuine avocations serving a presumptively useful social function. Tele-workers, their much-heralded vanguard, thus need to be given due place in the sun of political rhetoric, although, at the outskirts of the information economy, telecentres—the pits of the post-industrial era—continue to demonstrate the indispensability of trade unions, employment rights and other mainstays of labourism and the welfare state.

The great advantage of the Rawls-Tawney synthesis is that its basic architecture is constructed at a sufficiently high level of abstraction for it to be capable of absorbing all these changes in employment figures and related economic variables. Justice as fairness is pledged to raise the position of the lowest socioeconomic systact, but it is not referentially invariable and it does not have to denote the industrial working class or any other special class. If members of the worst off group in advanced nations are now statistically unlikely to work in factories, are more likely to wear white collars or no collars or to have time-travelled back into domestic service, or to be unemployed or underemployed, then such persons *ipso facto* become the new centre of political attention for Rawlsian-inspired social democracy. And the aim can still be Tawney's classless society, even though the agency of emancipation has broadened out beyond his beloved industrial heartlands.

Information technology, the second major vector of informatisation, impinges on social democracy in innumerable ways. Only one theme will be touched on at this point, by way of example: its impact upon leisure. If the restructuring of work is one inescapable trend, another that the Rawls-Tawney synthesis must address is the expansion of non-work. Tawney's critique of industrial capitalism included the charge that that system's drive for wealth left little time for leisure; this was part of the sickness of the acquisitive society. The only people who enjoyed free time, and they of course had far too much of it, were the functionless, idle aristocrats and capitalists— the Veblen class. However, Tawney did not foreground leisure in his theory; on the contrary, when hymning the likes of Mr Dubb he sometimes steered perilously close to the Marxian conceit that true freedom can only be found *in* work. *A Theory of Justice* does not contain a theory of leisure either, and Rawls never responded to Walzer's postulate (1985: 185) that leisure is 'a central issue of distributive justice'. To be accurate, Rawls did later offer one or two brief comments, taking an opportunity in *Justice as Fairness: a*

Restatement (Rawls 2001: 179) to growl that government is under no obligation whatever to support types who 'surf all day off Malibu'. But whatever normative theories of industrial society had to say or not to say, leisure
is unavoidably a *post-industrial* issue, and a contemporary Rawls-Tawney
synthesis needs to stress it. Utopian nonsense about a post-scarcity era can
be discounted, but the potential for a greater quality as well as quantity
of 'down-time' is undoubtedly built into the post-industrial circumstances
of justice. Labour-saving was, after all, one of the great original promises
of informatisation, from at least as far back as 'automation' in the 1960s
(Duff 2006a). Indeed, the freeing-up of human time is arguably the rationale of most technology. Thus far, sadly, the promise has been entirely broken, a failure not of the technologies themselves but of the political will to
socially-shape their deployment. Yet the information society of tomorrow
ought to be about reducing drudgery, not ushering in a neo-feudal regime
of 24/7/365 connectivity. There are many other ways in which ICTs can be
harnessed to the cause of social democracy, but surely nothing is quite as
overdue as this.

However, the principal task for an informatised theory of social democracy lies at its conceptual core, and this cannot be postponed any longer.
The third dimension of informatisation is the exponential growth of data
stocks and flows, the so-called information explosion. The normative
theory of the information society needs to respond to this multifaceted,
ubiquitous reality by somehow acknowledging *systematically* the emergent
societal significance of information. Of course, everyone knows that information can be extremely valuable. One need only think of winning lottery
numbers or nuclear missile launch-codes; or, to use Renée Marlin-Bennett's
(2004: 103) striking although now dated example, the geographical coordinates of Osama bin Laden. However, data of this epistemic order have
always been at a premium; knowledge of predators' whereabouts was, to
be sure, critical for Stone Age survival. What is different today, in the Castellsian Information Age, is the *scale* of information's valorisation and its
salience in society. Modern intellectual history has already registered two
seismic conceptual changes. The nineteenth century revered information
as an instructional and educational force; that remains a prime dictionary
meaning. The twentieth century reduced information to a technical category, not only, legitimately, in information theory, but also, perniciously,
in propaganda, where information's semantic content was largely distorted.
But now, in the twenty-first century, a new paradigm is being fought for, a
new battle for its soul is taking place: information as either commodity or
utility, product or amenity. And the skirmishing is past; the explosion of
information flows across all realms demands a proper response at a politico-philosophical level. The question is how.

Certain general solutions immediately present themselves. Information
could be cast as a new 'public good', in the conventional classical-economics
sense, thereby joining fresh air, national defence, municipal parks and the

like. 'The quality of the information environment which makes citizenship possible', Venturelli points out (1998: 71), 'would easily qualify for public good status'. 'Information', confirms eminent sociologist of knowledge Nico Stehr (1994: 120; cf. Stehr 2005), 'has attributes assuring that it constitutes, certainly to a greater extent than is the case for knowledge, a public good'. But what does this approach imply institutionally? Does it mean that corporate information activity should cease, that the state must appropriate all means of information and set up a giant information utility? Probably not. Less drastically, information could perhaps be made part of a new-look 'social welfare function'. But does it then have to observe Pareto-optimality, the classicist's clever veto on radical redistributions? Such issues will have to be left to classically-oriented experts in information economics, the Nobel Prize-winning field ploughed by Kenneth Arrow (e.g. 1996) and Joseph Stiglitz (e.g. 1994). A very different manner of conceptualisation would be for an 'information theory of value' to somehow replace the 'labour theory of value' and its associated 'theory of surplus value', an approach that has already been to some extent forged by Marxian philosophers such as Krippendorff (1993). Fully state-owned means of information and communication would presumably be their policy brief. However, I do not intend to pursue any of these leads. They may well offer ways to import at least a proportion of an information perspective into normative theory, but they are not the best point of entry for the conception of ethical social democracy under construction here.

In the opening chapter of this book, information was focused definitionally as a social, semantic and factual category. Now the need is to demonstrate exactly how information in this robust sense can enter the Rawls-Tawney synthesis, and the way to do it is actually obvious. If we are serious about the information society thesis, then we must accept that information is now a *basic* resource, that is, in Rawlsian terms and therefore also in terms of the Rawls-Tawney synthesis, a 'primary good'. To recall, primary goods are 'things that every rational man is presumed to want': rights, liberties, powers, opportunities, income, wealth and the bases of self-respect (Rawls 1973: 62). To that bundle—the word is appropriate, since the list always looked unstructured and open-ended—the normative theory of the information society must now add *information*, thereby valorising it as an independent resource, a good in its own right. No longer hidden in other goods, it 'comes out' and declares its autonomy. So it will be a cornerstone of all the argumentation presented below that, if there is anything significant in the information society thesis, it follows that information must finally qualify as an entitlement, along the lines of other basic rights. It is a decisive way of philosophically, and, by corollary, politically, accommodating all those myriad intuitions and insights, assertions and aspirations, about the centrality of information in the post-industrial epoch. The claim is not that information was unimportant in the industrial era, but that in the post-industrial era, where a large measure of informatisation has occurred, information has elevated itself to primary good level. We have, then, our answer to the question political philosophers (e.g. Knowles 2001: 206) are fond of asking: 'equality of what?'.

This conceptual move, natural for a modernised theory of social democracy built around the framework of Rawls-Tawney, does not claim originality. A growing band of commentators, roughly describable as neo-Rawlsians, has crossed the same Rubicon. An important early marker was Jorge Schement and Terry Curtis's *Production and Distribution of Information in the United States*, which argued that information is 'the key social component of the new infrastructure' and that it should be counted as 'a clause in society's definition of basic welfare' (1995: 159). The work registered that arguments for access to information to be included in 'universal service', a stance already becoming common in progressive telecommunications policy circles, were often inspired by Rawls (Schement and Curtis 1995: 160). Since the turn of the millennium, there has been a wave of similar testimonies. Don Fallis (2004b: 81) opines that 'although Rawls himself does not explicitly discuss *knowledge*, it is clearly such a primary good'. Douglas Raber (2004: 120) holds that 'a national information infrastructure is now part of the basic structure of a just society'; hence, 'central to a truly innovative liberal argument for support of universal service as a necessary component of social justice is the establishment as fact that participation in and use of a national information infrastructure is what Rawls calls a primary good—an essential aspect of the total system of liberties and necessary for the full exercise of meaningful liberty'. 'To create a just society in which everyone is able to work, consume, save, produce, take part in politics and socialise to whatever extent they desire', write O'Hara and Stevens (2006: 88–89) following a discussion of Rawls, 'it is surely essential that everyone has sufficient access to ICT, and the skills involved in leveraging that access'. For them, 'ICT is now undoubtedly part of the vital mix that enables everyone in a society to pursue their own idea of the good life' (O'Hara and Stevens 2006: 88–89).

'In an information society', echo van Dijk and Hacker, implying a general adoption of Rawlsian ideas, 'information *is known* as a so-called primary good' (2003: 324, italics added). The roll-call also includes Britz (2004), Nissenbaum and Introna (2004), Collins (2007), and van den Hoven and Rooksby (2008), among others; and I have already quoted Wilhelm (2004). Indeed, it is probably safe to infer that it is now majority opinion among scholars acquainted with political philosophy as Rawls seminally recast the discipline, that information qualifies as a primary good. However, while this Rawlsian turn is welcome, the way that the theory of justice has been coopted thus far is problematic. The referent even in the quoted texts varies between knowledge, information, information infrastructure and ICTs, none of which are co-extensive. There has also been, on the whole, a rather limited grasp of the intricacies of Rawls's position, not to mention a reluctance to negotiate the mountainous secondary literature it has generated.

We lack, as a result, a finalised set of propositions stating precisely how the positing of information as a primary good facilitates an informatising of the theory of justice and democracy. Several major hermeneutical issues will need to be dealt with immediately.

The central question of the referent can actually be despatched with very rapidly. For the normative theory of the information society the issue is not ICTs, nor the information or telecommunications infrastructure. These are relevant only in a secondary, derivative sense, namely only insofar as they materially affect the social distribution of information. Our target is not the medium but the message (and only *some* messages), not the technology but the intractable hinterland that stretches out behind technology, the contours of information-access and -utilisation that help to make up the social fabric. Knowledge too is not the focus. Knowledge is a higher-order construct than information and it needs separate treatment, for example by incorporation into theories of justice in education and theories of social epistemology. We are concerned with the more elementary matter of information, and factual information to boot. And, according to the final section of Chapter 1, the vast majority of communications flows are not even in the frame of the normative theory of the information society. Indeed, is it not preposterous to suggest that all information, on the anything-goes, computing conception—the five exabytes discovered by information scientists at Berkeley (University of California 2003), for example—qualifies in any conceivable normative sense? That is like saying the whole biosphere should be given 'greenbelt' status. Most 'information' is not information in the true sense, what I have called the journalistic sense, and of that which is, most is trivial, outdated, irrelevant, repetitive, redundant, or otherwise arbitrary from a moral and political point of view.

It is not, in a word, justiciable. Some information, however, *is* justiciable, but now another basic interpretative dilemma of great significance immediately presents itself. Again glossed over by many neo-Rawlsians, it is whether justiciable information belongs to the first or second principle. If it belongs to the first, then we are saying that information is integral to political liberty and must be distributed strictly equally, as in one man, one vote. If the second, we are saying that it does not require lexical prioritisation or arithmetic equalisation, but is still important enough to be an object of differential distributive justice. Raber proposes the national information infrastructure as 'an essential aspect of the total system of liberties and necessary for the full exercise of meaningful liberty'. Since Rawls, as we saw above, distinguished liberty (first principle) from the material basis for the meaningful exercise of liberty (second principle), this formulation seems to be having it both ways. Van den Hoven and Rooksby make a very lucid case (2008: 384) that 'access to information is best treated as a basic liberty'. Their position will be discussed in detail below. Most neo-Rawlsians, however, appear to prefer to place information, or whatever cognate they are using, under the second principle. For example, Britz recognises (2004:

202–3) that certain information inequalities, as accommodated by copyright, for example, can contribute to overall wellbeing and the alleviation of information poverty. Fallis (2004b: 82) explicitly supports a 'Rawlsian distribution', meaning 'a distribution of knowledge where the information have-nots have as much knowledge as possible'. He suggests that such a distribution is compatible with 'very large' disparities, although he seems to feel that such an outcome is tolerable (Fallis 2004b: 83).

The approach that will be followed here is very different. Instead of treating information as monolithic and saying or implying that all of it should be subject to one or other of the principles, I wish to argue that information is heterogeneous from an ethical-political point of view and that, therefore, different kinds of information must have a different logical relation to social justice. This is an extrapolation of the bank of intuitions which informed both Rawls's and Tawney's theories of social democracy. Broadly speaking, as Ronald Doctor pointed out (1992: 55–56), we—meaning, in the present context, regular members of post-industrial societies—tend to have egalitarian norms about political information and inegalitarian norms about economic information. In addition, we have, I would add, no norms of justice at all about most types of information. It follows that some categories of factual information fit better under the first principle, while others should go under the second; whereas the remainder, since they fall under no principle of justice, can be safely left to market forces as regards their production, distribution and consumption. I propose to systematise these nuances in what I wish to call the Rawls-Tawney Theorem (cf. Duff 2011). This theorem is an informatised restatement of the two Rawlsian principles of justice, with a 'Tawney proviso' appended as a third clause of the second principle. The wording is as follows:

The Rawls-Tawney Theorem

First Principle of Information Justice

Each person has the same indefeasible claim to all information essential for the exercise of a fully adequate scheme of equal civil and political liberties, which scheme is compatible with the same scheme of liberties for all

Second Principle of Information Justice

Inequalities in the social distribution of categories of information required for social and economic functioning are to satisfy three conditions:
  (i) they are to be attached to an information infrastructure equally accessible to all (the equal opportunity clause);
  (ii) they are to be to the greatest benefit of the least advantaged members of society (the difference principle); and

(iii) they should not be so extensive as to generate class distinctions (the Tawney proviso)

It might be helpful at the end of this chapter to summarise where we have arrived with terminology. The Rawls-Tawney Theorem is a prescriptive formula for the social distribution of information, with information defined by the journalistic conception. The theorem is part of, but not coterminous with, the Rawls-Tawney synthesis, which covers also a doctrine of social morality, classified earlier in the chapter as a social deontology. The social deontology is logically prior or upstream in the synthesis; the theorem, downstream. The Rawls-Tawney Theorem, thus positioned, tries to offer something superior to both utopian socialism and the woolly centrism of recent editions of social democracy. In the next chapter, the details of the theorem will be spelled out. However, the overarching point so far, the headline, is that information has moved very visibly onto the radar of social justice, after centuries of obscurity and neglect. In our post-industrial, computerised epoch, information becomes every bit as justiciable—if the pun can be forgiven—as money or power; and, if the theory of social democracy outlined above is convincing, the distribution of socially-valuable information, as of other primary goods, must be brought into line with the principles of fairness crystallised in the Rawls-Tawney Theorem.

3 On the Social Distribution of Information and News

The central claim that has emerged during this exercise of recapturing the ideas of Rawls and Tawney as a potential solution to the normative crisis of the information society is that future statecraft should embrace a prescriptive approach to the social distribution of the asset of information. This proposition is predicated on a traditional, social democratic conception of political and economic justice, one whose applicability to the modern world has been widely impugned, and which needs therefore to be updated to, in Tawney's phrase, 'make sense of changing realities'. In this way, the focus of social democracy can switch from industrial-style economic politics to post-industrial information politics, and to the conventional remit of material distributive justice can be added aspirations for non-material, epistemic justice. To summarise the state of the art very crudely, the problem of power was dealt with by liberalism and the problem of poverty was addressed by socialism, but information has not yet been vouchsafed, on anything like the same intellectual or political level, its own doctrine, its own 'ism'. Of course, information has been touched on *tangentially* countless times, often wrapped up in the concept of knowledge, by all sorts of classical theories and disciplines negotiating the political, economic and cultural realms, but it is only in the past few decades, as a result of the sharp growth of consciousness of the informatisation process, that arguments for information justice, for a genuinely social epistemology, have started to find insistent expression. Information technology, as a disruptive if not revolutionary principle of innovation, has forced societies, and indeed world society insofar as that exists, to revisit issues of justice that were lying dormant in the late-autumn of industrialism. How should all this new-found or revalued booty—intellectual property, very broadly conceived—be shared out? It is as an answer to that post-industrial puzzle, in the shape of a recombinant social democracy, that the Rawls-Tawney Theorem has been positioned. What needs to be done now is to tease out the precise implications of the theorem.

FIRST PRINCIPLE OF INFORMATION JUSTICE: AN OPEN POLITY

So let us begin with the first part of the Rawls-Tawney Theorem, the liberty principle as transmuted into a first principle of information justice:

First Principle of Information Justice

> Each person has the same indefeasible claim to all information essential for the exercise of a fully adequate scheme of equal civil and political liberties, which scheme is compatible with the same scheme of liberties for all

'To live effectively', declared cyberneticist Norbert Wiener (1989: 18) 'is to live with adequate information'. Social justice demands that the facilitation of an effective, informed citizenship should be the overriding duty of a democratic polity in the information age, as it was, or should have been, in the industrial era. The basic rule, that liberty comes first, is not available for negotiation. The problem, though, is to identify the special meaning of civil-political liberty in the information age; or, to be more exact, and to keep faith with the moderate version of the information society thesis, to ask how post-industrial liberty *both* maintains *and* transcends the liberties hammered out in the industrial age. In what ways do the industrial liberties need to be recast in light of the information society thesis? And are there any wholly new basic liberties peculiar to the information society—that is, anything additional to freedom of speech, the rule of law, periodic elections, etc—about which liberal democracy (of which, I have argued, social democracy is a variant) *now* needs to be thinking? The paragraphs below try both to reconstruct aspects of the industrial scheme from an information perspective and also to extract some innovative deliverances of the first principle of justice. I shall designate this module of the normative theory of the information society the 'open polity'.

The interpretation of the first principle of information justice principally involves the selection of those special bodies of information for which it is the responsibility of the state to ensure an equal entitlement. They include, but are not necessarily restricted to, the following:

Categories of First-Principle Justiciable Information

   i. Constitutional, statutory and electoral information
  ii. Administrative and other official information
 iii. Personal information

Information of type (i) must be at the top of any inventory of the data demanded by democratic participation. Put the other way round, deprivation of the knowledge of one's basic rights of citizenship is the most clear-cut manifestation of information poverty. Who is in power nationally, regionally, locally? Which parties are standing for parliament and on what platforms? How do I actually exercise my right to vote? What is the law of the land? Where are the boundaries of my freedom of religion, expression, association? What are my options if indicted? Am I entitled to make a citizen's arrest of this football hooligan or that war criminal? How do I emigrate? Can the Supreme Court or the European Court of Justice help me in my hour of need? If I cannot answer these questions, then I lack the necessities of contemporary citizenship. But to answer them I must possess specifiable sets of accurate information. For example, information needed for rational choices in a general election is a condition of representative government. Therefore, such data must be guaranteed under the first principle of information justice. It is not enough to say that citizens in post-industrial societies enjoy unprecedented access in 'today's information-dense environment' (McNair 2000: 138), even though the observation is certainly true, because it is not only a question of totals or averages. Equity in such cases demands arithmetic egalitarianism. Constitutional, statutory and electoral information should be diffused among the citizenry absolutely equally, or as near thereto as humanly possible.

Even that is not enough today, however. The information-citizenship nexus has become tighter than ever before. Of course, links were to some extent visible throughout industrialisation, the era in which modern democracy was consolidated. Indeed, they were becoming evident even in the late-agrarian era, as James Madison, at least, testified. 'A popular Government', he wrote with majestic beauty, 'without popular information or the means of acquiring it, is but a Prologue to a Farce or a Tragedy; or perhaps both. Knowledge will forever govern ignorance; and a people who mean to be their own Governors, must arm themselves with the power which knowledge gives' (quoted in Strickland 2005: 549). However, the manner in which 'popular information' has been understood in the past will no longer pass muster for the present or the future. In our information age, a much more extensive right to political information must obtain. This can be expressed in the proposition that there is now an indefeasible right to category (ii) information, that is, administrative and other official information.

Hence the first principle implies that democratic polities ought to continue to travel in the direction of freedom of information. While limited disclosures of this kind have always been part of democracy, the idea of a general formal right to government information has rarely been explicitly recognised, still less rigorously expounded or justified, in the liberal tradition. Indeed, political democracy has existed without *soi-disant* FOI for hundreds of years—seemingly quite contentedly. FOI may be a close cousin of democracy and freedom of expression, but it has not been considered essential. If it had been, Sweden, which, commendably, legislated the 'right to know' back in 1766, would have been the only free nation in the world until 1966, when the US finally passed its own FOI statute. However, while it would be wrong to claim that FOI has been a necessary condition of political liberty in the past, that does not mean that it will not be so in the future, or that we should not be pressing for it in the present. On the contrary, an open polity, in this expanded sense, is the proper ideal of a post-industrial constitution. Such is the unavoidable political logic of the information society thesis, a thesis about the centrality of information—journalistically conceived—in the polities, economies and cultures of advanced societies.

The Rawls-Tawney Theorem needs to be cautiously handled in this respect, because the base in primary sources proves quite slender. The cornerstone of Tawney's entire philosophy was 'the infinite difference between what is false and what is true' (1972: 43). At a more mundane level, it is evident throughout his writings that he appreciated the political importance of factual public information. For example, he spoke that way as part of his influential argument for free secondary schooling in the UK. 'If an intelligent public opinion is to be formed on educational questions', he counselled (1923: 13), 'it is essential that full information with regard to the progress of education in the United Kingdom and other countries should be made regularly and easily accessible. At the present time such information is provided only in a piecemeal and haphazard manner'. However, Tawney seemed to have no inkling of the concept of a formal right to know. Rawls too could on occasion suggest that 'all citizens should have the means to be informed about political issues' (1973: 225) or refer to the need to find 'ways of assuming the availability of public information on matters of public policy' (1996: lviii). However, like Tawney, and with less mitigation, he did not anywhere set out a clear account of FOI or explain the significance of popular information for his philosophical system of liberal rights. This was one of the many loose ends that had to be taken up by students of his ideas (e.g. Carey 1985). The shortcoming, characteristic of liberal theorists even under mature industrialism, needs now to be made good. As society has informatised and, in some senses at least, transformed itself into an information society, FOI must graduate from luxury good to bare necessity—it must become a *normal* part of democracy.

Thankfully, the nature of information rights in the new landscape has been clarified by other analytical philosophers. Mark Bovens (2002) distinguishes several levels of government openness. The first, a straightforward negative liberty, is the absence of censorship of political information. The second, more positively, denotes the presence in the statute books of a formal right to government information. The third level is still more proactive, a duty of the state to publish information. However, there is a fourth level, one which few governments seem to heed, namely a duty of the state to actually secure a fair social distribution of information. 'A right of access to information', Bovens writes (2002: 333), 'is only a limited means to achieve a socially just distribution of information. From a socioliberal point of view on citizenship, therefore, it is an issue of social justice that the government also support citizens in gaining access to crucial societal information channels'. And this means access, as he vividly puts it, not only for the 'double-income, dual-career residents of the Amsterdam canal district, but also for the widow from Appelscha' (2002: 333), the latter apparently a stereotype, at least in Dutch telecoms circles, of the underprivileged user. It is at this highest level, I should like to add, that liberal democracy morphs into social democracy. For those categories of administrative and other official information covered by FOI, political justice requires a guaranteed egalitarian distribution, or an outcome as close to that as possible. It is a proactive matter, not merely the formal right to know but the state using its power to ensure that the information actually reaches every end-user, every member of the political community. This then is now one of the requirements of the first principle of the Rawls-Tawney Theorem.

Van den Hoven and Rooksby (2008) provide further elucidation, both by employing an overtly Rawlsian framework and by detailing the categories of information subject to considerations of justice. Having made a cogent case for information to be added to the index of primary goods, they conclude that 'access to information is best treated as a basic liberty' (van den Hoven and Rooksby 2008: 384). The content is specified as 'citizenship information' plus 'a great deal of scientific, academic, and commercial information'. The former unpacks into information on the following subjects: 'citizens' rights and responsibilities; jurisprudence; the quality of food and standards for its production; drugs; transport; the environment and pollution; housing; employment trends; health care standards and risks; national safety, crime rates; opportunities for political participation; educational opportunities; economic prospects; political processes and so on'. Like Bovens, they conclude that, in societies depending on 'often expensive and complex' ICTs—i.e. information societies—'ensuring a just distribution of information requires not only a just distribution of information liberties for all citizens, but also mechanisms to ensure that people's opportunities to exercise their information liberties are roughly equal' (van den Hoven and Rooksby 2008: 385). Thus the first clause of the second principle of justice—equality of opportunity—is brought into play, as well as the liberty principle, although the difference principle does not seem to figure in their account.

The inclusion of information on housing, health risks and the like, although it goes well beyond strictly political information, is surely correct. The architects of post-war social democracy in Britain, notably Tawney's brother-in-law William Beveridge, advocated energetic dissemination of precisely those kinds of welfare rights information (Leonard 2003: 37–49). And the case for extending arithmetic equality in such ways is highly plausible on Rawlsian premises, as the Rawls-Tawney Theorem implies. It does seem unfair if one citizen knows appreciably more than another about, say, tenancy rights in rented accommodation or the lethal risks of polio or AIDS, just as it is palpably a denial of the first principle of justice if party-political information is unevenly distributed at election time. If so, we are now referring to a much fuller canon of justiciable civil and political information, a right to several additional categories of data presumptively integral to healthy, knowledgeable membership of a modern polity. However, it is not so clear that all scientific, academic and commercial information also warrants first-principle treatment. While wide distributions of such are obviously desirable, and while it is important to avoid *vast* information gaps between different systacts, it may be an exaggeration to say that they deserve exact equality. Framing too many types of information divide as a civil rights issue on a par with the right to vote or to a fair trial, runs the risk of permanently devaluing the moral currency of rights (cf. Foster 2000: 451). Nevertheless, the larger point stands: civil-political information must at last take its place under the first principle of information justice, alongside other now uncontroversial basic liberties. This represents a significant enhancement of democracy, marking the arrival—by the *front* door—of information politics.

At the same time, however, that the Rawls-Tawney Theorem mandates open government, it asks, in a sense, for its antithesis—hence category (iii). Privacy was identified above as a prime site of normative crisis, and the defence thereof has become a major preoccupation of information politics. It may even be what theorists of agenda-setting (e.g. McCombs 2004) like to call the 'MIP'—most important problem—of the new century. For cliché or not, it is still worth being reminded that the information society, for all its benefits, makes much more real the threat of 'dystopia': telescreens in the bedroom, panopticons, anti-democratic reversions from *lex rex* (law is king) to *rex*—i.e. Big Brother, or perhaps Big Browser—*lex* (the king is law). In plain language, total information equals potential total surveillance, which could in principle translate into total loss of privacy for the individual. The nightmare scenario was there in seed-form at the beginning. Privacy was in fact the main social issue aired by the mentally alive in the early days of computing. But it can no longer be politically ignored. 'Something very big, new, and threatening is permeating our political life . . . For the snoops, the sneaks, the meddlers, data glut is a feast. It gives them exactly what [they] require', Roszak warned in his colourful *Cult of Information* (1994: 211). 'That', Day notes rather more soberly (2001: 49), 'a communications utopia is really a state of control is manifest in the very cyborg model that emerges out of cybernetics'. Vincent Mosco (2002: 264) suggests, with a characteristic slant, that 'the fight for personal privacy is part of a wider struggle against the expanding commodity'. And O'Hara and Stevens conclude brutally, but perfectly accurately (2006: 245), that 'privacy is a casualty of the information age. It seems that ICT is killing our personal space'. The claim that privacy is a normative information issue of great importance has been vindicated by authoritarian responses to political violence in both North America and Europe. Identity (ID) cards, biometric testing, dataveillance, etc: all such developments impinge on the personal space of citizens and thereby present an acute philosophical and policy problematic for the normative theory of the information society.

Yet neither mainstream philosophy nor conventional politics has seemed keen to uphold the right of privacy. In the formative period of liberal democracy, it was never systematically expounded. Close reading by Lucas Introna (1997: 261) revealed that the major liberal theorists, such as Locke, Rousseau and Mill, 'did not spend as much as a page on the subject'. Of course, it existed between the lines, nestled inside Locke's right of private property and Mill's emancipation discourse, for example, but entitlements that are left conceptually vague are unlikely to be regarded as watertight, still less to be converted into positive law. Nor did the US Constitution, one of the first genuinely liberal constitutions, contain an explicit right of privacy. Again it was present implicitly, lurking in the penumbra with FOI and other information principles (Braman 2006), but it was not constitutionally foregrounded. Thus the ethico-legal case for personal privacy has had to be gradually pieced together. A large step forward in the US was Samuel Warren and Louis Brandeis's *Harvard Law Review* article of 1890, which promoted (quoting a judge named Cooley) the 'right to be let alone'. But even in 2011, the right of privacy is still only partially recognised. In Europe, things seem rather better. Indeed, the European Data Protection Directive (European Union 1995) has established itself as something of a global benchmark for privacy and data protection. This diktat's content extends far beyond the negative right not to be interfered with, conferring on citizens a positive right of control over stocks and flows of personal information (e.g. Stein and Sinha 2002: 413–5). Yet no one would dare to say that privacy, either negative or positive, is safe in Europe, or anywhere else.

So this is another shortfall that needs to be addressed. In an information-based society, as distinct from the industrial democracies of the past, privacy—just as much as its antithesis, FOI—must assert itself as a component of a 'fully adequate scheme' of freedom (Rawls), as now one of the 'supreme goods of civil and political liberty' (Tawney). The first principle of the Rawls-Tawney Theorem is therefore to be cashed out in such a way as to protect the personal space of the individual. Needless to say, what is meant here is liberal privacy, not the 'enforced privacy' of veiled women and the like (Marlin-Bennett 2004: 183). In particular, there is an urgent need for safeguards in view of rapid developments in surveillance that result from the increasing scope and sophistication of ICTs (e.g. Anderson *et al.* 2009). Privacy-enhancing technologies (PETs) should be officially encouraged as part of any future-proofing agenda for civil and political liberty. Ultimately, however, the state, as final guarantor of the dignity of the individual, has to create a robust institutional and legal framework in which online privacy, no less than its offline parent, is fully respected. Of course, this raises a host of agonising dilemmas for the polity. Given the regrettable existence of violent anti-democratic forces, *some* state incursions into privacy may turn out to be justifiable. Justice, as Rawls (1973: 218) sagely pointed out, 'does not require that men must stand idly by while others destroy the basis of their existence'. Thus the first principle leaves open the question of encryption and other issues pertaining to government duties in the domain of national security. However, the default must from now on be the right of privacy. The minutiae of where legal boundaries should be drawn are matters for juridical interpretation in light of specific national traditions as well as changing technical circumstances; they need not be pursued here.

In addition to new entitlements to the three special categories of information, there are several traditional rights in need of reinforcement. Many scholars do not hesitate to place freedom of expression on the information policy agenda, even at its head (e.g. Maxwell 2003). There may be conceptual difficulties in so doing. The limits of free speech cannot be confined to speech that is information-based, nor even to coherent speech. The issue seems to belong more naturally to media or cultural policy, and those fields have routinely pronounced on it. It must be admitted, nevertheless, that information in all sorts of contexts is crucial to freedom both of speech and of other forms of expression, and that, therefore, the normative theory of the information society may be due its own say. An 'ideal speech situation' requires a clean information environment, after all (Habermas 1989). Moreover, this particular supreme good is in the nonideal world so gravely threatened currently that every cognate field perhaps ought to be dropping trivial pursuits and rallying to its cause. The first principle of information justice thus stresses that freedom of expression should also be fully honoured in a post-industrial polity. Its ideal is a global First Amendment, and to that end the principle will firmly remind any culture that freedom of speech stands or falls with the freedom to be counter-cultural. This does not mean that it will discourage sensible regulation for the sake of public safety or morality, but it does mean that it will jealously defend offensive speech—including anonymous modes—on spiritual, ethical, sexual, political, scientific and literary matters. It will protect satanic versifiers, but it will also curb those pressure groups which overplay their rights by trying to silence communities faithful to religion or traditional morality. These are the kinds of information-related battles that will intensify as the culture wars spread.

Finally, political justice in information needs of course to keep abreast of teledemocracy. This is not to claim a new category of 'virtual rights' (e.g. Fitzpatrick 2000), because, as already decided, the normative theory of the information society is resolutely medium-independent. The people's right is to information, not specifically to digital information. However, as the polity becomes digitised, and as mass migration online occurs, it becomes the responsibility of state authorities to take steps to ensure that citizens have equal access to relevant content and skills. So if, as the Rawls-Tawney Theorem postulates, citizens have an equal and inalienable right to electoral information, and if voting turns electronic, then citizens must have identical rights to any necessary technology. Similarly, as local and national government processes go virtual, in the whole domain of egovernment, citizens must be guaranteed the wherewithal to make use of them. This is all a matter for the first principle, for a strict egalitarianism modelled on political axioms like 'everyone is equal in the sight of the law' and 'one person one vote'.

However, while such areas as FOI, privacy and edemocracy present serious normative and policy challenges, they are at bottom generic issues for liberal democracy, rather than specifically *social* democratic matters. To a very large extent, they are not even a left-right issue. Privacy advocates, for example, have long realised that they must make common cause across party divides (Bennett 2008). As argued above, the normative theory of the information society has to concentrate on socioeconomic issues because those are the special burden of social democracy, its putative contribution to the enhancement of liberal democracy. If advanced nations are increasingly information-based, then it follows that we need to think about establishing information rights that go well beyond the horizon of democratic rights derived from the first principle of justice. Information has to be seen not only as an adjunct of political citizenship, as a condition of an open polity, but also as a strategic socioeconomic resource, one upon which people have justiciable claims of the kind that have traditionally animated discussions of 'distributive' justice. Thus, it is time now to exit the cultural politics of information and to enter the more divisive zone of information's economic politics.

SECOND PRINCIPLE OF INFORMATION JUSTICE: SHARING OUR WARES

'The concept of post-industrial society', Bell taught (1999: 483), 'is an *analytical construct*, not a picture of a specific or concrete society. It is a paradigm or social framework that identifies new axes of social organization and new axes of social stratification in advanced Western society'. 'Social structures do not change overnight,' he adds, 'and it may often take a century for a complete revolution to take place'. That construct is generally portrayed, at least in its dominant, optimistic form, as a world where information—unspecified, normally, in terms of content—is abundant, an age of access. Access and abundance, though, for whom? How will the new society be organised as a result of the new axes of stratification? Or is it really access for everybody, and, if so, on what time scale? But then precisely what species of information are or will be available, and how intrinsically valuable are they? Moreover, can anything be done to ensure that available, valuable information is effectively utilised by underprivileged systacts? This section focuses on how social stratification is affected by the information revolution, insofar as the latter has been played out and can be reliably expected further to play out in the foreseeable future, and what this means for ethical information policy. In other words, information here will be examined not as a constitutive principle of a well-ordered post-industrial polity but as a tangible good amenable to the socioeconomic paraphernalia of quantifications, curves and coefficients.

As noted in Chapter 1, a multidisciplinary literature on distributive justice in information and IT has existed for many decades, but the issue has reappeared with unprecedented academic and policy salience in the guise of worries over the 'digital divide', or, more accurately, 'digital divide(s)' (Barzilai-Nahon 2006; Golding and Murdock 2001). Indeed, we are faced with another veritable logorrhea. According to one estimate, the number of scholarly papers—merely one genre, albeit the one where real innovations are most likely to be reported—on the digital divide alone was upwards of 440 by 2005 (Vehovar *et al.* 2006: 279). There have also been numerous research monographs, such as those by Norris (2001), van Dijk (2005), Servon (2002), Warschauer (2003), and Mossberger *et al.* (2003), as well as the edited volumes of Compaine (2001c) and Wyatt *et al.* (2000), to cite a few of the best new-millennium offerings. In addition, numerous reports, both official and unofficial, have made significant contributions. As Blaise Cronin observes in his priceless opinion-piece collection *Pulp Friction* (2003: 62), there is nothing like alliteration for giving an issue momentum. ('Generation gap' had a similar effect on the media, public and policy agendas in the 1960s.) Simon Nora and Alain Minc's *Computerization of Society: a Report to the President of France* (1981) was a prototype of the influential information policy report. The National Telecommunications and Information Authority's *Falling Through the Net* (United States 1999) was pivotal in shaping official attitudes to the digital divide in the US, while *Beyond the Digital Divide* by UK think tank Futurelab (Selwyn and Facer 2007) is proof of the high calibre of recent work in this genre. The digital divide was even a major theme—was one of the main causes of—the World Summit on the Information society.

It is gratifying to see social justice in any shape or form back on mainstream agendas again. More than that, it is a seminal development and a matter for celebration that, perhaps for the first time since the end of the nineteenth century, we appear to have discovered another 'moral aspect of the economical problem' (Caird 1888). That is to say, information technology has not only provided a valuable entry-point for thinking about social justice again, it has transformed the very nature of the object about which we must exercise moral thoughtfulness. However, as far as the normative theory of the information society is concerned, none of the proffered policy approaches has been adequate, as a brief overview will attempt to show.

It is logical to begin with the school of thought that flatly denies the existence of digital divides. What one might call the 'Crisis?, What Crisis?' approach, this school's *laissez-faire,* anti-statist philosophy reflects the long-running economically conservative drift in western politics. Its defining moment came when Michael Powell, the Federal Communications Commission chairman responsible for key aspects of Republican information policy under George W. Bush, compared the digital divide to a 'Mercedes divide' (Stern 2001). By implying that information is just another disposable luxury item, such statements betray the right's limited grasp of the nature of deprivation and disenfranchisement in an information-centred society. Post-industrial people can live without Mercedes automobiles, but not without information. In its more credible forms, however, *laissez-faire* shades into another position that is capable of invoking a non-negligible body of relevant social-scientific research. This 'normalization' thesis (Norris 2001: 30–31) holds that, while the digital divide is morally deplorable, it is a temporary phenomenon which in the normal run of things can be expected to automatically resolve itself. Its chief exhibit is the 'S' (Sigmoid) curve, according to which, while the adoption of innovations may initially reflect social stratification, this 'early adopter' phase is sooner or later followed by relative price drops and consequent mass takeup, and ultimately by the bringing-on-board of 'laggards'. Moreover, the argument continues, the trend is an accelerated one in the case of those ICTs associated with the digital divide, especially the internet (Compaine 2000b; Schement and Forbes 2000). Benjamin Compaine, a lucid spokesman for the school, deduces that government interference in the diffusion process, if it must happen at all, should be confined to 'fine-tuning'; in short, he says, 'declare the war won' (Compaine 2001a).

Such a conclusion confirms, in the eyes of its supporters, some of the early optimism surrounding informatisation. Yet even if it is conceded that the pattern of diffusion that the curve plots is generally empirically accurate, there are still serious problems. The first is the situation of those who never—without intervention—adopt at all. On its own premises, the curve flattens at some point short of saturation. For example, even in affluent nations television has always fallen short of full household penetration and the internet, for all its marvels, is hardly likely to surpass the success of the 'magic rectangle' (Lewis-Smith 1995). Those without, some of whom belong to a permanent underclass, are easily lost from view. The second problem is that because of the continuous appearance of new types and versions of ICTs, gaps keep opening even as some older gaps more or less close, leaving certain groups invariably at a disadvantage. So even if internet household penetration were to achieve saturation, we can expect some further innovation then to have entered the field. While the cup might look half-full for optimists, for pessimists it is half-empty. Thus—as the 'stratification' model predicts (Norris 2001: 30–31, 71; cf. Katzman 1974)—information inequality can never be finally overcome. Moreover, the normalisation thesis, by concentrating on access or takeup, is prone to overlook other important factors, particularly the divergent types of usage different systacts make of ICTs.

Concerns such as these have prompted a dazzling display of philanthropic deeds. The colossal wealth accrued in certain quarters of the information economy has created a new order of 'digerati' anxious to mitigate the more visible defects of the curve. Private donations, voluntary sector initiatives, and foundations maintained by companies such as Microsoft, Intel and Hewlett-Packard, have all supported programmes to reduce forms of digital deprivation. Yet much philanthropy, as the Bill and Melinda Gates Foundation perhaps demonstrated in its equipping of public libraries with proprietary software, has ulterior motives, and can uncharitably be read as a cunning tactic of post-Fordist capital accumulation (Stevenson 2009). Its subliminal message seems to be that *state* interference, from which the rich and powerful have most to lose, is unnecessary. Yet the fundamental weakness of private philanthropy has been pinpointed since at least as far back as the socialist and left-liberal texts of the nineteenth century: such initiatives are inherently unsystematic and arbitrary, and tend in the long run to perpetuate dependency and social stratification. They should be warmly welcomed in the short run for their palliative properties, but they are no substitute for the systemic reforms accomplishable only through political action.

An imposing corpus of academic and official opinion deduces, therefore, that it is the business of the *state* to try to tackle the digital divide, to deal with its 'rough realities' (Luke 2000). There is much confusion about the goals of this branch of public policy, but it is possible to identify three main positions: poverty reduction, arithmetic egalitarianism and geometric egalitarianism, as defined in the previous chapter. By far the most politically popular, of course, is anti-poverty action. This involves simply identifying a post-industrial social class or systact suffering acutely and then training the big guns of state funding on it. The recipients might be informationally-deprived 'minorities' (Davis 2001: 186), perhaps 'the schoolgirl in Carthage, Tennessee' to whom Vice-President Al Gore's information superhighway rhetoric used to refer (Hundt 2000: 9). They might be widows from Appelscha or the retired ladies and other 'outsiders' described with great empathy by Elfreda Chatman (1996, 1999). Whoever they are, the state, acting as a result of interest-group advocacy, media agenda-setting or on its own initiative, steps in to relieve their information poverty, at least temporarily. But what it carefully avoids is any thought of pursuing equality.

O'Hara and Stevens have produced a competent philosophical articulation of this view. In 'prioritarianism', as they call it (2006: 112), 'the gap between the better off and the worst off is not morally salient as it is for egalitarianism'. Prioritarianism aims only 'to do enough to solve problems without engineering a complete solution' (O'Hara and Stevens 2006: 298). It is thus basically a form of what Venturelli (1998: 132) calls 'information-society policy as welfare economics', i.e. policy which will increase the wellbeing of the badly off only if it does not simultaneously reduce the wellbeing of anyone else, including the very rich. Or, in the older, biblical vernacular, prioritarianism holds that government is morally obliged to 'comfort the afflicted', but not to afflict the comfortable. However, from the perspective of the Rawls-Tawney Theorem, the narrow lens of this philosophy of state interventionism, its manner of hermetically sealing from one another the concepts of poverty and wealth, constitutes a fatal flaw. The welfare state, for all its merits—and it was the greatest political achievement of the twentieth century—is compatible with immensely unequal distributions of resources, including information. But contemporary social justice, if the preceding arguments are correct, is not only about absolute destitution but also about *relative* deprivation, the relationships between individuals and groups in a community, and this means that *both* ends of the socioeconomic scale must be addressed. While prioritising poverty, justice does not, to quote Tawney again, 'turn a blind eye on privilege'. In information society terms, it regards the luxuriating of an information elite as no less a social evil than the penury of an information underclass. So while attacking information poverty, progressive infopolitics also needs to strike into the established social system of entitlements and burdens. Information inequality, in the fine, Latinate language of another writer, is one of the 'gaps by which democracy we measure' (Schement 2001).

The goal for those who really wish to achieve a socially just distribution of information can be, as with any other primary good, arithmetic equality. While such strict egalitarianism is actually quite uncommon, and is more often found as a strawman in the minds of partisans of the economic right, it has occasionally existed in the real world. There are a few latter-day levellers who want to see an exact equality of information, just as their predecessors agitated for an equality of land, capital, disposable income, etc. In *Technics and Civilisation* (1934), Lewis Mumford, cited elsewhere as a key thinker for the information society (May 2003c), drafted a prototype for a basic communism of goods. More recently, Brian Martin's *Information Liberation* (1998: 50) spelled out plainly the central objective of this type of radical post-industrial politics: 'not just equality of opportunity, but equality of outcomes'. Everyone must not only start the race simultaneously but also end together. Yet the problems that have always beset this school of leftist thought remain. To recap the argument from Chapter 2, arithmetic equality can seem unfair, given the unequal efforts, skills and responsibilities of citizens. And even if it were fair, experience has shown that it tends both to compromise liberty and to dampen productivity and enterprise, with pernicious results for economic growth. Arithmetic socioeconomic equality in information, *if* it can be achieved, is therefore likely to be an equality of misery and one that leaves the polity grossly overcommitted, if not, indeed, totalitarian.

Such considerations have led to the procrustean bed of arithmetic information egalitarianism being increasingly avoided in favour of a more relaxed approach, some form of geometric equality that allows circumscribed spaces for differentials. Introducing an alternative terminology of 'vertical' *versus* 'horizontal' egalitarianism, Leah Lievrouw and Sharon Farb have helpfully applied such thinking to the information age. Vertical, i.e. arithmetic, egalitarianism, treats justice in information as a simple function of the distribution of social and economic goods, and aims in predictable manner for equal shares. 'From this perspective', they explain, 'greater equality of information access and use can be achieved by a more even redistribution of these goods among various groups' (Lievrouw and Farb 2003: 501). On the other hand, the more nuanced, horizontal perspective accommodates pertinent empirical knowledge, such as user studies research to the effect that people with similar social and economic traits may nonetheless vary widely in terms of their information needs. Thus it treats people differently, where appropriate. Appealing to both Rawls and Amartya Sen for philosophical authority, Lievrouw and Farb argue (2003: 501) that 'the fairness or *equity* of access and use, rather than the more or less equal distribution of information goods, may be a more useful foundation for studying inequities and formulating appropriate social policies'.

There can be no doubt that Lievrouw and Farb have accurately registered the general direction of post-industrial social democracy, in terms of both philosophy and electoral strategy. Mapping out the basic politico-philosophical terrain of progressive socioeconomic information policy, their article deserves to be, as it hopes, a 'starting point for a new and fruitful discussion' (Lievrouw and Farb 2003: 531). However, it is indeed only a beginning. They leave open the issue—'one of the most vexing questions in a post-industrial society' (Bell 1999: 451)—of what level of differential can be permitted by a democratic state that takes distributive justice in information seriously. In other words, the task remains of specifying a precise *formula* of differential justice. This is the thorny question that still dangles tantalisingly at the highest altitude of the digital divide literature, and it is as an answer to it that the second principle of the Rawls-Tawney Theorem has been devised. The second principle deals essentially with information which, while definitely within the orbit of social justice, is not so vital that it must be distributed exactly equally. To recall:

Second Principle of Information Justice

Inequalities in the social distribution of categories of information required for social and economic functioning are to satisfy three conditions:
 (i) they are to be attached to an information infrastructure equally accessible to all (the equal opportunity clause);
 (ii) they are to be to the greatest benefit of the least advantaged members of society (the difference principle); and
 (iii) they should not be so extensive as to generate class distinctions (the Tawney proviso)

It should be emphasised that the theorem is unwavering about the denotation of distributive justice: information itself, rather than digital media, or ICTs, or the telecommunications infrastructure, or the information superhighway. For the normative theory of the information society, the latter are significant only insofar as they impinge on the social distribution of information itself—information *qua* facts, reliable data, the building-blocks of knowledge and participation. Thus the digital divide is politically important primarily because of the way that it reveals the underlying structural issue of the unfair social distribution of hard information, the class stratification that turns some people into informed citizens while making others informationally illiterate and apathetic. It is this human hinterland, the sociological and psychosocial terrain *inland* of the digital hubs, teleports and access points, that festers in the absence of whole-hearted political ministrations, and that demands genuinely innovative thinking. A new edition of geometric/horizontal/differential egalitarianism, the second principle of the Rawls-Tawney Theorem is designed to achieve the correct public policy balance in addressing the fundamental problem *behind* the digital divide, namely, *unjustifiable* inequalities in the *social* distribution of *important* information in *post-industrial* societies. Now more flesh will need to be put onto its bones.

The first clause, expressing a conception of equality of opportunity, mandates equal access to information. It does not insist that every citizen ends up with the same amount, but that people should have—in practice as well as 'on paper'—an equal chance of having the same amount. In the field of education, where the principle has been very widely invoked, its import is now tolerably clear. Equality of opportunity means that all children should have roughly the same quality of primary and secondary schooling and thus the same prospects of entry into tertiary education. For social democrats, this in turn entails both the drastic improvement of many state schools and (although here some social democrats demur) the gradual integration of private schools—not least those which trade in the UK under the 'comically inappropriate' label of 'public schools' (Tawney 1923: 22; cf. Tawney 1943)—into a popular national educational system. But what would be the equivalent in information, as distinct from education? It is difficult to grasp the concept except by speaking in terms of institutions, for example a good public library system, a nationalised telecommunications network, or perhaps some wholly new type of information institution. I will pursue such details below; the point here is to establish that the second principle of information justice enshrines an ideal of equal opportunities in the substantive sense of equal access to information.

As we saw in the previous chapter, however, equality of opportunity is compatible with a very unequal society. While going further than relief of the information poor, equal access, judging by the prevalence of centre-ground political rhetoric paying homage to it, is not even controversial. Hence considerations of information justice spur real social democrats onwards and upwards, to a second clause, the difference principle. This states that inequalities of outcome are permissible as long as they maximise the information of the worst off group, that is to say only as long as the worst off group is better off under those inequalities than it would be if information were equally distributed. In this way and this way only, moderate differentials can be part of a fair society in the post-industrial age. What, though, *is* an unacceptable level of inequality in information outcomes? Let us be clear again that the aim is not merely to increase access for the information have-nots in absolute terms; it is to maintain a reasonably close social and economic relation between the informationally well off and badly off. We retain the concept, built into the theorem, of relative deprivation and its solvent of relational, interpersonal justice. And here the third clause, the Tawney proviso, provides calibration by specifying that an unacceptable level is being reached when there are signs that class divisions are forming. New castes and classes should not be allowed to materialise, nor old ones to linger. The theorem vetoes information elites as well as information underclasses.

The next theoretical task is that of stipulating which categories of information belong to the second principle of the Rawls-Tawney Theorem. Just as the previous section argued that only some orders of legal and political information—the data constitutive of participatory citizenship—merited the arithmetic distribution and lexical priority of the first principle, so this section needs to try to determine what kinds of information should be in the discursive frame if we wish to speak of *socioeconomic* justice in information. We know that to live effectively is to live with adequate information, and we know now what is necessary for political functioning, but what exactly is required for 'social and economic functioning' in the emergent socio-technical formation? It is absurd to suggest that *all* information is thus liable, even if information is defined as strictly as the journalistic conception demands. Indeed, that suggestion, not least the form of it which says or implies that all information must now be treated as a primary good liable to the difference principle, is not only philosophically unwarranted but actually serves to bring the enterprise of making information justiciable into disrepute: it devalues the currency of information justice. Thus the normative theory of the information society needs to name the categories of information which, while not paramount, are nevertheless important enough to deserve to be rescued from the swelling swamps of non-justiciable data.

It is submitted that the categories of information subject to the second principle of the Rawls-Tawney Theorem include the following:

Categories of Second-Principle Justiciable Information

   i. Hard news: domestic and foreign
  ii. Scientific, technical and medical (STM) information
 iii. Economic information
  iv. Religious information

The list is not exhaustive, but there is a persuasive social democratic case for these four at least to be among the information-types in an open set of second-principle justiciable information. Hard news, which enables the citizenry to be cognisant of political developments and other important current affairs both at home and abroad, has always been recognised as an important condition of well-informed democratic participation. STM information is of a very different order, yet the case for such intellectual wares to be widely distributed, rather than selfishly locked down by the intelligentsia, has become increasingly compelling. Bell's oft-repeated claim that 'theoretical knowledge' is 'axial' in post-industrial society is only part of a common persuasion that the contemporary citizen, and even more so the future citizen, cannot flourish without a basic grasp of innovations in science, medicine and technology. STM information is information that is not so crucial to citizenship that it belongs to the first principle of justice, yet is sufficiently important for its social distribution not to be left entirely to the vagaries of market forces or happenstance. Economic information—about jobs, interest rates, commercial opportunities—is also likely to qual-ify as a category that is subject to differential justice, such that, while all citizens need not have the same amount, the state should maximise the information level of the worst off group. Finally, to round off this starter list, the distribution of religious information, information so vital not only to the lifeworld of individuals, families and communities, but also to social peace itself, surely cannot be safely abandoned to the anarchy of worldly markets. Religious information would indeed have been considered first-principle justiciable in most premodern cultures; in post-industrial society its calling will have to be more modest.

The two ensuing sections will give more details of how the second prin-ciple of information justice might be able to work in practice. Before that, however, another hitherto postponed problem needs to be honestly faced, that of arriving at precise measurements of information levels. The Rawls-Tawney Theorem obviously cannot be used properly without such, but it has to be asked to what extent we can attain reliable knowledge of how much information an individual or group possesses. The problem is not so much at the lower end of the scale. Philanthropic and governmental initia-tives have meant that information poverty has often come under the micro-scope, resulting in many reasonably plausible forms of measurement (e.g. Childers 1975; Lumiers and Schimmel 2004). But what about information riches? If there really is such a state as information excess, as the theorem implies, how can it be ascertained in such as way that the problem can be politically addressed? While it might be a relatively straightforward matter to seek out and rectify the widow from Appelscha's ignorance of her con-sumer rights, say, is it also possible to quantify, or even talk meaningfully about, a surfeit of consumer information residing in the heads of her nem-eses, that well-heeled couple from Amsterdam's picturesque canal district? In short, is the idea of an information maximum viable?

Thankfully, there are grounds for hope that a positive answer will be forthcoming. We know from Japanese information flow censuses that the maximum psychological personal daily intake of information is approxi-mately 48,000 words; that insight, and much else in this neglected research tradition, can be enlisted to the cause (Duff 2000a, b). There is also the well-established western tradition of knowledge gaps research, which pos-its a 'ceiling effect', i.e. a limitation on how informed the well-informed can become on particular topics (e.g. Bonfadelli 2002: 67–68). What both research fronts, and no doubt others, seem to imply is that it is possible to get some kind of critical handle on the notion of information limits. Moreover, we can in any case always construct indicators which employ tangible variables as proxies of information wealth, notably, to take the most obvious example, legal ownership of information technology systems, broadcasting media or telecommunications networks. A few further comments apropos of the measurement issue will be offered in the next two sections, but this is really a technical matter which, once acknowledged, the normative theory of the information society will need largely to delegate. The main point is that it is not unreasonable to expect that, by some such means, the normative theory of the information society will be able to at least *approximate* its goal of specifying upper as well as lower parameters of permissible information appropriations.

Finally, it may be that the entire tradition of intellectual property rights management, a central concern of information policy research (e.g. Browne 1997a, b; Burger 1993), supports the general thrust of my argument. The classic justification of copyright or patents is that they promote general social wellbeing by incentivising the individual's production of more or better information (e.g. Moore 2001). At the same time, with its 'fair dealing' or 'fair use' clauses, and other qualifications, copyright looks after those outside the ownership circle. This seems to suggest both that the outline of the rationale behind the difference principle in information was visible hundreds of years ago and that it is *not* counter-intuitive that certain other categories of information should now, in an informatised society, be made into a primary good. Yet it does more than that. It appears to constitute evidence that the idea of numerical limits, of differentials and tradeoffs, is perfectly feasible in the special, in some ways abstract and rarefied, world of information. The task of identifying the optimal length and strength of a copyright or patenting regime, while obviously complex, has never been considered insurmountable. So neither should it be thought naive to want to apply precise values to the variables in the Rawls-Tawney Theorem. However, in order to establish more firmly some of these general points, the next section will cash out more plentifully the argument for the inclusion of one particular category of second-principle justiciable information: news-information.

ILLUSTRATION: DIFFERENTIAL ACCESS TO NEWS-INFORMATION

News has always been a unique epistemological species and one that understandably excites powerful emotions, allegiances and aspirations, but it has not often received attention as an object of systematic doctrines of distributive justice. Normative theories of the information society cannot avoid viewing it from this angle, however. Definitional clarity is invariably the essential starting-point of rigorous thought, and for the theory under development here, news will be restricted to 'hard' news, both domestic and foreign, of politics and current affairs. It will be contradistinguished, and this of course is itself a normative manoeuvre, from 'soft' news and other flows broadly classifiable as entertainment or advertising. The fact that these categories shade into one another does not at all mean that they are not intrinsically different, despite what some media theorists may allege. Everything is what it is, and not another thing. I will seal this distinction, first advanced in the final section of Chapter 1, by referring hereafter to 'news-information'.

News-information, then, has enjoyed a key role in the history of statecraft, both moral and Machiavellian, democratic and dictatorial (e.g. Allan 2004; Conboy 2011). On the one hand, governments have patronised its production. In one way or another, they have recognised that newspapers, for example, are not typical market commodities, not horse-shoes or tins of baked beans, and that they warrant, therefore, some kind of special dispensation. In a landmark study, Robert Picard (1985: 101ff.) demonstrated that political interventionism on behalf of the press is standard in the West, in such guises as tax advantages, reduced postal rates, varieties of loans, even cash grants. *The Times*, no less, was launched with a government handout, specifically as an organ of information to combat the radical press post-1789. This generalisation holds good even for that minimal-state bastion, the US, where, contrary to American self-images, the press is financially assisted by the federal government, albeit in ways that seem rigged in favour of the corporation-dominated status quo (Picard 1985: 145). On the other hand, government interest in mass media has also taken the very different form of censorship and regulation. Yet these too are back-handed ways of the state endorsing the proposition that it has a responsibility for the correct distribution of news-information. Nor are they are necessarily synonymous with authoritarianism. As Runciman (1997: 23) wisely points out, 'a liberal mode of persuasion is not defined by a lack of censorship in any form, but by the difference between the censorship of what is claimed (however unconvincingly) to be so libellous, seditious, or obscene as to be unacceptable to public opinion and a censorship which proscribes as heretical all views not directly in accordance with the doctrines and purposes of the incumbents of governmental roles'.

For their own part, information society theorists have also been quick to salute the centrality of news-information. Taking a long backwards glance, Youichi Ito (2000) portrays the spread of newspapers as integral to informatisation and modernisation, alongside other factors such as rising literacy rates, the existence of a book industry, and the ability of writers to live on royalties. Porat (1977: 213, 218) too was apprised of the importance of the mass media, what he billed as the 'publishing sector', in his primary information economy: 'the survival of national dailies' was—in the event of market failure—an issue for information policy even then. 'The press', according to another early votary of electronic technology, 'will play a critical role in setting the quality of life in an information society' (Pool 1977: 264). More recently, Trevor Haywood (1995) gave attention to the likes of News Corp in his commentary on inequalities of 'access and exchange in the global information society'. It is not just a question of the print-on-paper press, of course. Michael McCauley (2002) reminds us of the 'normative mission' of National Public Radio (NPR) in the US, while Gustavo Cardoso's Castellsian *Media in the Network Society* (2006) presents television as still—just—the principal 'meta-system' of news-information. And journalism practitioners themselves sometimes self-identify as gate-keepers of information age democracy. 'Our standard as journalists', opines Brian Richardson (2004: 54), 'must be to provide audiences what they need to know: accurate, contextualized information that will help them control the course of their own lives'.

Yet despite its obvious political and social importance—its determination of many of the 'pictures in our heads', of our 'pseudo-environment' (Lippmann 1922: Chapter 1)—news-information has always suffered from a gross problem of maldistribution. While no one would deny that there is an abundance of easily and cheaply accessible material today, there are still numerous indicators of a serious stratification issue, even in the kinds of advanced societies designated in the information society thesis. Ignorance of basic items of current information remains, as since time immemorial it has been, partly a function of social class. The most striking recent illustration is poll evidence that a large proportion of viewers of US television channel Fox News believed that Iraq had nefarious links with al-Qaida, the crucial misinformation-package sold by the Bush-Blair axis to justify the invasion of Iraq (e.g. World Public Opinion.org 2011). Given that a high proportion of Fox News viewers are relatively poorly educated, false information on the defining foreign-affairs issue of our generation is evidently concentrated among particular systacts. These are surely among the information-poor in America, even if they are not necessarily wanting in other primary goods. At the other pole, the on-average more educated users of NPR or the *Washington Post* are known to be aware that the Osama-Saddam nexus was always preposterous fiction. So what we have is a straightforward manifestation of an unjust as well as pernicious social distribution of news-information. It is precisely this kind of scenario that ethical information policy, ethical infopolitics, must be geared to combat.

If the idea of an information-abundant society is to have any real meaning, news-information, distributed in a fair manner, must be a prominent part of it. However, while it is possible to be confident that category (i) qualifies as a primary good, and while current patterns of consumption are clearly still not what they ought to be, news-information does not merit first-principle treatment. Social justice is indeed at issue, but in this case arithmetic equality is not the solution. There is no substantial body of intuitions to the effect that every citizen should have exactly the same quantity or quality of news-information. If more candidate-information were given to the rich than to the poor while campaigning or in the voting booth, our intuitions would certainly be offended, but we do not feel so vehemently egalitarian about information at a safer distance from pure electoral and constitutional matters. We do not feel outraged that some are information-ally better off in media consumption, so long as everyone has reasonable access to the major stories. Of course, news-information *could* be rationed out in identical slices to every citizen. Indeed, such has frequently been the avowed information policy of authoritarian regimes, and even occasion-ally of war-time liberal regimes. Yet arithmetic news-information equality as a steady-state is frankly abnormal. Politically-mature instincts militate against what might be called the '*Pravda* Paradigm', against the idea of the same paper (say) going to everyone, and this is the case whatever our beliefs may be about the content of the message.

Nor is news-information remotely comparable to vaccine information, which, civilised intuitions clamour, must go absolutely equally to absolutely everyone. However, those same intuitions also tell us that moral claims at some level *are* still operative, that the core business of journalism should to some extent be looked upon as a 'sphere of justice' (Walzer 1985). The basic rationale for news-information to be classed as a primary good is that, in all societies but especially information societies—where information has *ex hypothesi* become the prime resource—ignorance of up-to-date facts about the wider world is a deficiency which cannot be tolerated. So lest the distribution of news-information, a category self-evidently necessary to the proficient conduct of democratic citizenship, become too uneven, steps need to be taken to make sure that policy mechanisms work to produce, alongside a diversity of sources, a centripetal pressure on society and a mitigation of information inequality. Here, in other words, the difference principle can reign.

Roughly parallel arguments have been made by distinguished thinkers working from within different socio-philosophical frameworks. Garnham (1999: 121), representing the political economy of communication school, observes that 'one is not, in a sense, and feels oneself not to be, a full citizen if one is not able to be aware of the major stories in the papers'. He thinks that the object of social justice should not be conceptualised as a Rawlsian primary good but as a more rounded notion of 'capabilities' after the man-ner of Sen; this will supposedly get us away from 'superficial indexes of access or usage' (Garnham 1999: 120). I would suggest that the generic problem of indexicality cannot be pinned onto the specific move to make information a primary good. Moreover, it is possible that capability may itself be too amorphous a notion to fill the indexing slot in a feasible, veri-fiable theory of distributive justice. But the end-result is in any case simi-lar: the capabilities approach—like the Rawls-Tawney Theorem—'leads to policies of positive discrimination in the face of these [socioeconomic] bar-riers, if we are serious about equality' (Garnham 1999: 124). Significantly, Habermas too (2009) has recently spoken out in favour of state succour of the beleaguered German press, so as to ensure the social circulation of high quality information; the political logic, he believes, is not unlike the case for guaranteeing water or electrical power to all homes. The skewed social distribution of news-information has also long been a focus, and ethical concern, of knowledge gap theorists interested in media access (e.g. Bucy and Newhagen 2004).

What all of this points to is a news-information policy pincer movement. On the one hand, there need to be substantial 'information subsidies' to the poor, not in Oscar Gandy's (1982) depressing sense of press releases 'helping' journalists to fill their news holes, but in the more attractive sense of governmental underwriting of the dissemination of important, independently-produced, factual knowledge in the public interest. This must go further than what in telecommunications parlance is known as 'universal service' (Preston and Flynn 2000; Sawhney 2000) or 'universal access' (Sawhney and Jayakar 2007), noble goals though they be. There should of course be universalist public service institutions, of which NPR and the BBC are eminent current examples, dedicated to the promulgation of accurate domestic and foreign news-information. That much is obvious. And if we can accept broadcasting and telecoms subsidies, why not also, as Habermas says, newspaper subsidies? Beyond that, however, there need to be additional mechanisms for specifically targeting and 'raising' the information poor. How exactly this should turn out will presumably depend on the particular circumstances and traditions of different nations. For example, given the prevalence of 'tabloids' as a source in the UK, ethical information policy in this country might have to involve a media authority better able to monitor such papers *qua* news-information outlets. An accuracy norm may need to be effectively inculcated, by means of incentives or perhaps if necessary by sanctions. Of course, opinion and news are distinguishable and it is not being suggested that the likes of the *Sun* should not be wildly partisan in their op-ed pages. However, where news itself is being reported it is reasonable for an information society to query whether the deliberate and regular splashing of falsehoods can be compatible with a fair social distribution of information. The *Sun* might well vigorously repudiate this charge, perhaps even convincingly, but one need only return to my original example of its News Corp stable-mate, Fox News, to carry the general point.

Another scheme for developing the news-information system in line with the second principle of the Rawls-Tawney Theorem might be one-off government grants to fund long-range investigative reporting projects. It is well-known that investigative reporting is struggling. If we do not wish to lose this great social-epistemic tradition, the courageous exposures of Watergate, Thalidomide and the like, then perhaps radical measures need to be considered. The knee-jerk objection that the state cannot fund independent investigative reporting is as absurd as saying that there cannot be critical thought in public universities. Grants could be administered via a third party akin to the academic research councils. But the point here is that the Rawls-Tawney Theorem provides the philosophical support for progressive information policies. There could also be renewable state bursaries for foreign correspondents, another matter of urgency given the current near-total market failure in that vital department. Any number of solutions might be imagined and should be imagined. The fundamental need is to find where significant gaps lie and then to devise mechanisms which make good those defects in such a way as to ensure that the news-information system as a whole works for the benefit of the whole society, and particularly its worst off members.

At the other end of the scale, ways need to be found to effect reasonable constraints on the rights of information ownership. The information minimum must be raised, but—and this is where the Tawney proviso makes its mark—an information maximum must somehow also be established. Admittedly, it is not yet very obvious how this can be done. What *is* clear, though, is that wealth and power in the new millennium cannot be allowed to become so concentrated that the news-information system no longer serves the common good. It seems likely that the wings of media barons will have to be clipped if we are at all serious about creating fairer, in their informational aspects, twenty-first century societies. Hence it is probable that implementation of the second principle would push the overall ownership structure of the mass media in a leftward direction. Nevertheless, the idea of an information maximum should not be equated with a democratic socialist theory of the press like Picard's (1984), since there is nothing in the Rawls-Tawney Theorem to imply that socioeconomic justice is incompatible with private ownership of a reasonable, although not dominant, proportion of the media. In a just information society there can be capitalist owners, as well as intermediate actors such as cooperatives and trusts—the Scott Trust, owner of the *Guardian* and *Observer*, has been a more or less sustainable model of the latter—alongside the state utilities. It is not a question of taking all news-information media into common ownership, but of refashioning the system so that all things work together for good. And this will be brought about by smart social programming, not by Manichean politics or dogmatic economics.

So what we seem to be left with is a variant of the already familiar mixed economy of the media. Some modification of this time-honoured formula should continue to meet the requirements of socioeconomic right in the particular sphere of justice under discussion. For many categories of valuable but not paramount information, the trick is to avoid simplisticism, especially crude dichotomies and concomitant totalising political-economic narratives. It sounds impressive, but is ultimately unhelpful, to say that information should now be a public good—just as unhelpful as saying that it should be a commodity. Information is not uniform and homogeneous, and neither should be its philosophy, politics or economics. News-information should *in some respects* and *to some extent* be conceptualised as a public resource, but *in other respects* and *to other extents* be treated as a private commodity. There can be a synergistic relationship between the two pure modes, and between intermediate forms and either or both of the poles. So what is needed, in this as in many another application of the normative theory of the information society, is the classic prescription of social democratic thought: a balance between individualism and collectivism, in this case in the shape of a media pluralism wherein the state acts as a resistance movement against the might of the new Kapital, information—acts, in plainer terms, to compensate for the deficiencies of the free market— while not simultaneously killing the private-sector geese that lay the golden eggs of innovation and prosperity.

It should be emphasised that only news-information—a small fraction of total media flows—is subject to the second principle of justice of the Rawls-Tawney Theorem. The normative theory of the information society keeps returning to its moorings in the journalistic conception. Hard political and current-affairs news fits easily into this conception, but its main rival, pure entertainment, while an important and legitimate popular function of the mass media, does not qualify as an item for social justice. In a world of scarce resources, it should not generally concern policymakers that soap operas and game shows are not distributed within the latitude of inequality permitted by the second principle, or any other principle of information justice. Such flows can normally be left without compunction to market solutions, and if some systacts cannot afford them, so be it. The state has a duty to oversee distribution—not, to reiterate, by micromanaging it, but by setting up a system which, allowing a variety of competing modes of ownership and access, secures the public interest, and particularly the interest of the information poor—but it need do so only with regard to bona fide information. Having said that, it might be conceded that considerations of national cohesion, acculturation, and so on, can perhaps be persuasively adduced in favour of state support of the televising of some sporting events and the like. However, special cases such as these, subsisting at the margins of social justice rather than its core, cannot be pursued here.

Although not fully fleshed-out, the foregoing excursion has perhaps done enough to illustrate the way in which the second principle works out apropos of a single category of socially-valuable information, namely, news-information—category (i) on the list. I have argued that there is a solid case for thinking that the social distribution of such, in advanced, post-industrial nations, *is* justiciable, *not*, however, in a draconian egalitarian manner but in the milder sense inscribed in the second principle of the Rawls-Tawney Theorem. Hopefully the reasoning has been cogent, or is at least capable of being made so. It is, therefore, submitted that categories (ii) to (iv), *viz.* STM information, economic information and religious information, are susceptible of structurally-similar normative apologetics. A plausible case could be worked up for each of these important categories, and perhaps also for others that have not been mentioned.

INDICATIVE INSTITUTIONAL OUTCOMES
OF THE RAWLS-TAWNEY THEOREM

The second part of *A Theory of Justice* describes in Byzantine detail an institutional system that, in Rawls's eyes, satisfied his two principles. Most of the 'background institutions' of his ideal land, as he aptly calls them—background, because individuals not institutions belong in the foreground of any liberal ideal—were instantly recognisable as the stock furniture of western liberal democracies: for the first principle, separation of powers, multiparty politics, periodic free elections, and so on; for the second, progressive income tax, public utilities, a welfare system, etc. *Pace* his radical-left critics, this was not at all a weakness of Rawls's theory, or a manifestation of circular reasoning. Rawls never set off to be a social revolutionary. His mission, rather, was to identify and freshly justify what might already be right in the institutional status quo and therefrom to deduce which other institutions needed reform or abolition. This is entirely consonant with the left-liberal tradition. For Tawney, too, the principles of justice demanded a social order that built on the best achievements of the past, although he tended to favour a greater degree of reconstruction. Citing the National Health Service and other concrete achievements of the post-war Labour administration, Tawney concluded that social democracy was at last beginning to be implemented in his own country:

> Social solidarity has been strengthened as the essentials of civilisation, once the privilege of a minority, have increasingly become a common possession. Judged by the distribution of income, a more equalitarian society than existed in pre-war England, and than exists to-day in the Soviet Union or in the United States, is in the process of creation. 'Choose equality and shun greed' is, doubtless, a far from all-sufficient formula. In a world, however, where Communist social theory and American economic practice agree in repudiating it, it is not, perhaps, a misfortune that one more people has been added to the small number of those disposed to take it seriously. (Tawney 1949: 115)

That, however, was the industrial epoch. The next step of a normative theory of the information society is to start the process of thinking about the kinds of institutions that justice requires in a twenty-first, post-industrial century. The importance of translating principles into institutions has been recognised by other information society theorists (e.g. Braman 2006; Galperin 2004), as well as by institutional socioeconomists (Hollingsworth 2002), among others. In this volume, I have tried to articulate an informatised synthesis of Rawls's and Tawney's positions, and this abstract construct now calls for its own effort of translation. However, a major caveat must be given. The bulk of the casuistical labour, as it were, will need to be handed to others, because the primary role of a normative theory of the information society is not to spell out institutional details but to provide a convincing conceptual framework for those and other specifications—to put the whole show, as it were, on the road, and heading in the right general direction. Many of the institutional specifics simply cannot be decided *a priori* in any case, and so need to be thought out in connection with concrete problems in particular local contexts. Thus the most that can be offered here are a few indicative outcomes.

To begin with the first principle, then, what kinds of information institution would exist if the Rawls-Tawney Theorem were being fulfilled in the *polities* of a post-industrial society such as Scotland, the US or Japan? The answer to this question would appear to be threefold: some of the background political institutions of industrial-era liberal democracy should carry on largely as before; others would need to undergo significant revision; and there would also have to be a third category of new information institutions capable of fulfilling social functions wholly unanticipated by the status quo. The following suggestions briefly explore all these categories.

There are plenty of information-based industrial-era political institutions that ought to survive with, at most, minor modifications. Prominent among them are the weathered pillars of liberal democracy, namely parliamentary and congressional complexes, secret ballots, independent judiciaries, accountable intelligence agencies, legal trade unions, free presses, and traditional free-speech zones like London's Speakers' Corner or Kent State University's Sproul Plaza. Rather than be uprooted by post-industrialist zealotry, these marvels of the modern world need to be reinforced. They are a necessary condition of any kind of political justice, including political-information justice, and they deserve to remain intact in perpetuity. As we have seen, the right to know, in the emergent sense of guaranteed access to administrative and other official information, is another specific central requirement of the first principle of information justice. This right needs to be nurtured and developed, and institutionally it should cash out into a progressive—i.e. pro-disclosure—FOI regime. It should mean that the inner workings of the public bureaucracy, as well as decisions by central and local government, and possibly some private-sector organisations too, should come under effective, systematic scrutiny. In addition, it requires a robust, efficient, timeous and user-friendly institutional mechanism for ensuring compliance. Explicated for illustrative purposes in terms of what currently exists in the US and the UK, this strand of the first principle would demand the best of both worlds: applicability to as many organs of the state as possible, like the US regime, which covers even the Central Intelligence Agency and the Federal Bureau of Investigation, combined with an exemplary machinery of compliance, after the manner of the offices of the powerful Westminster and Scottish 'information commissioners'. Whatever they might be called, it is safe to deduce that independent information ombudsmen with wide jurisdiction are an essential institutional outcome of the Rawls-Tawney Theorem. And that would certainly mark a tangible improvement on the typical industrial-era polity.

Another axial institution of first-principle information justice, though perhaps a less riveting one, is the public library. A legacy in the UK of social movements that campaigned for the Parochial Libraries Act 1708 and later for the Public Libraries Act 1850 (Cawkell 2001: 57), and of parallel movements elsewhere, book-lending public libraries remain today a key information utility in many lands. To say that they are 'nothing less than the heart and the brain of the Information Society' (Batt 1998: 16) is to be in danger of hyperbole, but they are surely one vital organ in a healthy body politic. We should heed library professionals when they tell us that if our goal is a national information infrastructure, 'the NII must facilitate these public institutions rather than annihilate them' (Schaefer 1995: 10). However, parsimony is required. It is absurd to argue that information-lite genres such as crime fiction need to be distributed arithmetically equally among the mob. On the other hand, at least one aspect of public library provision does definitely find itself in non-negotiable first-principle territory: reference works. Electoral rolls, biographical directories, encyclopaedias, statistical series, a range of daily and weekly newspapers—all the mainstays of the 'For Consultation Only' section of any self-respecting library—should be available to everyone regardless of geographic or socioeconomic coordinates. Libraries are to that extent as necessary a condition of political democracy as the right to vote, and the first principle therefore mandates their survival, including, as a logical consequence, financial support for the institutions of library and information science (LIS) education. Admittedly, some information society theorists prefer to advise that the concept of the public library is obsolescent, or try to marginalise it by prescribing information kiosks in other venues, such as doctors' surgeries, public houses, even hairdressing salons. However, it is a sign of technological determinism to make the information infrastructure synonymous with digital networks, to want to reinvent the access wheel for its own sake. Einstein once observed (1954: 6) that the problem with Prohibition was that by closing pubs the authorities removed an important site of cultural and political discussion. It would be the same with public libraries. The unglamorous truth is that a country with a library in every village would be far closer to a fair information society than a library-less society awash with computers.

Nevertheless, while it is probably safe to assert that an informatised, first-principle compliant society will for the foreseeable future include proximity to libraries as physical establishments, the first principle does also seem to call for some new information institutions. Something important appears to be missing in the information infrastructure as presently constituted. Even where an FOI law enjoins upfront disclosure, as in the 'publication schemes' in the Westminster and Scottish statutes, and even where public libraries housing vital political and social information abound, these do not yet produce an optimally information-conscious citizenry. Nor, I suspect, would special projects along the lines of the Digital Public Library of America envisaged by the Librarian of Harvard

(Darnton 2011), admirable though they may well be. There is a deeper missing link, something that has the ability to give people a decisive hoist up the informatisation scale. And it is becoming obvious in what general direction the answer is to be found.

What seems to be required for the twenty-first century polity is a network of institutions that disseminate key information *individually* and *proactively*. The UK's Citizens' Advice Bureaus (CABs) and Norway's Citizens' Information Centres may be prototypes of such, as some information society commentators have already recorded (e.g. Murdock and Golding 1989: 185; Baruchson-Arbib 1996: 27; Steele 1998: 178–9). Funded at least partially by the state, these agencies seek to empower the citizenry by dispensing legal and consumer advice at point of need. Yet their geographic presence and societal impact have always been modest. They have undoubtedly helped the unemployed miner, the bewildered widow and many other individuals in informational dire straits, yet they have not succeeded in establishing themselves as central information-age institutions. So new thinking, guided by the Rawls-Tawney Theorem, is needed. One possibility worth exploring would be the incorporation of citizen-information outfits into the public library system, combining the customised legal-advocacy skills of the former with the erudition, professional accreditation and high-street presence of the latter. Even if that particular scenario were to prove unfeasible, it at least suggests the kind of synergistic institutional solution for which the information society of tomorrow is yearning. This, at any rate, is one major blank that will need to be filled in.

Personal privacy also needs to find more stable institutional embodiment in the twenty-first century. While public consciousness of privacy rights has improved in recent decades as a result of the ongoing critical reflection on the consequences of informatisation, the practical process of institutionalisation is still unfinished. As noted above, the European Union has positioned itself as a global standard-bearer on data protection. Its rules are often interpreted with risible pusillanimity, for example when schools are too frightened to display examination results in case this violates putative rights of low achievers, but they have, in very general terms, served well the legitimate ethical core of the privacy cause. They are proactive, not just reinforcing the proverbial right to be left alone, but also giving data subjects positive rights of control over information flows. The small print cannot detain us here, but one special feature of the European system stands out. In many Union states, the strength of the regime derives largely from the existence of a dedicated privacy commissioner, another independent ombudsman with significant powers. He or she is able not only to protect the individual from invasions of privacy but also to speak ex cathedra on broad privacy-relevant developments. For example, a recent privacy commissioner won headlines and sparked a brief national debate by claiming that British citizens have managed to 'sleep-walk into a surveillance society' (BBC News 2006). The sociopolitical value of such interventions should not be underestimated. As with information czars, therefore, it is safe to stipulate that the office of privacy commissioner should be a standard institutional outcome of the first principle of information justice.

A state-funded telecasting facility is another information institution that merits the strict rule of arithmetically-egalitarian distribution. The reasoning can be briefly rehearsed. For representative democracy to work properly, the citizenry must make properly informed decisions. If so, every citizen has a right to an equal share of undistorted political information. At election time, especially, it cannot be the case that some sections of society know less than others about the policies and personalities on offer. But television, as explained by Cardoso (2006), remains for the time being a vital source of information as well as entertainment. If so, the state has a direct duty to support society-wide distribution. An exemplar of such universalism throughout much of the last century was the party political broadcasts mediated by the BBC, telecasts charged with itemising and elucidating specific manifesto policies. This state of affairs should continue. Of course, totally pure electoral information is an ideal that can never be fulfilled, but to allow election broadcasts to be abandoned or even watered down would only harm democracy; in particular, people should not be subjected to facile replacements in the form of political advertising, overt or subliminal. What this entails is either a government-funded independent broadcasting utility such as the BBC, or some other kind of subsidised and regulated electoral-information mass media system. Similar arguments underpin the BBC World Service and other services; and countries throughout the world might well be able to point to comparable information institutions of equal importance in their own cultures.

These then are some—albeit a mere fraction—of the kinds of institutions required by the first principle of information justice. Our intuitions about citizenship information are indeed sternly egalitarian, and we would find it unacceptable if access to public libraries, to information or privacy commissioners, to legal advice bureaus or to electoral broadcasts, were anything less than identical. However, I have argued that not all information calls for such strict fairness. The Rawls-Tawney Theorem does not demand socioeconomic-information equality or a fully socialised information economy, only that there should not be excessive gaps between information rich and poor. Thus many categories of information can be treated under the more lenient second principle, not to mention the innumerable other categories that can be safely left out of the orbit of social justice completely. It is this Aristotelian mean, rendered in economic parlance as the mixed economy, that the second principle of the Rawls-Tawney Theorem has been designed to capture. The principle translates into a variety of publicly-owned information institutions operating under the dispensation, familiar to the social democratic welfare state, of free at point-of-need—in this case information need. However, there is certainly also scope for an array of private information networks and organisations, so long as these are regulated in such a way that they too ultimately comply with the norms of distributive justice. There is no sense in legislating universal access if the economic system has removed any incentive to produce new information. We still need Silicon Valley and Silicon Glen.

The previous section anticipated some of the institutions that might satisfy the second principle with regard specifically to the category of news-information. So let us focus on some other categories now. As with news, STM information can invoke a compelling case for second-principle treatment, i.e. a case for information subsidies on the one hand and a cap on information ownership on the other. I have already suggested, *pace* advocates of wholesale information liberation (e.g. Martin 1998), that patents, copyright and other intellectual property modes must remain secure in the information society, but if we are serious about fair differentials then they certainly need to be adjusted. Institutionally, the second principle implies not just generous 'fair dealing' clauses and exemptions for public libraries, educational institutions and the like, but also lower limits on terms. The trend to ever-lengthening copyrights, in many regions of the world already extending to death of author plus 70 years, needs to be arrested if not reversed. It is difficult to see how anything longer than death of author, or at most death of author plus one generation, would not contravene the ideal of an information maximum that is enshrined in the Rawls-Tawney Theorem. Patents as currently constituted also seem to be working against the theorem. If scientific and medical breakthroughs are to maximise the position of the worst off, they need to be shared more widely and more expeditiously. This is about more than just a welfare state in information, it is about a fairer overall system which reduces excesses as well as supports those with less.

While, as with the first principle, such prescriptions may seem like a mere tweaking of the current information order, at least in the context of advanced democracies, that does not mean that the second principle of the Rawls-Tawney Theorem is superfluous. The key requirement is to firmly establish the principle that the transfer branch of government should switch not just money but also our new post-industrial currency, hard information, across systacts, especially from the rich to the poor. If the principle can help in any degree either to shore up or to improve valuable information institutions already in existence, that surely represents a useful contribution. Given the vulnerability of all social democratic-style institutions to the prevailing winds of neo-conservative reaction, not least in their witch-like garb of 'global forces', any assistance can only be welcome.

In any case, the next proposal marks a serious rupture with the status quo. Since the epidemic of privatisations of national telecommunications monopolies in the 1980s and 1990s, the concept of competition, or, more realistically, oligopoly, in the telecommunications infrastructure, has become naturalised. The Rawls-Tawney Theorem counters this specious orthodoxy. The basic intuitive case for state or municipal control of the information superhighway has never changed. Although the consensus took a century or more to finalise, the industrial era eventually accepted that the great transport system that it had produced could not be safely entrusted to private interests. It would be tedious to spell out the normative and technical arguments that inspired generations of political idealists in this regard. At the same time, however, while almost everyone believed that railways, roads and air space should be public utilities, almost no one was so aghast at the idea of private ownership of trains, airplanes or, at any rate, automobiles. Now a largely analogous bundle of intuitions points in favour of social ownership and control of data communications networks. Telephone handsets and myriad other peripheral networks and devices can be part of the competitive economy, but the core infrastructure, the Autobahn itself, should be publicly owned. It is precisely this public-private permutation that the second principle of the Rawls-Tawney Theorem implies once it is applied to telecommunications. Although it amounts only to a return to an historically familiar (at least in western Europe) settlement, the renationalisation of the telecommunications system represents today a very radical policy outcome of the second principle.

'The reduction of major inequalities', Ian Miles and Jonathan Gershuny wisely counselled (1987: 222), 'should be explicitly incorporated as a goal in the design of information society'. There are many other possible institutional implications of the inequality-reducing, but not equality-insisting, second principle of information justice. These might include, but would by no means be confined to, the following: school, college and adult education programmes in information and media skills; state provision of sustainable social networking sites and other cyberspaces catering to the business, artistic and spiritual public spheres; research and development in the fields of medical expert systems, community robotics and popular artificial intelligence; large-scale public information exhibitions; and explicit information society drives, including regional and global summitry. The task of teasing out the details of a new normative settlement cannot be engaged any further here, but the guidelines to follow when doing so should by now be very clear: equality of access, the information age's distinctive rendition of equal opportunities; maximin, the Rawlsian principle of maximising the welfare of the worst off group; and fellowship, Tawney's 'social solidarity'. All of these must find mutually compatible, as well as civil and political liberty-friendly, expression in the background institutions of the twenty-first century.

One final implication, however, cannot go unmentioned. There needs also to be a higher order institutional mechanism—an information meta-institution—for overseeing the operation of the numerous strands of information policy required by both principles of the Rawls-Tawney Theorem. Leon Trotsky once said that a capitalist society is one where each man thinks for himself and no one thinks for all (quoted in Bell

1980b: 539), a role he no doubt envisaged for himself in his communist utopia. It was the stuff of totalitarianism, of course, but there is certainly a case for a democratically-accountable office charged with the monitoring, coordinating and auditing of the justiciable institutions of an information society. This should not take the form of an omnicompetent commissar—after all, there will already be powerful independent information and privacy commissioners—but rather of a special civil service agency of some description, perhaps as part of a revamped department for constitutional affairs. It is significant that the top recommendation of Porat's report (1977: 10) was that 'in response to emerging horizontal [i.e. spread out across the whole economy] information policy issues, the Executive Branch should establish an appropriate organization to coordinate interdepartmental policy formulation'. 'This compact group', he elaborated (1977: 241), 'should serve as policy coordinators rather than policy formulators, policy monitors rather than policy implementers. Its job is to encourage communication between the mission agencies, to alert those that are on a collision course, to facilitate interdepartmental planning and cooperation'.

The Poratian priority was to make sure that information production, the new engine of the post-industrial economy, would operate smoothly under a largely free-market order. The overriding concern of the analytical capability required by a normative theory of the information society, on the other hand, is not economic efficiency but social equity. Its job would be to secure a coherent overall pattern in the system of independent information institutions, such that the polity would be able to say with confidence that, while liberty, including economic liberty, is flourishing, everything is working together for the good of society—and particularly its worst off members.

Information is resource, commodity, force, phenomenon, even cosmological principle, all of these and more. While there may be quite different ways of gathering it into the fold of social justice, of operationalising our new primary good, this section has essayed to do so by presenting a preliminary itemisation of a viable scenario of informatised social democracy. To summarise: the institutional setup, defined broadly as the universe of information utilities, corporations and intermediate entities, should include revitalised reference libraries, reinvented citizens' advice bureaus, pro-disclosure FOI statutes, powerful information and privacy commissioners, uncommercialised public service broadcasting systems, investigative newspapers, end-user-friendly patenting and copyright regimes, and national (and possibly international) telecommunications utilities. The case has been made throughout for a mixed economy, with the state acting not as panopticon but as part-owner and chief regulator in a diversified, pluralistic information economy. Together, these mechanisms and institutions can be made to generate a reasonably fair social distribution of information, and thereby to help us to edge towards the nirvana that Steve Fuller (2005: 265–66) calls 'epistemic justice'. In our own terms, an answer has been provided to the question of what information justice requires, namely an open set of institutions compatible with the Rawls-Tawney Theorem. Now, however, it is necessary to say more about how exactly such an ambitious *telos* can be achieved, to shed light not on the destination but on the road to the more bounteous information land.

4 Social Engineering
Industrial and Post-Industrial

The Rawls-Tawney Theorem contains what Nozick (1974: 156) disdainfully labelled 'patterned' principles, that is, detailed prescriptions for reshaping the social distribution of resources. In response to the empirical information society thesis, the normative theory of the information society analytically isolates a new site of distributive justice in the whole sphere, overlooked in the history of political thought, of information—the infosphere. It then proceeds on the unexceptionable premise that, while information is indeed superabundant in post-industrial societies, it is to a large extent unequally distributed. If the reasoning in the foregoing chapters has been cogent, or is capable of being made so, an informatised mode of quasi-egalitarian social democracy represents the ideal pattern towards which policies for the post-industrial age should be geared. The Rawls-Tawney Theorem, specifically, posits that, for social justice to be satisfied, some categories of political information should be distributed exactly equally, or as close thereto as humanly possible, and other categories of information, pertaining to the socioeconomic realm, moderately unequally. It should never be forgotten, however, that information is only one dimension of social justice. The information society thesis correctly construed does not involve the maximalist claim that information society has totally abrogated industrial society and thereby caused the social problems of industrialism suddenly to vanish. It suggests, to the contrary, that information society is overlaid upon industrial society, thickening the texture of the social fabric and thereby adding new twists to old problems as well as creating new information-related dilemmas. Information is a late addition to the Rawlsian index of primary goods, not a replacement of it, and the administration of its distribution should be understood as a further weight upon the already-burdened shoulders of a progressive polity.

We must resist the temptation, into which some critical theorists have fallen, to dismiss the information society as a relatively minor sideshow to the fundamental emergency of proletarian unfreedom and class stratification in late capitalism. The unfair social distribution of information is an important issue in its own right and deserves to be treated as such. Yet there is a kernel of truth in the critical theorists' stance. Information injustice does in numerous complex ways mesh with already existing layers of physical injustice, presenting a deeply convoluted situation. 'In countries like the US and the UK, where the Gini of inequality is already out of the bottle', John Myles (2006: 149) remarks, 'the time horizon for getting it back in again is probably a long one'. And that is even *before* one factors in information inequality. Moreover, there is the whole subterranean problem of apathy. Chatman's ethnographic work (1996: 199, 204) found that 'information of the most critical kind was not being asked for or shared' among marginalised groups, that 'there is a stratification of information acquisition and use'. To the sociologist's famous adage, 'tell me your social class and I will tell you what party you vote for, what sport you enjoy, what beverage you drink, etc', it seems that we can now add, 'and what kinds of information you do and do not seek'. The task is thus to try to penetrate these psychosocial depths, to discover ways to counteract the currents which make for inequality of motivation in the quest for objectively-useful political and socioeconomic information. In this respect the situation is actually worse than for other primary goods. Few egalitarians have met reluctance on the part of the disadvantaged to benefit from a redistribution of land, wealth or power, although they might have had great difficulty in selling the political means purportedly to that end. Yet with information, the end itself is sometimes shunned. Too many persons do not use hard information simply because they do not want it, or at least think that they do not want it.

What then can be the political path to the ideal society, that is, to the combination of revitalised and new information institutions required by the Rawls-Tawney Theorem? Which methodology of social change can provide a practical means of sustainable reconstruction? In this final chapter, I wish to try to locate that master key, to find, borrowing another felicitous phrase from Tawney's *Equality* (1964b: 119), a 'strategy of equality'. And I will argue that what is needed, and what most commentary, even by the most alert, informatised thinkers, has studiously avoided, is a recognition that the problem of inequality in all its dimensions, not least information inequality, cannot be fully solved by a democratic politics operating in beginner or even intermediate mode. Advanced mode is essential. The nature and scale of the issues comprising the normative crisis of the information society, the strength of the vested interests at stake and the (in a sense to be expounded below) false consciousness that accompanies all major technological innovations, together imply that the portfolio of instruments required for progressive twenty-first century policymaking will necessarily range into nothing less than social engineering. Social engineering, as a political methodology operating at a level above the quotidian preoccupations of normal policy, embraces a strategic, rather than merely tactical, approach to social goals, and it is only this, I believe, that can convert a reloaded social morality into effective norms, thereby making possible a new information and communication order.

The time for a reappraisal could hardly be riper. 'Social and economic "engineering"', Jean-Claude Burgelman (2002: 50) argues, 'surrounded the breakthrough, growth and success of the Internet'. A positive technology climate, or at least IT climate, continues to spread around the globe, including Britain (e.g. Dutton *et al.* 2009). The web has already delivered the ancient dream of the Alexandrian Library and performed many other astonishing feats. However, it is not just the technology. That whole sense of being in interstitial time, at a turning-point in history, first picked up fifty years ago in Bell's manuscript on post-industrial society (Waters 1996: 106 citing Bell 1962), begs a new openness in how we think about the good society and the mechanisms for achieving it. There is a growing scientific, not merely science-fictional, interest in the future, a futures-orientation that sets apart post-industrial society from the immediacy of industrialism. Thus social engineering seems well-suited to the conditions that the fluent prognosticator described, where 'society itself becomes a web of consciousness, a form of imagination to be realized as a social construction'. 'Inevitably, a post-industrial society gives rise to a new Utopianism', he continued (1999: 488), 'both engineering and psychedelic. Men can be remade or released, their behavior conditioned or their consciousness altered. The constraints of the past vanish with the end of nature and things'. Bell himself—and only to this extent was he a neo-conservative—evinced antipathy towards anything redolent of vanguard politics, towards, as he put it, the 'hubris' of venturing to 'cross the gap and embody the ideal in the real'. However, the fact remains that with every evolutionary step in the direction of the information society, the potential for experiments in social engineering increases.

My aim then is clear. It is to restore social engineering to the agenda of information policy and therein to defend the role of an intelligent democratic state as agency in the betterment of society. I begin by dispelling some myths and then present a brief case study of successful social engineering. A general argument for governmental interference, what I shall call the proactive state, is then advanced. Finally, there will be some final reflections on the ultimate objective of post-industrial political action, its teleology. Those remarks will conclude this attempt to set forth a normative theory of the information society.

THE TROUBLED SOUL OF SOCIAL ENGINEERING

Social engineering is normally dismissed as a concept beyond the pale of respectable political agency, like torture or anti-semitism. The very term strikes like an oxymoron. Engineering involves forcing physical matter into shape and belongs to the realm of determinism and inflexible scientific laws. Society, human communities, on the other hand, are not an invention but rather, so intuitions inform us, a natural development based on mutual help and advantage. The two cannot mix without a category mistake—and calamity. Analytical philosopher Gordon Graham judges social engineering untrustworthy, because of its supposed lack of a reliable body of scientific knowledge upon which to rest, as well as because society is too complex; he concludes, speaking for many, that trying 'to engineer not just this or that society but "the good society" now seems to be a ridiculously optimistic undertaking' (Graham 1988: 176). And in what is still one of the few doctoral-level studies devoted explicitly to information policy, Robert Burger's sole allusion (1993: 166) to social engineering is likewise highly critical, linking it to a 'technicist' mode of reasoning and 'the diminution of the dignity and potential of human action in human affairs'; he contrasts it with properly-constituted information policies, that is to say liberal democratic, market-friendly ones. Wherever one looks in the academy, in fact, it is hard to find endorsements. The late Adam Podgorecki, who defined it in glowing terms as, at its best, a 'paradigm of efficient social action' dedicated to 'just and rational social changes' (1996: 24, 54) was a conspicuous exception; some of his contributions will be discussed below.

Social engineering has recorded a vast range of techniques and instruments, including legislation, mass media, education, advertising, investment, subsidies, and one-off events such as grand exhibitions. Since some of these are common to other forms of social policy, we need to determine what exactly differentiates social engineering. The most obvious answer is its scale, demographic and temporal, and with that an unusual degree of irreversibility in its outcomes. Notwithstanding informal talk of social engineering in office politics and other interpersonal fields at the micro- and mesolevels, social engineering proper has a scale threshold and operates primarily at the macrolevel. While the ordinary social planner is typically thinking of a particular systact, the social engineer has in mind entire social classes, if not the whole population. And the social engineer, unlike the normal policymaker, does not think only for the near future; she thinks in terms of a whole generation or several. Moreover, unlike the mere politician or statesman, the social engineer aims for a fundamental change in both behaviour and attitudes. Like John Reith, first director-general of the BBC, her aim is to make the good popular and the popular good (Reith 1924; cf. McIntyre 1993). Her goal is paradigm shift, an alteration of people's world view, a new normality. Such factors help to explain why the idea of social engineering has become so badly tarnished, tied in most people's minds with unacceptable meddling by powerful agencies, particularly the absolutist state.

There is a further crucial difference. Unlike most forms of public policy, social engineering does not observe the reassuring convention that its central proposals should be intuitively acceptable, at least not initially. On the contrary, it typically strives for counter-intuitive ends. It does not seek to be presentable or electable, and it is precisely this assaulting of intuitions that gives the practice its hard engineering edge. It suggests the idea of a stratagem which gets populations from epistemic point A to epistemic point B without their fully understanding or willing the transition. This can happen in either of two ways. First, there can be pure coercion, a forcing of people to do what they do not want to do. Secondly, and more characteristic of most of the social engineering occurring outside of authoritarian regimes, there is an element of deception, something done behind human backs, a tricking of people into doing something that they would not do autonomously. And, of course, both modes are prima facie infringements of deontological morality. Social engineering would thus appear to clash with the charter Rawls-Tawney axiom that the rights secured by justice are not subject to political bargaining or the calculus of social ends.

Put another way, social engineering feels distinctly undemocratic. Informed consent is central to the concept of democracy, but informed consent is by definition not a high priority of social engineers, even the most benevolent. Even at its best, social engineering's tough image—policy not in the agonistic register of the liberal but in the decisive register of the revolutionary—leaves a sense that, while people may be persuaded, they are not necessarily convinced. It is this, rather than the scale or the irreversibility, that most troubles the democratic soul, for in democracy, not least in its Habermasian, deliberative forms, everything is meant to be both transparent and procedurally impeccable. Many of these negative connotations are illustrated perfectly by the manner in which social engineering has entered the lexicon of cyberspace: it is the term used for duping someone into revealing their password. Taken together, such features certainly make social engineering unique. Nevertheless, the case against is not quite as cut-and-dried as people like to think.

There has undoubtedly been an incalculable quantity of pernicious, inept and indeed unconscionable social engineering and any attempt at rehabilitation must begin by conceding this fact. Fascism does not merit even a word of dismissal. Communism, some of whose ends are arguably desirable, is a different matter. It is primarily Marxists, specifically Marxist-Leninists, Trotskyites and Maoists, who are to blame for the perception that social engineering is a deranged form of political idealism that sanctions violations of people's rights for their own putative good. However, it is not only authoritarian polities that have damaged the brand, as some interesting scholarly case studies have demonstrated. For example, war-time experiments by the 'Commission on Training Camp Activities' to 'make men moral', occasioned by the spread of venereal disease among recruits, were undermined by their blatant exclusion of Blacks; they failed as progressive social engineering because of their pursuit, as Nancy Bristow (1996: 216) expresses it, of a 'false and forced homogeneity'. One might say that such racism was typical of the US during that era, but even Sweden, often seen as a hub of enlightened values, was not above reproach. Recent scholarship suggests that its inter-war 'A-child competition', part of an undertaking to cultivate healthy, intelligent children, had overtones of the eugenics being developed not far away in Germany (Habel 2002: 224). Given the negative associations etched seemingly indelibly on western consciousness, it will not be necessary to add further illustrations of palpably 'dark' social engineering (Podgorecki 1996: 27).

However, while all of the foregoing must be acknowledged, there has also been 'light', as well as effective, social engineering. Dodgy competitions aside, mid-twentieth century Sweden is probably destined to go down in history as a benchmark of socioeconomic justice and political peace. A persuasive case has also recently been made that the large-scale programme of public library construction in Britain in the nineteenth and early-twentieth centuries was a bona fide exercise, and a tangibly successful one, in social engineering (Black *et al.* 2009). The next section will highlight the major Fabian role in the engineering of a fairer society on these shores. But surely even the Bolshevists' record is not entirely to be disowned. For example, their abolition of patriarchal excesses in Central Asia—child brides, marriage-by-abduction, wife-killing, full veils (Podgorecki 1996: 29–30)—was, in principle, both necessary and right, although the actual *praxis* was no doubt characteristically brutal. Moreover, the post-1979 one-child policy in the People's Republic of China, harsh though it too may seem, has at least banished the spectre of famine and mass destitution there; the Indian subcontinent, much of Africa, etc, might even wish to consider imbibing the same make of social-engineering medicine. And whatever is morally respectable in the whole tradition of liberal imperialism rests largely on a doctrine of benevolent social engineering. Even today, the erection of co-educational schools and other modern amenities deep inside pre-industrial communities arguably constitutes an example of a justifiable pitting of informed agency against moribund structure, of new polity against flawed ancient culture.

In any case, it is misleading to depict a stark Kierkegaard-style 'either-or' (1959) scenario, since the issue is to some degree one of trade-offs. Social engineering is without question an elitist exercise. It involves one group thinking that it knows the good and imposing its putative knowledge on everyone else. Not, of course, that everything coercive in long-range policy equals social engineering: compulsory vaccination visited upon a whole population is not social engineering because it does not aim at a major transformation of conduct or consciousness. However, to say that social engineering is always trumped by human or civil rights is to grossly oversimplify. It is a question, rather, of which presumptive rights must be upheld absolutely and which others can be ethically waived or limited, perhaps temporarily, for the sake of a specified and duly weighted long-range good. And that good might well be the rolling-out of civil liberties, as in the Central Asia example. It is because communities, especially their potentates, in such situations would reject political truth if suddenly confronted with it that they sometimes have to be in some respects coerced. The good might also be the achievement of socioeconomic justice, a prize that arguably can be worth the attenuation of certain freedoms, notably those of immodest property ownership and inheritance.

Even from a pure liberal-democratic perspective, there is an issue as to what extent controversial policies should be afforded salience on society's discussion agenda, in the shape of formal public consultations and the like. Exhaustive debate may be the default position for democratic opinion- and will-formation, but it is not necessarily the best solution in all cases in a nonideal world. According to Ithiel de Sola Pool, 1950s America discovered that the wisest way to integrate was simply to throw facilities open to non-Whites, because if integration was flagged up in advance opposition quickly coalesced to prevent its implementation. 'The decisions that get made with wide public consultation may conceivably be better ones', he comments (1998a: 299), 'but one cannot avoid the fact that bringing everyone into the discussion is a costly, time-consuming process that often generates stalemates'. Pool does concede that to move the race issue to a national stage required at some juncture the raising of consciousness of the general moral question of the role of Blacks in US society. However, he advised that only a small number of such highly-politicised issues could be tolerated; too many and society would tear itself apart. Ironically, Pool, whose *Technologies of Freedom* (1983) is often cited as a pioneering information-age text, made these remarks as part of his case against planning, yet they tend inexorably in the opposite direction. The core case for social engineering is precisely that people on occasion need to some extent to be bounced into being free. The intrinsic tension in the concept of liberal social engineering, that it is long-range in time logic and elitist in political logic, while electoral politics are populist in political logic and short-term in time logic, is a 'bug' with which democratic programmers of social justice must always struggle.

The instinct to anathematise social engineering also fails to see that social engineering has always been a fact of political, economic and cultural life. We are all always being socially engineered in innumerable ways. A great deal of activity by the state which does not declare itself as social engineering, not excluding minimalist states ideologically opposed to statism, is in fact exactly that. Strategic measures in fields such as crime prevention, health promotion and educational provision are typical instantiations. To take a topical example, draconian anti-smoking campaigns across the free world, based as they are upon both coercion (it is now illegal in Britain to run a private cigar club for consenting adults) and deception (there is no medical evidence that after-dinner cigars kill, or even harm, anyone), clearly fall into the category of social engineering. In the international arena, too, social engineering is obviously a staple of state actors, the most obvious evidence being the Pentagon's record in working by hook or crook to produce 'friendly' regimes in Latin America and the Middle East. Even leaving aside state actors, social engineering is immanent and inescapable. Podgorecki (1996) is emphatic that private as well as political entities sponsor and implement social engineering. Advertising, for example, has always been a major field of application. As Veblen recognised, modern capitalist industry is based on the practice of manufacturing new wants while claiming that they satisfy old wants, a mode of 'adaptive preference formation' (quoted in Fuller 2007: 104). It is no accident that the founder of behaviourism, John B. Watson, gained employment in Madison Avenue after his dismissal from Johns Hopkins University: behaviourism represents the ideal theoretical cover for the advertising industry. We should also think of entryism by computer companies in the classroom as a form of social engineering. And apart from all this 'soft compulsion of consumption training' (Habermas quoted in Webster 2002: 167), there is the rapid, surreptitious development of dataveillance in the workplace and elsewhere, which has happened largely without popular, political or judicial oversight.

There is also the social engineering, in some cases on as great a scale as anything encompassed by the state, of philanthropic agencies. Foundations of course have a societal impact in the US that lacks an equivalent in European countries and two of the greatest, the Carnegie Corporation and the Rockefeller trusts, have featured in a recent study of social engineering. Worthy philanthropic ends in both cases were accompanied by an unmistakable sub-text to the effect that the improvement of the masses required central control and a paternalistic ordering of the blue-collar labour force. The Rockefeller-funded Yale Institute of Human Relations, for example, was dedicated to a goal of social control through behaviourism. Sponsored to the tune of half a billion dollars in current terms, the Institute's first director, Beardsley Ruml, *'defined* the social sciences for the first time as a collective entity capable of social and human engineering' (Lemov 2005: 48). And out of these sciences, as Rebecca Lemov puts it (2005: 46–47), 'have emerged many of the measuring and engineering techniques that American society, more than any other, has experimented with and adopted: advertising techniques, public relations strategies, therapy movements, propaganda campaigns, focus groups, emotional management devices, human resource sciences, "crunching" knowledge from data processing, data mining'. 'These social-science-bred techniques', she concludes, 'take the measure of what is human, and in so doing they change it'.

Social engineering, even more dangerously, is increasingly intertwined with genetics. It is difficult to see the patenting of strands of human code as anything other than social engineering in the hands of a spectacularly brazen form of predatory capitalism, as the epitome of Tawney's sickness of an acquisitive society. Arguably, indeed, the entire trend towards commodification of information and knowledge can be interpreted as the creeping privatisation of social engineering. Some at least of this commercial enterprise has far stronger connotations of hubris and anti-humanistic control than the statist social engineering proposals that will be floated below. So if the twentieth century was the age of social engineering, the twenty-first is not going to be any different. The choice, therefore, will not be between social engineering and no social engineering, but between state-led, and hopefully democratic, social engineering and an unaccountable, privatised form. Hence it is absurd to write off statist social engineering as the province of mad mandarins and devilish dictators. But I should like to go further than that and postulate that most of the gigantic social problems of industrialism would never have been solved or even significantly ameliorated without social engineering. Moreover, this is equally true of *post*-industrial issues, not least the information inequality highlighted here. The trick, as ever, is to turn necessity into freedom. The following sections attempt to make good that claim by revisiting social engineering in a reasonably systematic manner, beginning with a case study of some great British social engineers of yesteryear.

CASE STUDY: THE BRITISH SCHOOL OF SOCIAL ENGINEERING

It is quite wrong to think that extremism has enjoyed a monopoly on social engineering. The record shows that the social democratic tradition has been as active in this regard as Marxism-Leninism and other expressions of political maximalism. One is tempted to invoke again the political miracle that was twentieth-century Sweden, but this has already received specialist treatment (e.g. Heilbroner *et al.* 1991; Habel 2002). However, it is unnecessary to stray from the shores of Albion to find an equally serviceable case of successful statist social engineering informed by left-liberal goals. The present section focuses on the role of the Fabian Society, one of the main 'think tanks' of the Labour Party. For friend as well as foe, the Fabians made themselves virtually synonymous in Britain with social engineering. The Society's leading lights, Sidney and Beatrice Webb, may even have coined the term. According to Karl Popper (1966 vol. 1: 201), whose important critique of social engineering will be addressed later, while the jurist Roscoe Pound definitely used the term in 1922, 'the Webbs almost certainly used it before 1922'. One might thus with some justification call this the British school of social engineering. I hope to show here that information played a central part in the Fabian approach to social engineering, that Fabian social democracy was, indeed, information-powered. This is one of the factors that make even a brief case study highly relevant for the normative theory of the information society.

The Fabian Society claims to be Britain's oldest extant socialist society, as well as the world's first think tank (Fisher nd: 1; Katwala 2004: 1). It was founded on 4 January 1884 in the drawing-room of London stockbroker Edward Pease, by a group of earnest Victorians burdened with the thought that they needed to do something about what was quaintly referred to as 'the social problem'—essentially the unchecked inequality between rich and poor. They quickly settled that their aim was to 'help on the reconstruction of society' and to 'obtain information on all contemporary movements and social needs' (MacKenzie and MacKenzie 1979: 27). Their outlook was socioeconomically left-wing, but their leftism had at least one pecu-liarity. Named after Quintus Fabius Maximus 'Cunctator' ('Delayer'), the Roman general who defeated the numerically superior forces of Hannibal by postponing pitched battles until he judged the time right to strike hard, the Fabians did not argue for the immediate reconstitution of society but for single, staggered reforms, using the slow horses of persuasion and par-liamentary democracy. Their favourite motto, 'the inevitability of gradual-ness', was glossed by a contemporary wit as 'don't be in a hurry, but when you *do* go it, go it thick' (quoted in Pugh 1984: 10). Committed to socialist ends but opposed to the insurrectionary means of Marxists, they proceeded on the optimistic premise that the public use of reason and evidence would eventually unlock the rigidly hierarchical status quo.

Rather like the 1960s, the late 1800s were marked by widespread ideal-ism, a social atmosphere in which the Fabian Society could be expected to expand. It soon attracted some significant personages, such as Sidney Webb and the affluent beauty Beatrice Potter, who married to become the 'firm' that presided over the Society for much of its early and middle periods. They were joined by George Bernard Shaw, who would be Britain's leading playwright, in his own estimation the greatest since Shakespeare, although to Lenin, Shaw was just a 'good man fallen among Fabians' (quoted in Shaw 1982: xl). The first literary landmark was *Fabian Essays in Socialism* (Shaw 1889), a set of articles by Shaw, Sidney Webb and others that was destined to 'hold the field for a very long time' (Cole 1961: 27). Another notable early recruit was H. G. Wells, who joined in 1903 shortly after the publication of his *Anticipations of the Reaction of Mechanical and Scien-tific Progress upon Human Life and Thought* (1901); that book's 'vision of a future society run on collectivist lines by a managerial elite was very close to Fabian thinking' (MacKenzie and MacKenzie 1979: 323). Many other important Fabian names could be mentioned, including Emmeline Pankhurst, Mahatma Ghandi, Rupert Brooke, Clement Attlee, Bertrand Russell and Jerome K. Jerome. Most of the leading figures in Labour poli-tics have been Fabians, including both recent 'old' Labour standard-bearer Tony Benn and 'new' Labour adventurer Tony Blair. It is an impressive roster by any standards

The Fabians seemed to think that the future of civilisation lay on their shoulders. They lectured, researched, wrote books and pamphlets, set up provincial groups, helped progressive-minded candidates in national and municipal elections, agitated, organised, founded the London School of Economics and other educational establishments, launched the *New Statesman* magazine, and much more; on occasion they even managed to make a success of summer schools in Scotland (Pugh 1984: 244). While initially keen to influence or 'permeate' all political parties—even Win-ston Churchill was courted—a growing association with the nascent Labour Party, which indeed some of them helped to create, came to seem natural. The Fabian Society eventually sought formal affiliation with that party and served, at least until the rise of other left-leaning research institutes, as its main source of policy ideas. It is through Labour governments of the twentieth century that many of the Fabians' most important prescriptions were implemented, including national health care, comprehensive education, public utilities, nationalised industries and adequate pensions. These are still largely the background institutions, the social furniture, of Great Britain.

Fabianism as a school of political thought is best known for its gradualism (e.g. Scruton 1983: 164). Here, however, I wish to highlight another feature, as much their hallmark as the inevitability of gradualness, namely the privileging of facts. This is not an entirely new interpretation. 'What the Fabians can claim', advises Margaret Cole, historian of the Society, 'is to have established a tradition of tolerant discussion within Socialist circles, to have insisted on laying a *foundation of fact* for all assertions' (1961: 328, italics added). I should like to call this their informationalism. Of course, such a characterisation could be misleading since all schools of socialism, including the most emotional or ideological, utilise information in myriad ways. Even Marx, high priest of dialectical materialism, is popularly pictured poring over statistical tables in the reading room of the British Museum. However, I am suggesting that information played a significantly greater role in Fabianism, that its ratio of information to other discursive elements was much higher than average, and that this goes a long way towards explaining the Society's strong and mainly felicitous impact.

There is ample evidence to support the claim. I have already quoted their charter objective to 'obtain information on all contemporary movements and social needs'. But as is often the case, the most memorable evidence is anecdotal. Webb was once asked about his concept of a university. His terse, typical response: 'I don't have one. Here are the facts' (quoted in McBriar 1966: 73). There is colourful correspondence too. Shaw describes in a letter to fellow-author William Morris how he had fled from the police during a botched political demonstration in London. 'We *skedaddled*', he recalls, 'and never drew rein until we were safe on Hampstead Heath or thereabouts . . . It all comes from people trying to live down to fiction instead of up to facts' (Shaw 1982: xiii). However, the chief evidence must be the Society's famous series of policy pamphlets. The 'Fabian Tracts' commenced in 1884 and have continued in unbroken sequence down to this day; they are as closely associated with the Fabians as polemical sermons were with seventeenth-century Reformers and websites are with present-day anarchists. One of the first was *Facts for Socialists* (Tract 5, 1887). According to the *Encyclopaedia Britannica* (Cole 1977: 712), this was 'the first concise expression of the Fabian conviction that public knowledge of the facts of industrial society was the essential first step toward the reform of that society'. The titles of other first-generation tracts are also proof of a straightforward factualism: *Why are the Many Poor?* (Tract 1, 1884), *Figures for Londoners* (Tract 10, 1889), *Questions for Poor Law Guardians*

(Tract 20, 1890), *State Education at Home and Abroad* (Tract 52, 1894), and *The Case for State Pensions in Old Age* (Tract 73, 1896).

The Fabian conception of facts was technical, inductive and centred on discrete items rather than holistic structures. Their epistemology, like their political strategy, can perhaps be summed up as *modular*. Commenting on one of the Webbs' works, Norman and Jeanne MacKenzie (1979: 212–13) observe that 'narrative came before analysis, and the narrative was constructed like a jigsaw puzzle, piece by piece, from the file cards which contained the facts'. 'This piecemeal approach', they explain, 'was similar to the Webbs' belief that reforms could be separated into discrete packages each of which was intrinsically sound. . . . By recording each fact on its own card and then shuffling the cards in different categories and sequences (a crude anticipation of modern factor analysis and data processing) they could arrive at the principles of organization underlying the facts'. Naturally, then, the Fabians valued the social role of organised information institutions such as libraries, and they took immediate steps to ensure that their great academic creation, the LSE, became a repository of the world's social-scientific and official literature. 'Town councils and government agencies as far apart as Calcutta and Elmira, New York', it is noted (MacKenzie and MacKenzie 1979: 227), 'were surprised to receive letters asking them to deposit their publications at the library'. Wells would even envisage a 'world brain' housing Alexandrian Library-style the accumulated knowledge of mankind (Wells 1964: 302–309; cf. Rayward 1999; Schuler 2001).

Information was indeed at the core of the official Fabian manifesto for the future of Britain. The *Constitution for the Socialist Commonwealth of Great Britain* ends with a section entitled The Need for Knowledge, where the message could not be clearer:

> There is no need so imperative to-day as increased economic and political science. There is no peril so dangerous as the failure to get community of education among all classes. . . . But our present failures are to be ascribed, not merely to deficiencies in knowledge, but also to the impossibility with our existing institutions, of bringing into play such knowledge as is available. . . . We want to get rid of the 'stuffiness' of private interests that now infects our institutions; and to usher in a reign of 'Measurement and Publicity'. (Webb and Webb 1920: 354, 356)

That tradition has continued. Almost every modern Fabian Tract is still rich in factual content and circumspect in prescription, the obverse, one might say, of a typical newspaper opinion column (Duff 2008b). On a wider front, the late Michael Young, another Fabian stalwart, co-founded the peerless consumer-information magazine *Which?* as well as the much-cloned Open University (Briggs 2001). It is no wonder that Cole (1961: 86) could speak of 'a Fabian vision of Britain in which every Important Person would have an anonymous Fabian at his elbow . . . trained very thoroughly in information'.

Fabian informationalism extended to an official agnosticism. Proud to cast themselves as pragmatists whose sole allegiance was to common sense, they expressly rejected the proposition that political principles need to be derived from an holistic world view. This distinguished them from their main rivals, Marxists and Christian socialists. Marx had insisted in works such as *Theses on Feuerbach* (1978) and the *Communist Manifesto* (Marx and Engels 1978) that socialism be grounded in historical materialism, specifically in his own Hegel-inspired version; and he ensured that the first clause in cadre rulebooks was compulsory atheism. And in *Old Worlds for New* (1917: 32), the Christian socialist Penty criticised what he called 'the prejudice of the modern intellectual against all reasoning which is not based on material facts'. 'The difference between the Fabian and the mystic', he continued (Penty 1917: 34), 'is not that the Fabian has an eye on facts, and the mystic has not, but that the Fabian sees only the material fact while the mystic sees its spiritual significance'. Yet that was to miss the point. Fabianism did not depend on philosophical materialism after the manner of Marx, it did not require any metaphysical base at all. Individual Fabians were entitled to believe anything they liked about spiritual significance, as long as their beliefs were compatible with this-worldly socialism. In essence, the early Fabians anticipated Rawls's position, expounded most powerfully in 'Justice as Fairness: Political Not Metaphysical' (1999a), that social justice should be treated as a purely political conception. Modern Fabians can still be heard arguing that 'we should not put off potential adherents by suggesting that to be a socialist you have to accept extravagant and implausible philosophical assumptions' (Barry 1996: 115).

The early Fabians' cautious, fact-laden approach was received by many contemporaries as a welcome antidote to the emotional rhetoric and rash truth-claims in which much politics of that era indulged. Of course, many now would dismiss it as simplistic, as epistemologically primitive. 'Facts', according to a representative statement from the sociology of knowledge (Knorr-Cetina 2005: 175), 'are not something we can take for granted or think of as the solid rock upon which knowledge is built'. John Hall specifically tackles (1977: 355) Sidney Webb for his belief that 'information provided to those at the centre of politics, the powerful and influential who inhabited the world of Westminster and Whitehall, would provide influence on the simple supposition that knowledge was power'. 'This approach', in Hall's eyes, 'betrays an unconscionable ignorance of politics. Political life is concerned with choices between different images of society; knowledge is usually an aid to realizing such images, not an independent variable in its own right'. There is of course something in this, but it is equally arguable that the foregrounding of facts as a political dynamic served to point progressive British politics in basically the correct direction. And surely if today we do not believe that information is to some extent an autonomous social force, and ceteris paribus a beneficent one, then we would have to abandon the information society thesis, if not the whole future of rational politics. At any rate, the Fabians' story can only corroborate the version of the information society that has been put forward in the present study, i.e. the information society as informed society. Their basic conception of information-powered social democracy was, and I believe still is, profoundly valid.

It is not being suggested that the Fabian model is perfect. In practice, they did not always live up to their informationalism, frequently evincing a deeply ideological mindset. Indeed, such is surely betrayed by that very slogan about the inevitability of gradualness. For what can be the basis of inevitability, if not some supervening principle, force or deity? *Constitution for the Socialist Commonwealth of Great Britain* can be taken as an illustration. Part 1 is a fairly detailed, although largely unreferenced, description of the workings of British political and social institutions. Part 2, entitled The Co-operative Commonwealth of To-morrow, is a profile of what the Webbs thought Britain should look like, and, moreover, they were certain, *will* look like. Yet they never supplied any justification for the convenient escalation to a future tense, and no such justification is logically available on the strictly empiricist premises to which they subscribed. In the end, their arguments resemble nothing so much as the Marxian historicism that they professed to despise. This determinism still vitiates Fabian thinking today, as we have already had cause to notice with regard to expositions of the Third Way. The insurmountable fact is that one cannot read off normative or teleological propositions from a critical analysis of social reality, no matter how brilliant.

There was a much more serious flaw in early Fabianism, however. Elitism, vanguardism, the agency of what Wells (1905) memorably called 'the new Samurai', I have conceded, is an unavoidable part of progressive social engineering, but it can be taken too far. Several of the leading early Fabians possessed a distinctly authoritarian streak, and it soon became clear that their ultimate goal was the same as that of the hard left, i.e. a totally transformed society with no room for dissent. 'Within wide limitations', the Webbs wrote (1920: 99), 'we can mould our institutions so that they may produce the society that we desire'. The desirables included abolition of the market economy, comprehensive nationalisation, splitting of the polity into separate political and social parliaments, eradication of all differences in wealth and income, and suppression of the private press. The scenario is one of ultra-statism, of absolutism, a major topic to which I shall return in the next section.

The Fabians' autocratic gene eventually surfaced in its final monstrous form in their endorsement of the Soviet Union. Mesmerisation was evident as early as Wells's eulogy 'The Dreamer in the Kremlin', which draped Lenin in phrases like 'this amazing little man' (Wells 1927: passim). Shaw (1982: 475) also strongly backed the regime, justifying its very worst deeds, such as the murder of the czar's family—'certainly the most humane regicide in history'—and the Moscow show trials. *Soviet Russia: a New Civilization* (Webb and Webb 1944: passim) was, however, the nadir. The book initially came out with a question mark after the title, but later editions expunged even that concession to objectivity. Its defence, in travelogue-style prose, of virtually every facet of Stalinism is breathtaking. Beneficiaries of the white-wash included the one-party state ('*a study of the facts* suggests that there is no alternative to the One-Party system with its refusal to permit organised political opposition', emphasis added), the secret police, the treatment of Jews ('they suffer not as Jews but as shopkeepers and money-lenders'), and militant state atheism ('there is, in the USSR to-day, nothing that can prop-erly be called persecution of those who are Christians'). Trotsky is duly denounced as a counter-revolutionary, but conveniently he was murdered, assert the Webbs, 'by one of his own followers'.

All of this, of course, is false. To take the last-quoted, the truth about the dissident author of *The Revolution Betrayed* and *The Stalin School of Fal-sification* (Trotsky 1937a, b) is that he was liquidated, like countless others, on Stalin's orders. It is difficult to know what to make of such mendac-ity. One might begin by asking where the assertions leave all the Fabians' other, hitherto non-suspect, facts. That, however, would be uncharitable. Alternatively one could suggest, as some have done, that the Fabians just reflected their troubled times, not being the only intellectuals in the 1930s who 'took it for granted that Social Democracy was pretty well played out' (Martin 1980: 84). Surely that, though, would be to implicitly devalue the achievement of contemporaries—Orwell, Tawney and Russell among them—who, at the price of being politically unmodish, did remain loyal to social democracy. Of course, it can be partly explained by the totalitarian temptation, by what Bell (1988: 444–45) called the 'ideological caul that envelops people and makes the rest of the world opaque'. But there was a more fundamental weakness, a void in their basic social ethic. 'This is where', according to Tawney (1972: 46), 'the Fabians are inclined to go wrong. They seem to think that you can trick statesmen into a good course of action, without changing their principles, and that by taking sufficient thought society can add several cubits to its stature. It can't, as long as it lives on the same spiritual diet. No amount of cleverness will get figs off thistles' (1972: 46). What Tawney saw, perhaps more clearly than any other thinker of the twentieth century, is that progressive politics have to be nourished in a wholesome moral culture, a normative public philoso-phy of the right order. Because the Fabians altogether lacked that kind of anchor, their allegiances eventually drifted into foreign waters, into glis-tening, but lethal, political/philosophical seas. They lacked, in essence, a social deontology.

These lapses, however, should not make us doubt the contribution of the Fabians to British social engineering. On the contrary, judging by their domestic record alone, they offer a model from which much can be learned.

They provide solid evidence in favour of the proposition that social engineering can 'work', in the sense of effecting a gradual approximation to a just society *within* a parliamentary framework. Most of the institutions that they either set up themselves or persuaded Labour governments to set up are still in existence in a more or less recognisable form, a stubborn reality over which politicians of the right have often despaired. This is no mean feat; indeed, it is an astounding achievement. In *Educate, Agitate, Organize: 100 Years of Fabian Socialism*, Patricia Pugh (1984: 277–78; cf. Duff 2006b), herself a non-Fabian, ends a panoramic review with the conclusion that the Fabian Society's impact on the social reconstruction of Britain between 1884 and 1984 was incalculably vast. It implies that for the most part they did, indeed, build on a 'foundation of fact'. Thus while the Fabians were locked in their industrial paradigm, and while they made serious mistakes, they nevertheless provide excellent resources for those of us today who seek to put together a doctrine of social engineering as the final module of a normative theory of the information society.

THE PHILOSOPHY OF THE PROACTIVE STATE

The subtitle of Loader's *Cyberspace Divide—Equality, Agency and Policy in the Information Society* (1998)—catches perfectly the key themes of the normative theory of the information society, and what has not been adequately addressed so far in the present study is that pesky middle term, agency. The thesis directly above was that social engineering, like the proverbial poor (although social democracy wishes to retire that particular proverb), is always with us, making the question not so much whether social engineering should be done, as who will do it. Surely the most plausible answer is that it ought to be conducted primarily by the democratic state. Politicians enjoying an electoral mandate, and relying upon sound information, should be allowed to plan certain long-range social goals and then to take resolute action to achieve them. This form of agency would involve confronting various kinds of harmful barrier embedded in social structures, not just by passing laws to that end but by dissolving the normative lumps which underpin them. The next section will try to forge a morally sound post-industrial theory of social engineering, but in order to clear the way, it is necessary first to make a few general remarks in defence of the state. For the assertion that the democratic state should be rehabilitated as chief agency in the high politics of social engineering immediately runs into the pervasive flak of antistatism. Loss of confidence in big government—albeit a pathology that has precisely *never* been reflected in the actions of politicians or their academic apologists when they have desired state-dependent objectives in either domestic or foreign policy—is, in fact, an important symptom of the normative crisis of the information society. Yet what I wish to call a *proactive* theory of the state—the state not just as active but as genetically in *favour* of being active—must be upheld today, for the simple reason that the infosphere is as much in *need* of interventionism as were many spheres of industrial society. At any rate, the Rawls-Tawney Theorem, and its accompanying policies and institutions as commended above, are entirely predicated on a vigorous, although not omnipotent, state.

At the heart of the panic about social engineering is a negative perception of the state, a fairly firmly-held intuition about the limits of state interference in the economic and social fabric of the nation. Popper was the intellectual standard-bearer of this view. The two volumes of his *Open Society and its Enemies* (1966) contain what is regarded as the classic attack on totalitarianism and all its works, including, especially, social engineering. However, a close reading actually throws up some revealing ambiguities. Popper was clearly wanting to be socially-progressive, but he simultaneously wished to propound the conservative proposition that the state is intrinsically suspect and that the only legitimate end of government action is individual freedom. This negativism—the state as beast that must indeed be captured for the sake of political power but whose scope is then limited to the protection of formal political rights—while a minority report at the end of the Second World war, has become, of course, prevalent. And there are many today who have taken hastily-articulated doctrines of internationalism, discourses about transfers of sovereignty away from the nation state, or even simply the existence of the word 'globalisation', as irrefutable proof that state power can no longer be called upon by democratic governments to anything like the extent imagined by socioeconomic progressives of yesteryear. This so-called 'hollowing-out of the state' has affected even social democrats. But even those who do not believe in any sense in the sanctity or eternity of the state should be able to see that this is too quick an inference. The heretical position that will be sketched here is that the state continues to be the prime site of *de facto* as well as *de jure* power, and that it therefore remains the correct agency for overseeing the decisive steps towards a just information society.

The apologist's ABC for the state depends upon a simple, universal instinct, tested in schoolyards and other situses of the lifeworld across time and space, that intervention by legitimate authority is the normal way of combating oppression. Government is political authority with a monopoly on the legitimate use of force; that is its 'grammar' (Winch 1972: 17). Yet, as in St Augustine's cheeky formulation, such an authority when it fails to pursue justice is merely large-scale piracy. Hence, government is ultimately responsible for everything that happens within its jurisdiction, whether famine, lynchings, crime waves, or inequalities, both legitimate—such as those sanctioned by the second principle of the Rawls-Tawney Theorem, or the inequalities resulting from retributive justice—and illegitimate. The Judeo-Christian tradition has been invoked, perhaps ad nauseam, in this book, but no one expressed the Augustinian axiom better than Muslim caliph Umar, when he said that if even one camel starved in his dominions,

Allah would hold him responsible. A wide experiential canvas supports the intuition that social welfare is a core duty of the state. For example, India has enjoyed a constitutional liberal democratic polity for over half a century, for most of it run by the party of Gandhi, yet it is still utterly disfigured by massive destitution alongside vulgar wealth, by a premodern caste system, and by failures in cultural development which entail that widows in some rural areas are still burned alive upon their husbands' funeral pyres. It should be clear to any unclouded mind which agency is ultimately at fault for such moral catastrophes. The ethical-political case for statism flickers in those fires, that is, in the basic truth that what Indian policy sorely lacks is major federal social engineering in accordance with the norms of justice. One could of course single out numerous other nations.

This insistent intuition has been marginalised by several departments of contemporary social and political theory, but it was not ever thus, as a brief recapitulation of the state's various phases will confirm. The modern state, that is, liberal polities resting on consent rather than force, struggled to emerge from a miserable medieval matrix of authoritarianism, obscurantism and privilege. Until at least the end of the eighteenth century, government, in its inward-looking aspect, denoted merely the panoply of private ownership, the night-watchman state alert and cruel to those who transgressed property rights of the rich, yet dead to the oppression of the weak and exploitation of the poor. A more positive outlook emerged during the nineteenth century, not least as a trend within political liberalism, which eventually saw that freedom could not be secured without a somewhat more interventionist state. No one expressed this new understanding with greater profundity and conviction than the British Idealist Green (1986b: 97), for whom, famously, 'the state is an institution for the promotion of a common good'. It is needful, he continued, 'to point out the directions in which the state may remove obstacles to the realisation of the capacity for beneficial exercise of rights' (Green 1986b: 162). In particular, since this was the central issue of economic politics in the Victorian age, the state must to some extent interfere with market forces, an argument Green (1986a) also outlined in his seminal lecture, 'Liberal Legislation and Freedom of Contract'. It was still authentic liberalism, in that its point of departure was the doctrine of limited government, but it was a novel liberalism, pollinated by socialism, one which recognised that true liberty would never be attained for the populace by mere *laissez-faire* (cf. Boucher and Vincent 2000; Ulam 1951). While it was overlaid and, arguably, enhanced by Christian sacerdotalism (Jones 1968; Norman 1987), the essence of its moral case was that the state is obliged to underwrite the educational and material conditions in which alone the formal rights of citizenship can be put to efficacious use. Utilitarian liberals such as J. S. Mill arrived at the same statist conclusions from their own very different premises.

At the same time that mainstream liberalism was rethinking its mission, anti-establishment movements, articulating more directly the rage of the people, emphasised the moral imperative to grow the state. This was not a universal view on the left. Some, notably syndicalists and anarchists, claimed that the state is a necessarily corrupt institution and thus scorned the view that it could enjoy sufficient neutrality to be an effective instrument of social progress. Such was the Marxian position too, although Marxists conceded that the state was needed temporarily as a weapon of the proletariat, prior to its withering away. However, for the great majority, for whom socialism was, to quote some deservedly celebrated slogans, 'a cry of pain, sometimes of anger, by those who feel most keenly the injustice of the social order' (Emile Durkheim), or a 'broad movement on behalf of the bottom dog' (G. D. H. Cole), or even 'a resistance movement against the destruction of love in social reality' (Paul Tillich), the state served as the principal, and enduring, agency of worldly justice. No socialist ever thought that the state can be entirely neutral or denied that it is a site of political contestation and manoeuvring, and few have denied that it would inevitably be to some extent captured by its own bureaucratic cadre, if not by elements of the better off systacts. But the inference that the state is inherently evil was recognised to be false, for the good reason that it is false. In any case, a manifold doctrine of political interventionism in the socioeconomic realm gradually became the norm in mainstream progressive, that is, left-liberal and democratic socialist, circles. And, to cut a long story short, by the middle of the twentieth century, some measure of belief in the welfare state had come to represent conventional wisdom across much of the political spectrum, including even the centre right. In *The Good Society* (2005: 3), Walter Lippmann, America's finest political columnist, identified the proposition that 'through the power of the state men can be made happy' as the 'dominant dogma of the age'. Thus, in less than a hundred years a total paradigm shift had occurred.

Positive ideas of the state are integral to the philosophies of Rawls and Tawney, who represented so well, as we have seen, the right and left poles of the twentieth century's social democratic vision. Yet statism, while ascendant in Tawney's day, had by Rawls's era come again under serious assault. The development of economically neo-conservative, what specialists call libertarian, thought, expounded by philosophers of the calibre of F. A. Von Hayek (e.g. 1960), Murray Rothbard (e.g. 1982) and Robert Nozick (1974), resurrected the case for small government. Libertarianism takes various forms, but essentially its thesis is that statist solutions contravene inalienable rights of the individual. Nozick's *Anarchy, State, and Utopia* set up the stall with unrivalled lucidity and aplomb. 'Our main conclusions about the state', he wrote, 'are that a minimal state, limited to the narrow functions of protection against force, theft, fraud, enforcement of contracts, and so on, is justified; that any more extensive state will violate persons' rights not to be forced to do certain things, and is unjustified; and that the minimal state is inspiring as well as right' (Nozick 1974: ix). Moreover, as we have already had cause to observe in connection with official responses to the digital divide, neo-conservatives argue that statism, though perhaps well-meaning—*ergo* 'nanny' state—typically makes the badly off even worse off. They basically revert to 'invisible hand' arguments, as originally given in Adam Smith's *Wealth of Nations* (1977) and *Theory of Moral Sentiments* (1976). Perhaps the reason why the hand is invisible, observes Stiglitz sardonically (2003: 6), 'is that it is simply not there—or at least if it is there, it is palsied'. Nevertheless, libertarian philosophy was enacted in the 1980s with such conviction by politicians like Margaret Thatcher and Ronald Reagan that, while no longer at high tide, it is still the default in policymaking across much of the world.

Such, in the coarsest of brush-strokes, has been the modern career of the state, insofar as the state is potentially pertinent to the question of social engineering. But how has the state fared specifically with regard to information issues? The answer yields no surprises: the state's career in information is a microcosm of its overall career. Over the late nineteenth and first three-quarters of the twentieth century, the state was increasingly interventionist in the information and media domain. The magisterial *Cambridge History of Libraries in Britain and Ireland* details, for example, how its expansion was bound up with the growth of literacy, reading and public libraries in one corner of Europe (Black and Hoare 2006). The result was, as it were, a welfare state for mind as well as body. Jean-Guy Lacroix and Gaetan Tremblay (1997: 94), speaking for much of the Continent and beyond, argue that 'while [the welfare state] manifested itself with some force in the areas of labour, education, and health, it was also present in the cultural and communication sectors'. Welfarism in this realm translated into a public service ethos underwritten by government commitment 'to guarantee all citizens access to honest information' (Lacroix and Tremblay 1997: 97). Computerisation also coincided with the golden era of twentieth-century statism, a circumstance reflected in Bell's optimistic, technocratic writing on the advent of post-industrial society. 'When I am weary or nasty', one of his critics commented mordantly, 'I sometimes remark that the post-industrial society was a period of two or three years in the mid-sixties when GDP, social policy programmes, and social research and universities were flourishing' (Miller 1975: 28). In France, Nora and Minc's report (1981) led directly to Minitel, the first national distribution of household computers. Across the world in Japan, governments, in characteristic league with industry and academia, devised and executed firmly *dirigiste,* and highly successful, plans of informatisation. 'In the advanced countries', judged the Japan Computer Usage Development Institute (1974: 175; cf. Morris-Suzuki 1988), 'de-industrialization is now underway, and the world is generally and steadily shifting from the industrialized society to the information society'. Its recommendation was unequivocal, and robustly statist—'the establishment of a new national target: Realization of the Information Society'.

More recently, however, as on the larger stage, an antistatist mood has prevailed. The growth of the 'global information society' was 'hampered by different visions of the role of the state' (Marsden 2000: 5), particularly the minimal-state vision. Few authors in the information field have exhibited detailed knowledge of libertarian political philosophy, and rigid designators are rare, although citations of Hayek, and even Nozick, can occasionally be spotted (e.g. Chadwick 2006: 35). But the mood itself was growing. Pool defied the 1960s zeitgeist by arguing early on for the rolling back of the state, as part of his claim that computers comprised a new technology of individual freedom. He predicted that the nation state 'will decreasingly be an effective unit of planning and action in the world that is being created by electronic communication of messages and money, as well as by efficient transport and intelligent machines' (Pool 1998b: 232). Now there is a much more prominent anti-state stance. Esther Dyson *et al.* (2004: 37) declare that 'Third Wave' governments should be 50 percent or more smaller than 'Second Wave' governments. May calls this the 'Californian ideology', a replacement of the welfarism of Flower Power and an expression of the individualistic, libertarian ways of Silicon Valley. 'The information age (and specifically the internet)', he notes (2002: 117), 'represents a chance to sideline government and reconstitute a voluntary society'. While *laissez-faire* is never consistently followed in either information society theory or practice, it is now the default mentality, just as in other domains.

In addition to the influence of the normative philosophy of libertarianism, information society thinking is marked by purportedly empirical propositions about the demise of the state. Bell himself claimed (1999: lxxxi) to have coined the slogan about the nation state being 'too small for the big problems of life and too big for the small problems'. Stehr (1994: 105) suggests that while 'the horizon of human action and potential social action expands considerably in a knowledge society', this 'applies first and foremost at the intermediate level of action, that is, at the level of small groups, social movements, smaller corporations and not necessarily at the so-called institutional level of social action, referring for example to the state agencies, the political system, the economy, the educational system, or even society and the nation-state'. The difficulty of patrolling 'borders in cyberspace' (Kahin and Nesson 1997) supposedly signals insuperable difficulties for state sovereignty. Empirically-oriented post-statism has also been perpetuated in the accounts of commentators evidently sympathetic to social democracy. Echoing Bell, Castells (2004: 337) finds that the evidence 'seems to support the popular saying according to which national governments in the information age are too small to handle global forces, yet too big to manage people's lives'. 'At the dawn of the information age', he concludes (2004: 419), 'a crisis of legitimacy is voiding of meaning and function the institutions of the industrial era. Bypassed by global networks of wealth, power, and information, the modern nation-state has lost much of its sovereignty'. 'The state', lament Lacroix and Tremblay (1997: 105), 'no longer views itself as the representative and defender of a specifically socio-cultural point of view vis-à–vis commercial interests'. And Braman (2006) identifies a brand new form of polity. While her 'informational state' might not be powerless, it is, crucially, something that supercedes the welfare state. Bell, Pool, Castells, Stehr, Braman: the state's obituary seems to have been written by more or less everyone on the 'A-list' of information society studies.

Such contributions exemplify the generic crisis of confidence in the feasibility, if not the moral validity, of government largesse. However, a sober audit by no means yields such an unequivocal verdict. To start with the minimalist's main comfort zone, we do not see any diminution of state power in the military field. For example, the US, with personnel in perhaps 70 percent of the countries of the world and invasive adventures or ambitions on several continents, most of them unjustifiable, enjoys more global power today than any nation of the industrial epoch. This putatively neo-conservative entity constantly spins minimal, moderate or maximal modalities of agency, as it pleases; its recurrent protectionism proves that it is not even economically minimal-statist in a consistent manner. In information warfare, moreover, it excels in a new post-industrial form of power, a complement to industrial forms (Cronin 2005). Domestically, the spread of governmental surveillance is monitored by Privacy International and other civil society organisations; it is safe to assume that they would be rather reluctant to sign off obituaries of the state. Many less exotic areas of information policy—copyright, data protection, health records and so on—are equally subject to an expansion of pure political power. So May (2002: 131) is correct to infer that rapid developments internationally in the enforcement of intellectual property rights can only be understood as 'a radical widening and institutionalization of state authority'.

Furthermore, it is bordering on disingenuous to obscure the fact that, even in the socioeconomic realm where there has at times been a deliberate reduction of state involvement, all has been orchestrated from above. Non-state actors, especially large corporations, may at times be permitted to occupy spaces vacated by the state, for however long the state deems expedient, but there is never really any overall loss of political control. It would be tedious to multiply such evidence. Of course, there have sometimes been voluntary, at least at official level, transfers of specific powers upwards to regional and global agglomerations, but post-industrialism on the whole is not witnessing a withering away of the state, any more than did industrial polities. So notwithstanding the chorus to the contrary, the state is as powerful as ever.

No doubt, some will still say that any advocacy for statist social engineering is futile, that it sounds fine in theory but would not work in practice. However, there are no available proofs to the effect that moderate egalitarian politics, progressivism without the 'falsehood of extremes'

(Caird 1897: 20), such as the newly-minted brand expressed in the Rawls-Tawney synthesis, are necessarily electorally unfeasible. Some evidence may point that way, but other recent research suggests that there is still public support for more equality (e.g. Myles 2006: 145). Marxian social-ism, certainly, has failed; it was never even a serious psephological proposi-tion in the flagship nation, America (Bell 1967a; Tawney 1979). However, as regards social democracy we have undeniable success stories, measured not just in years but in decades. The Scandinavian tradition of innovative social democracy has already been hailed. Sweden, a country with almost every household online, attributes its information society achievements to 'political intervention', including a tax discount on computer buying and infrastructure investment, all deriving from 'policy visions', such as 'An Information Society for All' (Olsson 2006). Similarly, Castells and Himanen have argued that Finland represents a desirable trajectory very different from the Singaporean and US models, being a land where the Gini coefficient remains low, although rising (Patomaki 2003). They mar-shal ample data to support their conclusion that 'the Finnish model com-bines a dynamic informational economy with stronger social justice and a collective protection of labor—the old tasks of the welfare state—than the global trend'. Finland is indeed an 'informational welfare state' (Cas-tells and Himanen 2002: 87). The goal of informatised social democracy does not appear to be the stuff of extreme utopianism.

Moreover, informatised social democracy cannot allow itself to be fazed by globalisation arguments, that modern form of fatalism magicked up to excuse myriad governmental and commercial shortcomings. There are outright dissenters from the whole orthodoxy that internationalisation is greater than in the past (some cited in Henten and Skouby 2002: 321). Such dissent may be misplaced, in that globalisation has been a key accom-paniment to the information society thesis in many of its stronger forms, including that of Castells, but also in the more modest form endorsed above (cf. Alvarez and Kilbourn 2002). However, it can be, and typically is, over-stated, especially in much information policy literature. Pessimistic argu-ments from global market forces were hurled at the Swedes in the 1930s and coolly refuted over the following half-century. Indeed, European social democracy as a whole arose amidst concerns about the putative attrition of state sovereignty. 'The issues at the heart of the contemporary globalization debates', Berman observes (2003: 141), 'are in fact very old . . . Then, as now, the political environment was dominated by a belief in the primacy of economics and unfettered markets, and yet marked by a longing for some type of societal control and communal solidarity'. The power of interna-tional capital, of transnational corporations and the like, has no doubt increased since the middle of the twentieth century, but there is still plenty of wriggle room for national social justice. Is it really so naive to agree with Marc Raboy (1999: 296) that 'globalization should be viewed as a pol-icy challenge rather than a justification for the "end of policy" arguments presented in neoliberal, deregulationist discourses'—and presented in some defeatist forms of contemporary social democracy too?

There may be a case, as Braman argues at length in *Change of State* (2006), that the state has to a degree metamorphosed from the 'bureaucratic welfare state' into the 'informational state'. She forensically extracts information-related elements in the US Constitution, copyright clauses and so on, deducing that what was implicit then is now more salient, indeed definitive, in the behaviour of the polity. And on a larger canvas, she points to certain developments which taken together imply that the modern state is different in nature from its industrial predecessor. The argument is to some extent convincing, but it is also important to emphasise that the johoka state has not, in either an empirical or a normative sense, *supplanted* the welfare state. It is rather an *additional* principle of development, a new dimension that increases the complexity of governmental agency and thickens the texture of state power. The key social-moral themes of welfarism— not bureaucracy, which was only ever a necessary evil, but human need, universalism, the procedural as against the punitive theory of poverty, etc—will run ahead, and ought so to do, into the next phase of the life of the democratic state.

No, 'the politics of the information age are not about getting rid of the state but rather deciding how states and governments can help facilitate and deliver the sort of society we want' (May 2002: 147; cf. Rau 2009). In addition, I maintain that social democracy still offers the best theory of the state, preferable to both the monopolistic collectivism of the far left and the hedonistic individualism of the neo-conservative right. In the social democratic perspective, as expounded above with special reference to the work of Rawls and Tawney, the state is neither deified nor anathematised; instead, it is instrumentalised. 'The State', as Tawney (1949: 124) pronounced in characteristically stentorian tones, 'is an important instrument; hence the struggle to control it. But it is an instrument, and nothing more. Fools will use it, when they can, for foolish ends, and criminals for criminal ends. Sensible and decent men will use it for ends which are sensible and decent'. The British social democratic state might not have attained perfection, but it had, at least 'set its face towards the light' (Tawney 1949: 126). This is still the right way for progressive politics to be understood. The core liberal belief in limited government, in the open society, should be tempered by a recognition of the duty of the state to secure the common good, within a deontological schedule of entitlements and rules. The polity cannot be confined to policing property: state 'interference', that is, intervention, remains feasible as well as legitimate, in such expansive modes as regulation, investment, ownership, subsidy, new ministries and public bodies, and redistributive taxation. Such a conception of agency, which I am dubbing the proactive state, can serve as a stable platform from which a concluding case for mild social engineering can be mounted.

COMPUTOPIA: RUDIMENTS OF POST-INDUSTRIAL TELEOLOGY

This final section attempts to outline a post-industrial theory of social engineering. To restate the obvious: any treatise containing elements of prescriptive social theory would be incomplete without some account of the road to the destination, which, for a social democracy inspired by the great Tawney, translates into an updated 'strategy of equality'. What the foregoing argumentation basically points towards is a new paradigm that has broken with indefensible assumptions of the industrial era. I will concentrate on setting out the main features of a positive approach to statist social engineering, based on what is valuable in the Fabian tradition and the philosophical theory of the state. As noted already, the industrial era saw social engineering in both good and bad forms, but the bad tended to crowd out the good, and even the good was inadequately underpinned by ethical thinking and was thus liable at any point to tip over into bad social engineering. Yet political idealism, that is, realistic utopianism, should never be abandoned. What is needed now instead of despair is a doctrine of social engineering that has learned its lessons from the past as well as teased out some of the extraordinary potentialities of the present.

While there is no generally accepted theory of social engineering, the benchmark text remains *The Open Society and its Enemies* (Popper 1966). Since Popper's strictures have overshadowed scholarly discussion, not just in the early post-war decades but also much more recently (e.g. Avery 2003; Croy 2005; Duff 2005), any project of reinvention must clearly start there. My contention is that Popper—a methodologist adrift, I think, in social philosophy—left mixed, if not mutually exclusive, messages. Popper's chief burden was to ring-fence political freedom against the authoritarianism of the 1930s and '40s, and it is in that context of a defence of the open society that his animadversions on social engineering must be understood. His target was specifically what he called 'utopian social engineering', a set of practices whose purported justification he located in the unlikely pair of Plato and Marx. The utopian approach to politics, according to Popper, holds that 'we must determine our ultimate political aim, or the Ideal State, before taking any practical action'; it is based on a 'blueprint' (Popper 1966 vol. 1: 157). Thus armed, utopian social engineering eschews half-measures and aims at 'the reconstruction of society as a whole' (Popper 1966 vol. 1: 162). There were two main problems with this approach. First, its methodology was flawed, in that it was predicated, prematurely, on the possession of 'sociological knowledge' (Popper 1966 vol. 1: 162). And underneath this unwise predication lurked 'historicism', the false belief that social evolution is determined by knowable inexorable laws. The second serious shortcoming was political: utopian social engineering necessitated the massive concentration of political power, 'a strong centralized rule of a few' (Popper 1966 vol. 1: 159). Believing, wrongly, that they were privy to positive knowledge of the correct shape of the future, social engineers fancied that they had the right to dictate and even use violence to achieve their ends. Thus, utopian social engineering was inherently totalitarian, which is why it had found favour with both German fascists and Russian communists, but not with rational politicians (Popper 1966 vol. 2: 335). 'Few serious minds', echoed *The End of Ideology* (Bell 1988: 402), 'believe any longer that one can set down "blueprints" and through "social engineering" bring about a new utopia of social harmony'.

Yet, for all that, and this nuance is often missed, Sir Karl was by no means a foe of every form of social engineering. He observed that within the social engineering camp there resided another type, which he called 'piecemeal', i.e. small-scale, and which he judged 'methodologically sound' (Popper 1966 vol. 1: 161). According to Popper, a truly scientific politics would not be deterministic but would consist simply of 'the factual information necessary for the construction or alteration of social institutions' (Popper 1966 vol. 1: 22). Piecemeal social engineering, being incremental, is less risky than the utopian variant. It can be reversed; it is falsifiable. It struggles 'against the greatest and most urgent evils of society, rather than searching for, and fighting for, its greatest ultimate good' (Popper 1966 vol. 1: 158). Such an approach, what today would be classified as negative utilitarianism, is also more likely to be popularly supported; it is elector-friendly social engineering. As regards blueprints, the piecemeal social engineer may or may not have one, but if he does he reckons it 'far distant' and thinks that all generations, including the present, 'have a claim', i.e. indefeasible rights (Popper 1966 vol. 1: 158). However, Popper had no problem at all with blueprints for single institutions, such as health care, unemployment insurance or educational reform. Indeed, in volume 2 he confirmed his support for 'economic interventionism' in terms which could serve as a one-line summary of the kind of social democracy I have been trying to promote throughout this work. 'We must', Popper wrote (1966 vol. 2: 125), 'construct social institutions, enforced by the power of the state, for the protection of the economically weak from the economically strong'. Thus he hailed 'the democratic interventionism of Sweden and the "Smaller Democracies" and the New Deal in America' (Popper 1966 vol. 2: 335). Popper also came out in favour of paternalistic interference by the state—i.e. *cultural* interventionism—in areas such as personal accident insurance, the sale of drugs, use of safety belts, and television broadcasting content (Pera 2006: 278). And yet his bottom philosophical line remained that interventionism is 'extremely dangerous', that government is a 'necessary evil', and that 'state interventionism should be limited to what is really necessary for the protection of freedom' (Popper 1966 vol. 2: 130).

Some of these claims are eminently reasonable, but it is also obvious that there are shortcomings in Popper's account, too much bundling of ideas, too much sheer inconsistency. He frames the entire debate unhelpfully, especially with that rigid dichotomy between utopian and piecemeal social engineering. No doubt utopian engineering in his sense, taken as a complete set of propositions, is intrinsically unsafe, and should be laid to rest. The idea of changing the whole of society—economy, culture, polity—in one fell swoop can be happily buried as an industrial-era conceit, alongside the dark satanic mills and general anarcho-capitalism against which social engineering was initially directed. But it is a *non sequitur* to deduce that social engineering has then to be merely perfunctory. The following paragraphs define a post-Popperian approach equidistant between his utopian and piecemeal stools. The normative theory of the information society requires a positive, post-Popperian doctrine of social engineering, one which pursues major future-oriented goals while also heeding procedural justice and the rights of the individual. It must incorporate the factualism and fallibilism that are strengths of Popper's philosophy, but it must also reaffirm the validity of working purposefully and systematically, albeit gradually, towards a comprehensive social ideal.

In light of what has been argued in Chapter 2, the paramount requirement of a post-industrial theory of social engineering, that is, one seeking consciously to supplant discredited industrial forms, is that it should connect to a social deontology; specifically, it must be founded on the axiom that 'the rights secured by justice are not subject to political bargaining or to the calculus of social interests' (Rawls 1973: 3–4). What this clearly means is that social engineering for the twenty-first century must observe non-negotiable limits on state action. So *pace* 1930s political poet W. H. Auden, there can be no such thing as a 'necessary murder' (quoted disapprovingly in Orwell 1962: 36); or, in the vulgar computing vernacular, certain things cannot under any circumstances be done to 'meatware'.

By way of illustration, the pursuit of so-called human 'enhancement' constitutes a prime domain where teleological, technologically-deterministic thinking needs to become subject to deontological values and vetoes. It is easily predictable that if the social engineering of the future does not maintain a credible distinction between the natural-born and the socially-constructed it will eventually fall foul again of the kind of eugenics that gave it a bad name in the first place. This is part of the danger in grandiose talk of manifestos for cyborgs, and the like. Some thinkers are already alive to the problem. For example, Fuller (2006: 203) explores an important nexus between social engineering and the sociology of cyborgs, while Tony Fitzpatrick (1999) cites social engineering during a discussion of social policy for such. Normatively, however, we must say that only *a priori* constraints rooted in the moral egalitarianism of the western tradition can truly protect the integrity of the person. At the less futuristic end, it is reasonable to assume that this tradition forbids the compulsory surgical implantation of surveillance and identification devices. However, the point here is not to produce a systematic bioinformatical dogmatics but simply to register the gravity and impending salience of the issues, and to proclaim the indispensability of basic moral markers. The function of a social deontology, as an integral component of a normative theory of the information society, is to act as a culturally-conservative, binding restraint on the political or market use of potentially oppressive socio-technical innovations. Fully specified, the social deontology would thus define the limits of an engineering standpoint.

Now it might at first sight seem that this is to tie social engineers' hands behind their backs before they even commence. Surely the one thing that any theory claiming Rawlsian support cannot entertain is social engineering, because is it not precisely the sort of consequentialist mindset implicit in social engineering that Rawls's whole counter-utilitarian project was designed to combat? However, while insisting that the right is prior to the good, and stipulating what cannot be done, there is no need to go further and foreclose on all forms of progressive teleological action. Industrial social engineering's cardinal error was indeed an excessive form of teleology, but it is absurd to infer therefrom that teleological action is proscribed *tout court*. Instead, rejecting a crude antinomy between the ethics of responsibility and the ethics of ultimate ends, the post-industrial theory of social engineering fixes the structure of its ethic so as to encourage teleological behaviour to the utmost limits of the deontological framework. Put another way, a new paradigm of social engineering does not require a Kierkegaardian (2005) 'teleological suspension of the ethical', but it does require that any wriggle room at all permitted by the social deontology be utilised to the full for democratically-decided ends—the teleological *extension* of the ethical, as it were. While we are obliged to set out an ethical context such that the dangers Popper imputed to utopianism can be averted, we need not be confined to the cramping negative utilitarianism of dealing only with manifest social evils.

To say that there is plenty of logical space for teleology inside the social deontology is to allow that the Ideal State can be a legitimate medium- as well as long-term political objective. The anathematisation of integrated social planning belongs to a mentality associated with economically right-wing politics, with the politics of merely staying afloat. Social democracy has always offered a more or less viable third way, in a generic rather than Giddensian sense, between both conservative pragmatism and revolutionary socialism, one that incorporates a form of social engineering neither utopian in any pejorative sense nor timidly piecemeal. Thus while post-industrial administrations should refrain from claims to omnicompetence, they can and should act from a social ideal, what Rawls, as we have seen, called a realistic utopia. The Scandinavian social democracies that even Popper found himself applauding were implementations of a joined-up political vision, exercises in realistic utopianism rather than mere piecemeal engineering. *Pace* Popper, we do need a blueprint of an Ideal State, and its content, I have argued, is supplied by the Rawls-Tawney Theorem cashed out into a concrete institutional setup. Somehow then we need to find an ethical path that is attuned to the circumstances of justice, yet sees that there are many promising technological developments which can be exploited.

The teleology appropriate to post-industrial statist social engineering differs from industrial teleology not only in its reduced status—inside, and thus ultimately subordinate to, the social deontology, rather than outside and sovereign—but also in its modality. This is evident in several inter-locking ways. The hallmark of post-industrial social engineering, naturally enough for a normative theory of the information society, is a heightened informationalism. This needs to be specified very carefully. The scientific politics of the would-be social engineer need a comprehensive basis of facts, according to Popper. Such a basis, he plausibly claimed, does not exist, with the supposed result that social engineering of the utopian variety can amount only to pseudo-science, so-called scientism. Indeed, he even suggests in *The Poverty of Historicism*, an influential methodological treatise which acted as a companion text to *Open Society*, that the method of utopian social engineering, 'so far from representing a high level or late stage in the development of thought, is characteristic of a pre-scientific stage' (Popper 2002: 69). Podgorecki too (1996: 46) comes to a very Popperian conclusion when he writes—and this is forty years or more after Popper—that, given the state of social-scientific knowledge, 'at present, a method-ologically reasonable sociotechnician [expert social engineer] would be reluctant to pursue macro-sociotechnical activities'. But such inferences are misleading as well as overly pessimistic. The major premise, that social engineering (and politics generally) should be based on factual information, is certainly correct. And, of course, the social engineering of the past often ran far beyond its informational warrant into perilous pseudo-science. The perfect example was Lysenkoism, the anti-Mendelian biology that propped up Stalin's stereotype of the compliant comrade and even bewitched one or two of the finest scientific brains in the West, including the logistic mas-termind of D-Day (Brown 2005: 304–9). But the real problem was never the facts nor their absence, and always the philosophies of history or other overarching metanarratives to which totalitarians, including some Fabians, as we have seen, succumbed. Informationalism in my sense is the antidote to such scientism, for scientism is exactly science minus hard information.

We incontrovertibly need, as the Fabians in their more lucid moments insisted, to lay a foundation of facts, and to build political architecture only on such. The social engineer thus requires at her side that expert in information, what we would call today an information scientist. However, it does not at all follow that factual knowledge cannot be used ambitiously or that macrolevel social engineering must be avoided. To begin with, there is far more informa-tion now. We certainly have more technical data, more societal information, more information flow across-the-board, as the Japanese and others have long since calculated. This is not to say that we enjoy perfect information, or even near-perfect information; indeed, our prospects of attaining such an episte-mological end-state will always be zero. However, we do now know enough about social problems, social institutions, social psychology and even social justice to enable a twenty-first century politics of social engineering.

Moreover, firm anchorage in information should not prevent social engineering from engaging in careful use of a variety of innovative fields and speculative techniques, what Bell (1999: 27), ever the coiner of apt labels, termed 'intellectual technology'. They include econometrics, game theory, maximin strategy, modelling, mathematical theory of choice, technological forecasting, and so on. Perhaps the most promising field for twenty-first century social engineers is cybernetics. It is important to be very clear here. There can be no single science of social engineering. Podgorecki (1996) envisaged what he called sociotechnics as such and, possessed of this unrealistic hope, despaired of any kind of radical social engineering. However, cybernetics, the science of control *via* feedback mechanisms, would be the most obvious candidate for any such title. 'To live effectively', to quote again its left-liberal pioneer, 'is to live with adequate information, so communication and control belong to the essence of man's inner life, even as they belong to his life in society' (Wiener 1989: 18). It is wrong to associate cybernetics in any way with inhumanity; on the contrary, Wiener demanded the human use of human beings, a 'humanistically inscribed social determinism' (Day 2001: 51). What such intellectual technologies can do is help to remove the baggage from normative thinking, making it more precise. So long as they operate within the parameters of the social deontology, they should be regarded as legitimate aids to social engineering.

A cognate update, contributing to the paradigm shift that the theory of social engineering now demands, is also required in the conceptualisation of communication. The industrial-era paradigm assumed the 'hypodermic needle' or 'bullet' model, which portrayed messages being fired from source to audience in an unstoppable, one-way direction. Influenced by information theory and prevalent in one shape or another in the heyday of twentieth-century social engineering, the model allowed for no deviation, no responsiveness to impact, no conception of feedback. It was not only the crass utopian engineering of the dictators that followed this 'propaganda model', as it became known; it was also to some extent evident in the practice even of social democrats and others committed to progressive change inside the envelope of a liberal polity. Marxists are notorious for it, but, as noted previously, the Fabians were for their part sometimes guilty of thus modelling the 'masses'—a revealingly inert term. 'It is', as Castells (2000: 363–64) justly observes, 'one of the ironies of intellectual history that it is precisely those thinkers who advocate social change who often view people as passive receptacles of ideological manipulation, in fact precluding the notions of social movements and social change except under the mode of exceptional, singular events generated outside the social system'.

Thankfully, however, research programmes over several decades have been united in restoring agency to audiences in the construction of meaning, thereby rendering obsolete not only the propaganda model but also the primitive ideas about social engineering which it supported. What is coming through is some kind of helical model. Instead of the finite straight line of the needle, communication is depicted as circular, recursive, interactive. Messages, playing from receiver back to sender as well as from sender to receiver, are socially and institutionally embedded, in a multiplicity of complex, constraining ways. A richer and ultimately more human conception of communication emerges, more 'user education' than 'engineering of consent'. By systematically integrating feedback, this model enables teleological politics to follow a falsificationist methodology, requiring social engineers to act in such a way that policies can be to some extent revised in light of negative experience. However, I should leave detailed exposition to communication scientists (e.g. Dance 1970, 1997; Mattelart and Mattelart 1998; McQuail and Windahl 1981).

A revised granularity would also modulate the teleology of the future. Arguably, another basic error of industrial social engineering was its mistaken apprehension of its primary subject. Industrial social engineers worked from too personalised a script; they wanted to remake everybody according to their conception of the good citizen or worker, the new man. Post-industrial social engineering needs to operate at a coarser level of granularity, in the sense that its political-administrative focus should be institutions rather than individuals. Consciousness may be 'raised', but mainly by indirect means, through reforming or reinventing the social institutions that partly shape consciousness. This condition provides latitude to individuals, removing them from the intense pressures of teleological expectations, as well as upholding the requirements of procedural justice and the rule of law. Sometimes an image of the person might come into focus, for example if a governmental broadcasting campaign supporting the information poor has to delineate 'before' and 'after' scenarios, but the energising logic and general orientating framework of social engineering must seek to be resolutely institutional. Adherence to institutionalism, in this sense, would clearly reduce the risk not just of micromanagement but also of an unwelcome resurgence of messianic politics. It is bad enough that the cult of personality frequently accompanies identity politics and cultural politics—recall that it was these that Bell foresaw (1977, 1988), along with the revival of felt religion—without it also corrupting the fact-venerating politics of information.

Furthermore, however credible may be the case for post-industrial social engineering by the state in pursuit of the good life for the citizenry, a default of gradualism, what I have renamed modularism, must be maintained. This will always be the price that has to be paid for liberal democracy. Yet Lippmann, jettisoning his youthful Fabianism, overstated the problem in *The Good Society*. 'In so far as it seeks to administer the economy under a rational and coherent plan', he wrote (2005: 108, 110), '[the political system] must somehow prevent one majority from overriding the decisions of a previous majority. For if a plan is to be carried out, it must be adopted and the people must thereafter conform. . . . This is the insoluble contradiction of the gradual collectivist'. The response to this perennial charge, which basically conflates revolutionary and social democratic politics, is two-fold. To some extent, it can simply be asserted that modular engineering is not entirely irreversible, that long-range plans decided by one democratically-elected government can actually be mitigated, if not nullified, by subsequent administrations. It is not just social engineering, but all long-range projects, including, as imperialists are aware, foreign policy commitments, that are subject to policy shifts and happenstance. However, the other answer is a reiteration of the key point about the whole concept of social engineering. Even in its informatised, demassified and modularised form, there will inevitably be tensions with government by consent. There is no way of avoiding an element of vanguardism. Of course, it is desirable to have as much populism as possible, but it is naive, merely wheel-spinning, for information society conferences to declare that 'representatives of all members of the community should be involved', and that decisions 'should not be left to distant government decision makers and commercial technologists' (quoted in Patterson and Wilson 2000: 79). It sounds worthy but it is really a prescription for political paralysis. Some of the sting of the social appropriation of expertise can be removed, but never all. Nevertheless, the good society can and should be pursued, but only within the limits of the social deontology. That is how polity, culture and economy—the three realms—hang together in a well-ordered society.

Finally, of course, there is the computer, the information machine of information machines, the very icon and incarnation of our post-industrial epoch. It is now obvious that, in the old cliché, we have the (information) technology to remake the world. 'The development of a new intellectual technology', Bell wrote (1965: 121), '—game theory, decision theory, linear programming, simulation, information theory, cybernetics, systems analysis—all of it tooled by the computer, allows us now to construct models of the future'. The computer, indeed, 'plays a central role' in the 'social framework of the information society' (Bell 1980b: 500). This is not to say that computers offer a quick fix to social problems. Alvin Weinberg (2003) thought that technology could simply replace social engineering. Consider, he said, the case of how to stop war. The traditional social engineering solution would be somehow to teach people to love one another, Christian-style. But a much faster and more successful answer, he argued, is atomic bombs: they force people into peace because of the exorbitantly high price of war. Similarly, intrauterine devices are a better solution than trying to socially engineer population reductions through improved sexual behaviour. I believe that Weinberg's morally pessimistic counsel, typical of technologists, is profoundly wrong. Such solutions are inherently shallow, recklessly risky and generally short-lived. An enduring settlement at a higher level of moral consciousness must always be sought. In whatever way original sin is understood, it does not entail that humanity is incapable of justice, of some degree of self-restraint and altruism. And in any case, the choice Weinberg offers, like Popper's dichotomy of utopian or piecemeal social engineering, is false. People can be encouraged to love one another and to pursue purity, even as nuclear bombs and IUDs are institutionalised as part of a smart society's insurance policy for survival. That is how structure and agency should cohabit.

If the arguments in this book have been to any extent persuasive, the content of social engineering's *telos* is filled by the theory of informatised social democracy, specifically by the Rawls-Tawney Theorem. Post-industrial politics—that is, information politics—need to start being egalitarian: strictly egalitarian with respect to political rights and their informational adjuncts, mildly egalitarian regarding other social primary goods, including several key categories of socioeconomic information. Yet increasing access, or even underwriting the ideal of universal service and access, is comparatively easily achieved, by a mega-investment or the passing of a new statute. It is making people utilise the access that remains the major issue. Here the social engineer distinguishes herself from other policy actors by decisively rejecting the agrarian adage, you can take a horse to water but you cannot make it drink—she sees that as failing to take responsibility for the horse's welfare. She grasps the fact that, while social problems should of course be confronted openly, they must also be tackled strategically by slowly changing the background conditions that breed a low information consciousness. With its tool-box of computerised techniques, social engineering can now rise to the call of the post-industrial analogue of the glorious social democratic project of a classless society. What the world needs, in short, is a realistic utopianism assisted by informatics. Thus Yoneji Masuda, the Japanese visionary whose ideas have been the source of such mirth among western scholars, was right all along: our goal is nothing less than *computopia*.

Bibliography

Allan, Stuart (2004) *News Culture*, 2nd ed., Milton Keynes: Open University Press.

Alvarez, Isabel and Kilbourn, Brent (2002) 'Mapping the information society literature: topics, perspectives, and root metaphors', *First Monday* 7(1) [19 pp.] Available at http://firstmonday.org/issues/issue7_1/alvarez/index.html (accessed June 30 2011).

Anderson, Ross, Brown, Ian, Dowty, Terri, Inglesant, Philip, Heath, William, and Sasse, Angela (2009) *Database State: A Report Commissioned by The Joseph Rowntree Reform Trust*, York: Joseph Rowntree Reform Trust Ltd.

Armitage, John (1999) 'Machinic modulations: new cultural theory and technopolitics', *Angelaki: Journal of the Theoretical Humanities* 4(2): 1–16.

Arneson, Richard J. (2007) 'Equality, coercion, culture and social norms', *Politics, Philosophy & Economics* 2(2): 139–63.

Arnold, Thomas (1845) 'The Christian duty of conceding the claims of Roman Catholics', in *The Miscellaneous Works of Thomas Arnold, D. D., Collected and Republished*, London: B. Fellowes, pp. 3–78.

Arrow, Kenneth J. (1996) 'The economics of information: an exposition', *Empirica* 23(2): 119–28.

Avery, Thomas (2003) 'Popper on "social engineering": a classical liberal view', *Reason Papers: A Journal of Interdisciplinary Normative Studies* 26(Summer): 29–38.

Barber, Benjamin R. (1997) 'The new telecommunications technology: endless frontier or the end of democracy?', *Constellations* 4(2): 208–28.

Barbrook, Richard (2007) *Imaginary Futures: From Thinking Machines to the Global Village*, London: Pluto Press.

Barry, Brian (1996) 'Does society exist? The case for socialism', in Preston King (ed.), *Socialism and the Common Good: New Fabian Essays*, London: Frank Cass, pp. 115–43.

—— (2005) *Why Social Justice Matters*, Cambridge: Polity Press.

Barry, Norman (2000) *An Introduction to Modern Political Theory*, 4th edn, Basingstoke: Macmillan Press.

Baruchson-Arbib, Shifra (1996) *Social Information Science: Love, Health and the Information Society*, Brighton: Sussex Academic Press.

Barzilai-Nahon, Karine (2006) 'Gaps and bits: conceptualizing measurements for digital divide(s)', *The Information Society* 22(5): 269–78.

Batt, Chris (1998) *I Have Seen the Future and IT Works! (The Second Ameritech Information Society Lecture)*, Edinburgh: Merchiston Publishing.

Baynes, Kenneth (2006) 'Ethos and institution: on the site of distributive justice', *Journal of Social Philosophy* 37(2): 182–96.

BBC News (2006) 'Britain is "surveillance society"', November 2. Available at http://news.bbc.co.uk/1/hi/uk/6108496.stm (accessed June 30 2011).

Bekken, Jon (2002) 'Books and commerce in the age of virtual capital: the changing political economy of bookselling', in Manjunath Pendakur and Roma Harris (eds), *Citizenship and Participation in the Information Age*, Aurora, Ont.: Garamond Press, pp. 231–49.

Bell, Daniel (1962) *The Post-Industrial Society: A Speculative View of the United States and Beyond*, Unpublished Manuscript.

—— (1965) 'The study of the future', *The Public Interest* 1(Fall): 119–30.

—— (1967a) *Marxian Socialism in the United States*, Princeton, NJ: Princeton University Press.

—— (1967b) 'Notes on the post-industrial society (1)', *The Public Interest* 6(Winter): 24–35.

—— (1977) 'The future of religion (Hobhouse Memorial Lecture)', *British Journal of Sociology* 28(3): 419–49.

—— (1980a [1977]) 'Teletext and technology: new networks of knowledge and information in postindustrial society', in *The Winding Passage: Sociological Essays and Journeys, 1960–1980*, New York: Basic Books, pp. 34–65.

—— (1980b [1979]) 'The social framework of the information society', in Tom Forester (ed.) *The Microelectronics Revolution: The Complete Guide to the New Technology and its Impact on Society*, Oxford: Blackwell, pp. 500–49.

—— (1985) 'Gutenberg and the computer: on information, knowledge and other distinctions', *Encounter* 64(May): 15–20.

—— (1988 [1960]) *The End of Ideology: On the Exhaustion of Political Ideas in the Fifties*, with a new afterword, Cambridge, MA: Harvard University Press.

—— (1989) 'The third technological revolution and its possible socioeconomic consequences', *Dissent* (Spring): 164–76.

—— (1995a) 'Social science: an imperfect art', *The Tocqueville Review* 16(1): 3–24.

—— (1995b) 'The cultural contradictions of Newt Gingrich', *New Perspectives Quarterly* (Spring): 7–9.

—— (1996a [1978]) 'Foreword: 1978', in *The Cultural Contradictions of Capitalism*, New York: Basic Books, pp. xi–xxix.

—— (1996b) 'Introduction: reflections at the end of an age', in George T. Kurian and Graham T. T. Molitor (eds), *Encyclopedia of the Future*, vol. 1, New York: Simon & Schuster Macmillan, pp. xxi–xxxviii.

—— (1996c [1976]) 'Introduction/The disjunction of realms: a statement of themes', in *The Cultural Contradictions of Capitalism*, New York: Basic Books, pp. 3–30.

—— (1996d [1976]) 'The public household: on "fiscal sociology" and the liberal society', in *The Cultural Contradictions of Capitalism*, New York: Basic Books, pp. 220–82.

—— (1999 [1973]) *The Coming of Post-Industrial Society: A Venture in Social Forecasting*, special anniversary edition with a new foreword, New York: Basic Books.

Benhabib, Seyla (1986) *Critique, Norm, and Utopia: A Study of the Foundations of Critical Theory*, New York: Columbia University Press.

Bennett, Colin J. (2008) *The Privacy Advocates: Resisting the Spread of Surveillance*, Cambridge, MA: The MIT Press.

Berman, Sheri (2003) 'The roots and rationale of social democracy', *Social Philosophy & Policy* 20(1): 113–44.

Black, Alistair and Hoare, Peter (eds) (2006) *The Cambridge History of Libraries in Britain and Ireland, vol. 3: 1850–2000*, Cambridge: Cambridge University Press.

———— , Pepper, Simon and Bagshaw, Kaye (2009) *Books, Buildings and Social Engineering: Early Public Libraries in Britain from Past to Present*, Aldershot: Ashgate.

Bonfadelli, Heinz (2002) 'The internet and knowledge gaps: a theoretical and empirical investigation', *European Journal of Communication* 17(1): 65–84.

Borgman, Christine L. (2000) *From Gutenberg to the Global Information Infrastructure: Access to Information in the Networked World*, Cambridge, MA: The MIT Press.

Boucher, David and Vincent, Andrew (2000) *British Idealism and Political Theory*, Edinburgh: Edinburgh University Press.

Bovens, Mark (2002) 'Information rights: citizenship in the information society', *Journal of Political Philosophy* 10(3): 317–41.

Braman, Sandra (ed.) (2004) *The Emergent Global Information Policy Regime*, Basingstoke: Palgrave Macmillan.

———— (2006) *Change of State: Information, Policy, and Power*, Cambridge, MA: The MIT Press.

Briggs, Asa (2001) *Michael Young: Social Entrepreneur*, London: Palgrave Macmillan.

Bristow, Nancy K. (1996) *Making Men Moral: Social Engineering during the Great War*, New York: New York University Press.

Britz, Johannes J. (2004) 'To know or not to know: a moral reflection on information poverty', *Journal of Information Science* 30(3): 192–204.

Brooke, Heather (2005) 'Has anybody in Britain actually read *1984*?', *The Independent*, October 13.

———— (2007) *Your Right to Know: A Citizen's Guide to the Freedom of Information Act*, 2nd ed., London: Pluto Press.

Brown, Andrew (2005) *J. D. Bernal: The Sage of Science*, Oxford: Oxford University Press.

Browne, Mairead (1997a) 'The field of information policy 1. Fundamental concepts', *Journal of Information Science* 23(4): 261–75.

———— (1997b) 'The field of information policy 2. Redefining the boundaries and methodologies', *Journal of Information Science* 23(5): 339–51.

Bryant, Chris (1996) *Possible Dreams: A Personal History of the British Christian Socialists*, London: Hodder & Stoughton.

Bucy, Erik P. and Newhagen, John E. (eds) (2004) *Media Access: Social and Psychological Dimensions of New Technology Use*, Mahwah, NJ: Lawrence Erlbaum Associates.

Burgelman, Jean-Claude (2002) 'Integrating social sciences into information society policy', in Robin Mansell, Rohan Samarajiva and Amy Mahan (eds), *Networking Knowledge for Information Societies: Institutions and Intervention*, Delft: Delft University Press, pp. 47–53.

Burger, Robert H. (1993) *Information Policy: A Framework for Evaluation and Policy Research*, Norwood, NJ: Ablex.

Caidi, Nadia and Ross, Anthony (2005) 'Information rights and national security', *Government Information Quarterly* 22(4): 663–84.

Caird, Edward (1888) *The Moral Aspect of the Economical Problem (Presidential Address to the Ethical Society)*, London: Swan Sonnenschein, Lowrey & Co.

———— (1897) *The Present State of the Controversy between Individualism and Socialism (Inaugural Address to the Civic Society of Glasgow)*, Glasgow: Maclehose.

Callaghan, John and Tunney, Sean (2001) 'The end of social democracy?', *Politics* 21(1): 63–72.

Capurro, Rafael and Hjorland, Birger (2003) 'The concept of information', *Annual Review of Information Science and Technology* 37: 343–411.

Cardoso, Gustavo (2006) *The Media in the Network Society: Browsing, News, Filters and Citizenship*, Lisbon: Center for Research and Studies in Sociology.

Carey, Kevin (ed.) (1985) *Unveiling the Right: A Way Forward for Social Democracy Based on the Ideas of John Rawls*, London: The Tawney Society (John Rawls Creative Study Group).

Castells, Manuel (2000 [1996]) *The Information Age: Economy, Society, and Culture, vol. 1: The Rise of the Network Society*, 2nd ed., Oxford: Blackwell.

—— (2004 [1997]) *The Information Age: Economy, Society, and Culture, vol. 2: The Power of Identity*, 2nd ed., Oxford: Blackwell.

—— and Himanen, Pekka (2002) *The Information Society and the Welfare State: the Finnish Model*, Oxford: Oxford University Press.

Cawkell, Tony (2001) 'Sociotechnology: the digital divide', *Journal of Information Science* 27(1): 55–60.

Chadwick, Andrew (2006) *Internet Politics: States, Citizens, and New Communication Technologies*, New York: Oxford University Press.

Chatman, Elfreda A. (1996) 'The impoverished life-world of outsiders', *Journal of the American Society for Information Science* 47(3): 193–206.

—— (1999) 'A theory of life in the round', *Journal of the American Society for Information Science* 50(3): 207–17.

Cherry, Colin (1985) *The Age of Access: Information Technology and Social Revolution: Posthumous Papers of Colin Cherry*, ed. William Edmondson, London: Croom Helm.

Childers, Thomas (1975) *The Information-Poor in America*, Metuchen, NJ: Scarecrow Press.

Clift, Ben and Tomlinson, Jim (2002) 'Tawney and the third way', *Journal of Political Ideologies* 7(3): 315–31.

Cohen, G. A. (2001) *If You're an Egalitarian, How Come You're So Rich?*, Cambridge, MA: Harvard University Press.

—— (2008) *Rescuing Justice and Equality*, Cambridge, MA: Harvard University Press.

Cole, Margaret (1961) *The Story of Fabian Socialism*, Stanford, CA: Stanford University Press.

—— (1977) 'Webb, Sidney and Beatrice', in *The New Encyclopaedia Britannica, Macropaedia vol. 19*, Chicago: Enyclopaedia Britannica, Inc., pp. 711–13.

Collins, Richard (2000) 'Realising social goals in connectivity and content: the challenge of convergence', in Christopher T. Marsden (ed.), *Regulating the Global Information Society*, London: Routledge, pp. 108–15.

—— (2007) 'Rawls, Fraser, redistribution, recognition and the World Summit on the Information Society', *International Journal of Communication* 1: 1–23.

Compaine, Benjamin M. (2001a) 'Declare the war won', in Benjamin M. Compaine (ed.), *The Digital Divide: Facing a Crisis or Creating a Myth?*, Cambridge, MA: The MIT Press, pp. 315–35.

—— (2001b) 'Information gaps: myth or reality?', in Benjamin M. Compaine (ed.), *The Digital Divide: Facing a Crisis or Creating a Myth?*, Cambridge, MA: The MIT Press, pp. 105–18.

—— (ed.) (2001c) *The Digital Divide: Facing a Crisis or Creating a Myth?*, Cambridge, MA: The MIT Press.

Conboy, Martin (2011) *Journalism in Britain: A Historical Introduction*, London: Sage.

Consalvo, Mia and Ess, Charles (eds) (2011) *The Handbook of Internet Studies*, Chichester: Wiley-Blackwell.

Copley, Terence (2002) *Black Tom: Arnold of Rugby, the Myth and the Man*, London: Continuum.

Cort, John C. (2003) 'The death of a good philosopher', *Religious Socialism* 27(1): 6–7, 16.

Crick, Bernard (1972) Review of A Theory of Justice, *New Statesman*, May 5.

Cronin, Blaise (2003) *Pulp Friction*, Lanham, MD: The Scarecrow Press.

——— (2005) 'Intelligence, terrorism, and national security', *Annual Review of Information Science and Technology* 39: 395–432.

Croy, Marvin J. (2005) 'Social engineering', in Carl Mitcham (ed.), *Encyclopedia of Science, Technology, and Ethics, vol. 4*, Detroit, MI: Macmillan Reference USA, pp. 1804–7.

Dance, Frank E. X. (1970) 'A helical model of communication', in Kenneth K. Sereno and C. David Mortensen (eds), *Foundations of Communication Theory*, New York: Harper & Row, pp. 103–7.

——— (1997) 'Context's "culture": speech', in James L. Owen (ed.), *Context and Communication Behavior*, Reno, NV: Context Press, pp. 251–59.

Daniels, Norman (ed.) (1975) *Reading Rawls: Critical Studies on Rawls' A Theory of Justice*, Oxford: Blackwell.

Darnton, Robert (2011) 'Google's loss: the public's gain', *The New York Review of Books* LVIII(7) April 28–May 11: 10–12.

Davis, Allison (2005) 'Bridging the digital divide: leading the disenfranchised into the information age', in Tony Silvia (ed.), *Global News: Perspectives on the Information Age*, Ames, IA: Iowa State University Press, pp. 185–91.

Day, Ronald E. (2001) *The Modern Invention of Information: Discourse, History, and Power*, Carbondale, IL: Southern Illinois University Press.

Dearnley, James and Feather, John (2001) *The Wired World: An Introduction to the Theory and Practice of the Information Society*, London: Library Association.

De Mul, Jos (1999) 'The informatization of the worldview', *Information, Communication & Society* 2(1): 69–94.

Dennis, Norman and Halsey, A. H. (1988) *English Ethical Socialism: Thomas More to R. H. Tawney*, Oxford: Clarendon Press.

Doctor, Ronald D. (1992) 'Social equity and information technologies: moving toward information democracy', *Annual Review of Information Science and Technology* 27: 43–96.

Dretske, Fred I. (1981) *Knowledge and the Flow of Information*, Cambridge, MA: The MIT Press.

——— (2008) 'The metaphysics of information', in Alois Pichler and Herbert Hrachovec (eds), *Wittgenstein and the Philosophy of Information: Proceedings of the 30th International Ludwig Wittgenstein Symposium, Kirchberg am Wechsel, Austria, 2007, vol. 1*, Frankfurt: Ontos Verlag, pp. 273–83.

Ducatel, Ken, Webster, Juliet and Herrmann, Werner (2000) 'Information infrastructures or societies?', in Ken Ducatel, Juliet Webster and Werner Herrmann (eds), *The Information Society in Europe: Work and Life in an Age of Globalization*, Lanham, MD: Rowman & Littlefield, pp. 1–17.

Duff, Alistair S. (1998) 'Daniel Bell's theory of the information society', *Journal of Information Science* 24(6): 373–93.

——— (2000a) *Information Society Studies*, London: Routledge.

——— (2000b) 'Joho shakai: the Japanese contribution to information society studies', *Keio Communication Review* 22: 41–77.

——— (2001) 'On the present state of information society studies', *Education for Information* 19(3): 231–44.

——— (2004a) 'The past, present and future of information policy: towards a normative theory of the information society', *Information, Communication & Society* 7(1): 69–87.

——— (2004b) 'The sickness of an information society: R. H. Tawney and the post-industrial condition', *Information, Communication & Society* 7(3): 403–22.

——— (2005) 'Social engineering in the information age', *The Information Society* 20(1): 67–71.

——— (2006a) 'Informatisation: libraries and the exploitation of electronic information services', in Alistair Black and Peter Hoare (eds), *The Cambridge History of Libraries in Britain and Ireland, vol. III: 1850–2000,* Cambridge: Cambridge University Press, pp. 627–38.

——— (2006b) '"Laying a foundation of fact": Fabianism and the information society thesis', *Information, Communication & Society* 9(4): 515–36.

——— (2008a) 'Information liberation? The relations of knowledge and freedom in social-democratic thought', in Nico Stehr (ed.), *Knowledge and Democracy: A 21st Century Perspective,* New Brunswick, NJ: Transaction, pp. 199–215.

——— (2008b) 'Powers in the land? British political columnists in the information era', *Journalism Practice* 2(2): 230–44.

——— (2008c) 'R. H. Tawney', in William A. Darity (ed.), *International Encyclopedia of the Social Sciences, vol. 8,* 2nd ed., Detroit, MI: Macmillan Reference USA, pp. 271–72.

——— (2011) 'The Rawls-Tawney theorem and the digital divide in postindustrial society', *Journal of the American Society for Information Science and Technology* 62(3): 604–12.

Dupuy, Jean-Pierre (1980) 'Myths of the informational society', in Kathleen Woodward (ed.), *The Myths of Information: Technology and Post-Industrial Culture,* London: Routledge & Kegan Paul, pp. 3–17.

Dutton, William H. (ed.) (1999) *Society on the Line: Information Politics in the Digital Age,* Oxford: Oxford University Press.

———, Helsper, Ellen J. and Gerber, Monica M. (2009) *The Internet in Britain 2009,* Oxford: Oxford Internet Institute.

Dyson, Esther, Gilder, George, Keyworth, George and Toffler, Alvin (2004 [1990]) 'Cyberspace and the American dream', in Frank Webster (ed.), *The Information Society Reader,* London: Routledge, pp. 31–41.

Edelstein, Alex S., Bowes, John E. and Harsel, Sheldon M. (eds) (1978) *Information Societies: Comparing the Japanese and American Experiences,* Seattle, WA: International Communication Center, University of Washington.

Einstein, Albert (1954) *Ideas and Opinions,* trans. Sonja Bargmann, New York: Crown.

Elkin-Koren, Niva (2001) 'The privatization of information policy', *Ethics and Information Technology* 2(4): 201–9.

Emmet, Dorothy (1985) *The Moral Roots of Social Democracy,* London: The Tawney Society.

Erikson, Erik H. (1959) *Identity and the Life Cycle,* New York: International Universities Press.

——— (1968) *Identity: Youth and Crisis,* New York: W. W. Norton & Co.

Esping-Andersen, Gosta (1999) *Social Foundations of Postindustrial Economies,* Oxford: Oxford University Press.

'European Directive Compromise' (2001) *Library Association Record* 103(4): 191.

European Union (1994) *Europe and the Global Information Society: Bangemann Report Recommendations to the European Council,* Brussels: European Commission.

——— (1995) 'Directive 95/46/EC of the European Parliament and of the Council of 24 October 1995 on the Protection of Individuals with Regard to the Processing of Personal Data and on the Free Movement of Such Data', *Official Journal* L 281, 23/11/1995: 0031–50.

——— (2001) 'Directive 2001/29/EC of the European Parliament and of the Council of 22 May 2001 on the Harmonisation of Certain Aspects of Copyright and Related Rights in the Information Society', *Official Journal* L 167, 22/06/2001: 0010–19.

Fallis, Don (2004a) 'Epistemic value theory and information ethics', *Minds and Machines* 14(1): 101–17.

———— (2004b) 'Social epistemology and the digital divide', in John Weckert and Yeslam Al-Saggaf (eds), *Proceedings of Selected Papers from the Computers and Philosophy Conference (CAP2003), Canberra, Australia: Conferences in Research and Practice in Information Technology, vol. 37*, Sydney: Australian Computing Society, pp. 79–84.

Feather, John (2008) *The Information Society: A Study of Continuity and Change*, 5th ed., London: Facet.

Fisher, R. (ed.) (n.d.) *A History of the Fabian Society*, London: The Fabian Society. Available at http://www.fabian-society.org.uk (accessed June 30 2011).

Fitzpatrick, Tony (1999) 'Social policy for cyborgs', *Body & Society* 5(1): 93–116.

———— (2000) 'Critical cyberpolicy: network technologies, massless citizens, virtual rights', *Critical Social Policy* 20(3): 375–407.

Floridi, Luciano (2007) 'A look into the future impact of ICTs on our lives', *The Information Society* 23(1): 59–64.

Foerstel, Herbert N. (1999) *Freedom of Information and the Right to Know: the Origins and Applications of the Freedom of Information Act*, Westport, CT: Greenwood Press.

Forrester, Duncan B. (1997) *Christian Justice and Public Policy*, Cambridge: Cambridge University Press.

———— (2001) *On Human Worth: A Christian Vindication of Equality*, London: SCM Press.

Fortner, Robert S. (1995) 'Excommunication in the information society', *Critical Studies in Mass Communication* 12(2): 133–54.

Foster, Stephen P. (2000) 'The digital divide: some reflections', *International Information & Library Review* 32(3/4): 437–51.

Frankel, Boris (1987) *The Post-Industrial Utopians*, Cambridge: Polity Press.

Frost, Chris (2000) *Media Ethics and Self-Regulation*, Harlow: Pearson Education Ltd.

Fuchs, Christian (2008) *Internet and Society: Social Theory in the Information Age*, London: Routledge.

Fuller, Steve (2005) 'Knowledge as product and property', in Nico Stehr and Volker Meja (eds), *Society and Knowledge: Contemporary Perspectives in the Sociology of Knowledge and Science*, 2nd ed., New Brunswick, NJ: Transaction, pp. 243–68.

———— (2006) 'Notes towards a renaissance in British sociology: a response to Turner', *British Journal of Sociology* 57(2): 199–204.

———— (2007) 'Creativity in an Orwellian key', in Arnaud Sales and Marcel Fournier (eds), *Knowledge, Communication and Creativity*, London: Sage, pp. 97–111.

Galperin, Hernan (2004) 'Beyond interests, ideas, and technology: an institutional approach to communication and information policy', *The Information Society* 20(3): 159–68.

Gandy, Oscar H. (1982) *Beyond Agenda Setting: Information Subsidies and Public Policy*, Norwood, NJ: Ablex.

Garnham, Nicholas (1999) 'Amartya Sen's "capabilities" approach to the evaluation of welfare: its application to communications', in Andrew Calabrese and Jean-Claude Burgelmann (eds), *Communication, Citizenship, and Social Policy: Rethinking the Limits of the Welfare State*, Lanham, MD: Rowman & Littlefield, pp. 113–24.

———— (2000a) '"Information society" as theory or ideology: a critical perspective on technology, education and employment in the information age', *Information, Communication & Society* 3(2): 139–52.

———— (2000b) 'The role of the public sphere in the information society', in Christopher T. Marsden (ed.), *Regulating the Global Information Society*, London: Routledge, pp. 43–56.

Giddens, Anthony (1973) *The Class Structure of the Advanced Societies*, London: Hutchinson.

———— (1998) *The Third Way: the Renewal of Social Democracy*, London: Polity Press.

Golding, Peter (2000) 'Forthcoming features: information and communications technologies and the sociology of the future', *Sociology* 34(1): 165–84.

———— and Murdock, Graham (2001) 'Digital divides: communications policy and its contradictions', *New Economy* 8(2): 110–15.

Gore, William J (1996) 'Social democracy', in George T. Kurian and Graham T. T. Molitor (eds), *Encyclopedia of the Future, vol. 2*, New York: Simon & Schuster Macmillan, pp. 847–58.

Gorz, André (1980) *Farewell to the Working Class: An Essay on Post-Industrial Socialism*, London: Pluto Press.

Graham, Gordon (1988) *Contemporary Social Philosophy*, Oxford: Blackwell.

Graham, Phil (2006) *Hypercapitalism: New Media, Language, and Social Perceptions of Value*, New York: Peter Lang.

Green, T. H. (1986a [1881]) 'Lecture on liberal legislation and freedom of contract', in *Lectures on the Principles of Political Obligation and Other Writings*, ed. Paul Harris and John Morrow, Cambridge: Cambridge University Press, pp. 194–212.

———— (1986b [1885–8]) 'Lectures on the principles of political obligation', in *Lectures on the Principles of Political Obligation and Other Writings*, ed. Paul Harris and John Morrow, Cambridge: Cambridge University Press, pp. 13–193.

Gutmann, Amy (1980) *Liberal Equality*, Cambridge: Cambridge University Press.

———— (1989) 'The central role of Rawls's theory', *Dissent* (Summer): 338–42.

Habel, Ylva (2002) *Modern Media, Modern Audiences: Mass Media and Social Engineering in the 1930s Swedish Welfare State*, Stockholm: Aura.

Habermas, Jurgen (1984) *The Theory of Communicative Action, vol. 1: Reason and the Rationalization of Society*, Cambridge: Polity Press.

———— (1987) *The Theory of Communicative Action, vol. 2: The Critique of Functionalist Reason*, Cambridge: Polity Press.

———— (1989 [1962]) *The Structural Transformation of the Public Sphere: An Inquiry into a Category of Bourgeois Society*, trans. Thomas Burger, Cambridge: Polity Press.

———— (1996) *Between Facts and Norms: Contributions to a Discourse Theory of Law and Democracy*, Cambridge: Polity Press.

———— (2005) 'Pre-political foundations of the democratic constitutional state?', in Joseph Ratzinger (Pope Benedict XVI) and Jurgen Habermas, *Dialectics of Secularization: On Reason and Religion*, San Francisco, CA: Ignatius Press, pp. 19–52.

———— (2009) 'Media, markets and consumers: the quality press as the backbone of the political public sphere', in *Europe: The Faltering Project*, trans. Ciaran Cronin, Cambridge: Polity Press, pp. 131–37.

Hall, John A. (1977) 'The roles and influence of political intellectuals: Tawney *vs.* Sidney Webb', *British Journal of Sociology* 28(3): 351–62.

Haraway, Donna (2001 [1985]) 'A manifesto for cyborgs: science, technology, and socialist feminism in the 1980s', in David Trend (ed.), *Reading Digital Culture*, Oxford: Blackwell, pp. 28–37.

Haywood, Trevor (1995) *Info Rich, Info Poor: Access and Exchange in the Global Information Society*, London: Bowker.

Heilbroner, Robert, Barkan, Joanne, Brand, H., Cohen, Mitchell, Coser, Lewis, Denitch, Bogdan, Feher, Ferenc, Heller, Agnes, Horvat, Branko and Tyler, Gus (1991) 'From Sweden to socialism: a small symposium on big questions', *Dissent* (Winter): 96–110.

Henten, Anders and Skouby, Knud E. (2002) 'Information society and trade and industry policy', in Leah A. Lievrouw and Sonia Livingstone (eds), *Handbook of New Media: Social Shaping and Consequences of ICTs*, London: Sage, pp. 320–33.

Herman, Edward (2004) 'A post-September 11th balancing act: public access to US government information *versus* protection of sensitive data', *Journal of Government Information* 30(1): 42–65.

Hernon, Peter and Relyea, Harold C. (1991) 'Information policy', in Allen Kent (ed.), *Encyclopedia of Library and Information Science, vol. 48, suppl. 11*, New York: Marcel Dekker, pp. 176–204.

Higgs, Graham E. and Budd, John M (2004) 'Ethics of push technology and the emergence of norms', in Tom Mendina and Johannes J. Britz (eds), *Information Ethics in the Electronic Age: Current Issues in Africa and the World*, Jefferson, NC: McFarland, pp. 147–54.

Hitlin, Steven and Piliavin, Jane Allyn (2004) 'Values: reviving a dormant concept', *Annual Review of Sociology* 30: 359–93.

Hobhouse, L. T. (1922) *The Elements of Social Justice*, London: George Allen & Unwin.

Hollingsworth, J. Rogers (2002) 'On institutional embeddednesss', in J. Rogers Hollingsworth, Karl H. Muller and Ellen J. Hollingsworth (eds), *Advancing Socio-Economics: An Institutionalist Perspective*, Lanham, MD: Rowman & Littlefield, pp. 87–107.

—— , Muller, Karl H. and Hollingsworth, Ellen J. (eds) (2002) *Advancing Socio-Economics: An Institutionalist Perspective*, Lanham, MD: Rowman & Littlefield.

Honderich, Ted (1980) *Violence for Equality: Inquiries in Political Philosophy*, Harmondsworth: Penguin.

—— (2003) *On Political Means and Social Ends*, Edinburgh: Edinburgh University Press.

Hundt, Reed E. (2000) *You Say You Want a Revolution: A Story of Information Age Politics*, New Haven, CT: Yale University Press.

Introna, Lucas (1997) 'Privacy and the computer: why we need privacy in the information society', *Metaphilosophy* 28(3): 259–75.

Ito, Youichi (1981) 'The "johoka shakai" approach to the study of communication in Japan', in G. Cleveland Wilhoit and Harold de Bock (eds), *Mass Communication Review Yearbook, vol. 2*, Beverly Hills, CA: Sage, pp. 671–98.

—— (2000) 'Historical comparisons of the degrees of "johoka" ("informization")', *Keio Communication Review* 22: 3–29.

Japan Computer Usage Development Institute (1974) 'The plan for an information society: a national goal toward year 2000', *Ekistics* 226(September): 175–82.

Japan Ministry of Internal Affairs and Communications (2010) *Information and Communications in Japan: 2010 White Paper*, Tokyo: Ministry of Internal Affairs and Communications Economic Research Office. Available at http://www.soumu.go.jp/johotsusintokei/whitepaper/eng/WP2010/2010-index.html (accessed June 30 2011).

Jayasuriya, Kanishka (2000) 'Capability, freedom and the new social democracy', *Political Quarterly* 71(3): 282–99.

Jenkins, Timothy L. and Om-ra-seti, Khafra K. (1997) *Black Futurists in the Information Age: Vision of a 21ˢ Century Technological Renaissance*, San Francisco, CA: KMT Publications/Washington, DC: Unlimited Visions.

Jones, Peter d'A. (1968) *The Christian Socialist Revival 1877–1914: Religion, Class, and Social Conscience in Late-Victorian England*, Princeton, NJ: Princeton University Press.

Kahin, Brian and Nesson, Charles (eds) (1997) *Borders in Cyberspace: Information Policy and the Global Information Infrastructure*, Cambridge, MA: The MIT Press.

Katwala, Sunder (2004) 'Introduction', in Ellie Levenson, Guy Lodge and Greg Rosen (eds), *Fabian Thinkers: 120 Years of Progressive Thought*, London: The Fabian Society, pp. 1–5.

Katzman, Natan (1974) 'The impact of communication technology: promises and prospects', *Journal of Communication* 24(4): 47–58.

Keeble, Richard (2005) 'Journalism ethics: towards an Orwellian critique?', in Stuart Allan (ed.), *Journalism: Critical Issues*, London: Routledge, pp. 54–66.

Kierkegaard, Soren (1959 [1843]) *Either/Or, 2 vols*, Princeton, NJ: Princeton University Press.

——— (2005 [1842]) *Fear and Trembling*, London: Penguin.

Kim, Sangmoon and Nolan, Patrick D. (2006) 'Measuring social "informatization": a factor analytic approach', *Sociological Inquiry* 76(2): 188–209.

Kling, Rob (1994) 'Reading "all about" computerization: how genre conventions shape nonfiction social analysis', *The Information Society* 10(3): 147–72.

——— (2001) 'Learning about information technologies and social change: the contribution of social informatics', *The Information Society* 16(3): 217–33.

Knorr-Cetina, Karin (2005) 'The fabrication of facts: toward a microsociology of scientific knowledge', in Nico Stehr and Volker Meja (eds), *Society and Knowledge: Contemporary Perspectives in the Sociology of Knowledge and Science*, 2nd ed., New Brunswick, NJ: Transaction, pp. 175–95.

Knowles, Dudley (2001) *Political Philosophy*, London: Routledge.

Krippendorff, Klaus (1993) 'Information, information society, and some Marxian propositions', in Jorge R. Schement and Brent D. Ruben (eds), *Between Communication and Information: Information and Behavior, vol. 4*, New Brunswick, NJ: Transaction, pp. 487–521.

Kubin, Jerzy (1996) 'Social design methodologies *versus* efficient social action', in Adam Podgorecki, Jon Alexander and Rob Shields (eds), *Social Engineering*, Ottawa, ON: Carleton University Press, pp. 195–211.

Kumon, Shumpei (2006) *Key Concepts of Info-Socionomics*, Unpublished Manuscript. [19 pp.]

Kymlicka, Will (2006) 'Left-liberalism revisited', in Christine Sypnowich (ed.), *The Egalitarian Conscience: Essays in Honour of G. A. Cohen*, Oxford: Oxford University Press, pp. 9–35.

Lacroix, Jean-Guy and Tremblay, Gaetan (1997) 'The state's role in the sphere of culture and communication', *Current Sociology* 45(4): 93–113.

Lapinski, Maria K. and Rimal, Rajiv N. (2005) 'An explication of social norms', *Communication Theory* 15(2): 127–47.

Lash, Scott (2002) *Critique of Information*, London: Sage.

Lemov, Rebecca (2005) *World as Laboratory: Experiments with Mice, Mazes, and Men*, New York: Hill & Wang.

Lenk, Hans (1986) 'Socio-philosophical notes on the implications of computer revolution', in Carl Mitcham and Alois Huning (eds), *Philosophy and Technology II: Information Technology and Computers in Theory and Practice*, Boston, MA: D. Reidel Publishing, pp. 239–45.

Leonard, Penny (2003) *Promoting Welfare? Government Information Policy and Social Citizenship*, Bristol: The Policy Press.

Lewis, Justin (1997) 'What counts in cultural studies', *Media, Culture & Society* 19(1): 83–97.

Lewis-Smith, Victor (1995) *Inside the Magic Rectangle*, London: Victor Gollancz.

Lievrouw, Leah A. and Farb, Sharon E. (2003) 'Information and equity', *Annual Review of Information Science and Technology* 37: 499–540.

Lippmann, Walter (1922) *Public Opinion*, London: George Allen & Unwin.

——— (2005 [1937]) *The Good Society*, intro. Gary Dean Best, New Brunswick, NJ: Transaction.

Livingstone, Sonia (2005) 'Critical debates in internet studies: reflections on an emerging field', in James Curran and Michael Gurevitch (eds), *Mass Media and Society*, 5th ed., London: Sage, pp. 9–28.

Loader, Brian D. (ed.) (1998) *Cyberspace Divide: Equality, Agency and Policy in the Information Society*, London: Routledge.

Lucas, J. R. (1980) *On Justice*, Oxford: Oxford University Press.

Luhmann, Niklas (1995 [1984]) *Social Systems*, trans. John Bednarz, Stanford, CA: Stanford University Press.

Luke, Tim (2000) 'Dealing with the digital divide: The rough realities of cyberspace', *Telos* 118(Winter): 3–23.

Lumiers, Esther M. and Schimmel, Martijn (2004) 'Information poverty: a measurable concept?', in Tom Mendina and Johannes J. Britz (eds), *Information Ethics in the Electronic Age: Current Issues in Africa and the World*, Jefferson, NC: McFarland & Co., pp. 47–61.

Lyon, David (1983) 'Arthur Penty's post-industrial utopia', *World Future Society Bulletin* 17(1): 7–14.

——— (1988) *The Information Society: Issues and Illusions*, Cambridge: Polity Press.

——— (2005) 'A sociology of information', in Craig Calhoun, Chris Rojek and Bryan Turner (eds), *The Sage Handbook of Sociology*, London: Sage, pp. 223–35.

Machlup, Fritz (1962) *The Production and Distribution of Knowledge in the United States*, Princeton, NJ: Princeton University Press.

MacIntyre, Alasdair C. (1971 [1964]) *Against the Self-Images of the Age: Essays on Ideology and Philosophy*, London: Duckworth.

Mackay, Hugh, Maples, Wendy, and Reynolds, Paul (2001) *Social Science in Action: Investigating the Information Society*, London: Routledge in association with the Open University.

MacKenzie, Norman and MacKenzie, Jeanne (1979) *The First Fabians*, London: Quartet Books.

Mannheim, Karl (1936 [1926]) *Ideology and Utopia*, London: Routledge & Kegan Paul.

Mansell, Robin (1996) 'Communication by design?', in Robin Mansell and Roger Silverstone (eds), *Communication by Design: The Politics of Information and Communication Technologies*, Oxford: Oxford University Press, pp. 15–42.

——— (2006) 'Ambiguous connections: entitlements and responsibilities of global networking', *Journal of International Development* 18(6): 901–13.

——— (2008) *The Life and Times of the Information society: A Critical Review*, London: London School of Economics and Political Science. [26 pp.]

——— (ed.) (2009) *The Information Society: Critical Concepts in Sociology, vol. 1: History and Perspectives, vol. 2: Knowledge, Economics and Organization, vol. 3: Democracy, Governance and Regulation, vol. 4: Everyday Life*, London: Routledge.

Marlin-Bennett, Renée (2004) *Knowledge Power: Intellectual Property, Information, and Privacy*, Boulder, CO: Lynne Reinner.

Marsden, Christopher T (2000) 'Introduction: information and communication technologies, globalisation and regulation', in Christopher T. Marsden (ed.), *Regulating the Global Information Society*, London: Routledge, pp. 1–40.

Marsden, John (2004) 'Frederick Denison Maurice, Christian socialism and the future of social democracy', *Heythrop Journal* 45(2): 137–57.

Martin, Brian (1998) *Information Liberation: Challenging the Corruptions of Information Power*, London: Freedom Press.

Martin, Kingsley (1980) 'Shaw and Wells', in *H. G. Wells: Interviews and Recollections*, ed. John R. Hammond, London: The Macmillan Press, pp. 84–97.

Martin, Rex (2001) 'The essential indeterminacy of Rawls's difference principle', in Mark Evans (ed.), *The Edinburgh Companion to Contemporary Liberalism*, Edinburgh: Edinburgh University Press, pp. 101–12.

Marx, Karl (1978 [1845]) 'Theses on Feuerbach', in *The Marx-Engels Reader*, 2nd edn, ed. Robert C. Tucker, New York: W. W. Norton & Co., pp. 143–45.

—— and Engels, Friedrich (1978 [1848]) 'Manifesto of the Communist Party', in *The Marx-Engels Reader*, 2nd edn, ed. Robert C. Tucker, New York: W. W. Norton & Co., pp. 469–500.

Masuda, Yoneji (1981) *The Information Society as Post-Industrial Society*, Bethesda, MD: World Future Society.

—— (2004 [1990]) 'Image of the future information society', in Frank Webster (ed.), *The Information Society Reader*, London: Routledge, pp. 15–20.

Mattelart, Armand and Mattelart, Michele (1998) *Theories of Communication: A Short Introduction*, trans. Susan G. Taponier and James A. Cohen, London: Sage.

Maxwell, Terrence A. (2003) 'Toward a model of information policy analysis: speech as an illustrative example', *First Monday* 8(6) [18 pp.] Available at http://firstmonday.org/issues/issue8/_6/maxwell/index.html (accessed June 30 2011).

May, Christopher (2002) *The Information Society: A Sceptical View*, Cambridge: Polity Press.

—— (2003a) 'Digital rights management and the breakdown of social norms', *First Monday* 8(11) [28 pp.] Available at http://firstmonday.org/issues/issue8_11/may/index.html (accessed June 30 2011).

—— (2003b) 'Editor's introduction', in Christopher May (ed.), *Key Thinkers for the Information Society*, London: Routledge, pp. 1–11.

—— (2003c) 'Lewis Mumford', in Christopher May (ed.), *Key Thinkers for the Information Society*, London: Routledge, pp. 109–34.

McBriar, A. M. (1966) *Fabian Socialism and English Politics 1884–1918*, Cambridge: Cambridge University Press.

McCauley, Michael P. (2002) 'National public radio: the case for normative mission in the marketplace', in Manjunath Pendakur and Roma Harris (eds), *Citizenship and Participation in the Information Age*, Aurora, Ont.: Garamond Press, pp. 267–84.

McCombs, Maxwell (2004) *Setting the Agenda: The Mass Media and Public Opinion*, Cambridge: Polity Press.

McIntyre, Ian (1993) *The Expense of Glory: A Life of John Reith*, London: HarperCollins.

McNair, Brian (2000) *Journalism and Democracy: An Evaluation of the Political Public Sphere*, London: Routledge.

McQuail, Denis and Windahl, Sven (1981) *Communication Models for the Study of Mass Communication*, London: Longman.

Menou, Michel J. and Taylor, Richard D. (2006) 'A "grand challenge": measuring information societies', *The Information Society* 22(5): 261–67.

Miles, Ian (2002) 'Information society revisited: PICTuring the information society', in Robin Mansell, Rohan Samarajiva and Amy Mahan (eds), *Networking Knowledge for Information Societies: Institutions and Intervention*, Delft: Delft University Press, pp. 160–65.

——— and Gershuny, Jonathan (1987) 'The social economics of information technology', in Ruth Finnegan, Graeme Salaman and Kenneth Thompson (eds),
Information Technology: Social Issues: a Reader, London: Hodder & Stough-
ton/The Open University, pp. 209–24.

Miller, David (1998) 'Social democracy', in Edward Craig (ed.), *The Routledge
Encyclopedia of Philosophy*, vol. 8, London: Routledge, pp. 827–28.

Miller, S. Michael (1975) 'Notes on neo-capitalism', *Theory and Society* 2(1):
1–35.

Mills, C. Wright (1970 [1959]) *The Sociological Imagination*, London: Penguin.

Moore, Adam D. (2001) *Intellectual Property and Information Control: Philosophic
Foundations and Contemporary Issues*, New Brunswick, NJ: Transaction.

Morris-Suzuki, Tessa (1988) *Beyond Computopia: Information, Automation and
Democracy in Japan*, London: Kegan Paul International.

Mosco, Vincent (1996) *The Political Economy of Communication: Rethinking
and Renewal*, Thousand Oaks, CA: Sage.

——— (2002) 'Bridging the gap: processes of communication and institutions of
political economy', in Robin Mansell, Rohan Samarajiva and Amy Mahan (eds),
*Networking Knowledge for Information Societies: Institutions and Interven-
tion*, Delft: Delft University Press, pp. 260–64.

Mossberger, Karen, Tolbert, Caroline J. and Stansbury, Mary (2003) *Virtual
Inequality: Beyond the Digital Divide*, Washington, DC: Georgetown University Press.

Mueller, Milton, Page, Christiane, and Kuerbis, Brenden (2004) 'Civil society and
the shaping of communication-information policy: four decades of advocacy',
The Information Society 20(3): 169–85.

Mumford, Lewis (1934) *Technics and Civilisation*, London: George Routledge &
Sons.

Murdock, Graham and Golding, Peter (1989) 'Information poverty and political inequality: citizenship in the age of privatized communications', *Journal of
Communication* 39(3): 180–95.

Myles, John (2006) 'Do egalitarians have a future?', *Review of Income and Wealth*
52(1): 145–51.

Nagel, Thomas (1999) '"Justice, justice, shalt thou pursue": the rigorous compas-
sion of John Rawls', *The New Republic Online*. [12 pp.] Available at http://www.
tnr.com/archive/1099/102599/nagel102599.html (accessed June 30 2011).

——— (2003) 'Rawls and liberalism', in Samuel Freeman (ed.), *The Cambridge
Companion to Rawls*, Cambridge: Cambridge University Press, pp. 62–85.

Nissenbaum, Helen and Introna, Lucas D. (2004) 'Shaping the web: why the politics of search engines matter', in Verna V. Gehring (ed.), *The Internet in Public
Life*, Lanham, MD: Rowman & Littlefield, pp. 7–27.

Nora, Simon and Minc, Alain (1981 [1979]) *The Computerization of Society: A
Report to the President of France*, intro. Daniel Bell, Cambridge, MA: The MIT
Press.

Norman, Edward (1987) *The Victorian Christian Socialists*, Cambridge: Cambridge University Press.

Norris, Pippa (2001) *Digital Divide: Civic Engagement, Information Poverty, and
the Internet Worldwide*, Cambridge: Cambridge University Press.

Nozick, Robert (1974) *Anarchy, State, and Utopia*, New York: Basic Books.

O'Hara, Kieron and Stevens, David (2006) *Inequality.com: Power, Poverty and
the Digital Divide*, Oxford: Oneworld Publications.

Olsson, Tobias (2006) 'Appropriating civic information and communication technology: a critical study of Swedish ICT policy visions', *New Media & Society*
8(4): 611–27.

Ormrod, David (ed.) (1990) *Fellowship, Freedom and Equality: Lectures in Memory of R. H. Tawney*, London: Christian Socialist Movement.

Orwell, George (1962 [1940]) 'Inside the whale', in *Inside the Whale and Other Essays*, Harmondsworth: Penguin, pp. 9–50.

Overman, E. Sam and Cahill, Anthony G (1990) 'Information policy: a study of values in the policy process', *Policy Studies Review* 9(4): 803–18.

Parfit, Derek (2006) 'Normativity', in Russ Shafer-Landau (ed.), *Oxford Studies in Metaethics, vol. 1*, Oxford: Clarendon Press, pp. 325–80.

—— (2011) *On What Matters, 2 vols*, Oxford: Oxford University Press.

'Patenting Life' (2000) *The Guardian* Special Report, November 15. [12 pp.]

Patomaki, Heikki (2003) 'An optical illusion: the Finnish model for the information age', *Theory, Culture & Society* 20(3): 139–45.

Patterson, Rubin and Wilson, Ernest J. (2000) 'New IT and social inequality: resetting the research and policy agenda', *The Information Society* 16(1): 77–86.

Pels, Dick (2005) 'Mixing metaphors: politics or economics of knowledge?', in Nico Stehr and Volker Mcja (eds), *Society and Knowledge: Contemporary Perspectives in the Sociology of Knowledge and Science*, 2nd ed., New Brunswick, NJ: Transaction, pp. 269–98.

Penty, Arthur J. (1917) *Old Worlds for New: A Study of the Post-Industrial State*, London: George Allen & Unwin.

—— (1922) *Post-Industrialism*, London: George Allen & Unwin.

Pera, Marcello (2006) 'Karl Popper's "third way": public policies for Europe and the West', in Ian Jarvie, Karl Milford and David Miller (eds), *Karl Popper: A Centenary Assessment, vol. 1: Life and Times, and Values in a World of Facts*, Aldershot: Ashgate, pp. 273–81.

Perelman, Michael (1998) *Class Warfare in the Information Age*, London: Macmillan Press.

Picard, Robert G. (1985) *The Press and the Decline of Democracy: The Democratic Socialist Response in Public Policy*, Westport, CT: Greenwood Press.

Pierson, Chris (2001) 'Globalisation and the end of social democracy', *Australian Journal of Politics and History* 47(4): 459–74.

Podgorecki, Adam (1996) 'Sociotechnology: basic problems and issues', in Adam Podgorecki, Jon Alexander and Rob Shields (eds), *Social Engineering*, Ottawa, Ont.: Carleton University Press, pp. 23–57.

Pogge, Thomas (1999) 'A brief sketch of Rawls's life', in Henry S. Richardson and Paul J. Weithman (eds), *The Philosophy of Rawls: A Collection of Essays, vol. 1*, New York: Garland, pp. 1–15.

—— (2006) *Intellectual Property Rights and Access to Essential Medicines (Routledge Lecture in Philosophy)*, University of Cambridge, November 22.

Pool, Ithiel de Sola (1977) 'Technology and policy in the information age', in Daniel Lerner and Lyle M. Nelson (eds), *Communication Research: A Half-Century Appraisal*, Honolulu, HI: University Press of Hawai, pp. 261–79.

—— (1983) *Technologies of Freedom*, Cambridge, MA: The Belknap Press of Harvard University Press.

—— (1998a [1973]) 'Citizen feedback in political philosophy', in *Politics in Wired Nations: Selected Writings of Ithiel de Sola Pool*, intro. Lloyd S. Etheredge, New Brunswick, NJ: Transaction, pp. 291–303.

—— (1998b [1967]) 'The public and the polity', in *Politics in Wired Nations: Selected Writings of Ithiel de Sola Pool*, intro. Lloyd S. Etheredge, New Brunswick, NJ: Transaction, pp. 263–90.

Popper, Karl R. (1966 [1945]) *The Open Society and its Enemies, vol. 1: The Spell of Plato, vol. 2: The High Tide of Prophecy: Hegel, Marx, and the Aftermath*, 5th ed., London: Routledge & Kegan Paul.

—— (2002 [1957]) *The Poverty of Historicism*, London: Routledge.

Porat, Marc U. (1977) *The Information Economy, vol. 1: Definition and Measurement*, Washington, DC: US Department of Commerce, Office of Telecommunications.

Poster, Mark (1990) *The Mode of Information: Poststructuralism and Social Context*, Cambridge: Polity Press.

Preston, Paschal (2002) 'Knowledge or "know-less" societies?', in Robin Mansell, Rohan Samarajiva and Amy Mahan (eds), *Networking Knowledge for Information Societies: Institutions and Intervention*, Delft: Delft University Press, pp. 232–38.

—— and Flynn, Roderick (2000) 'Rethinking universal service: citizenship, consumption norms, and the telephone', *The Information Society* 16(2): 91–98.

Pruulmann-Vengerfeldt, Pille (2006) 'Exploring social theory as a framework for social and cultural measurements of the information society', *The Information Society* 22(5): 303–10.

Pugh, Patricia (1984) *Educate, Agitate, Organize: 100 Years of Fabian Socialism*, London: Methuen.

Qvortrup, Lars (1987) 'The information age: ideal and reality', in Jennifer D. Slack and Fred Fejes (eds), *The Ideology of the Information Age*, Norwood, NJ: Ablex, pp 133–45.

Raber, Douglas (2004) 'Is universal service a universal right? A Rawlsian approach to universal service', in Tom Mendina and Johannes J. Britz (eds), *Information Ethics in the Electronic Age: Current Issues in Africa and the World*, Jefferson, NC: McFarland, pp. 114–22.

Raboy, Marc (1999) 'Communication policy and globalization as a social project', in Andrew Calabrese and Jean-Claude Burgelman (eds), *Communication, Citizenship, and Social Policy: Rethinking the Limits of the Welfare State*, Totowa, NJ: Rowman & Littlefield, pp. 293–310.

Radice, Giles (1965) *Democratic Socialism: A Short Survey*, London: Longmans, Green & Co.

Rau, Zbigniew (2009) 'Human nature, social engineering, and the reemergence of civil society', *Social Philosophy & Policy* 8(1): 159–79.

Rawls, John (1973 [1971]) *A Theory of Justice*, Oxford: Oxford University Press.

—— (1996) *Political Liberalism*, New York: Columbia University Press.

—— (1999a [1985]) 'Justice as fairness: political not metaphysical', in *Collected Papers*, ed. Samuel Freeman, Cambridge, MA: Harvard University Press, pp. 388–414.

—— (1999b [1987]) 'Preface for the French edition of A Theory of Justice', in *Collected Papers*, ed. Samuel Freeman, Cambridge, MA: Harvard University Press, pp. 415–20.

—— (1999c [1987]) 'The idea of an overlapping consensus', in *Collected Papers*, ed. Samuel Freeman, Cambridge, MA: Harvard University Press, pp. 421–48.

—— (2001) *Justice as Fairness: A Restatement*, ed. Erin Kelly, Cambridge, MA: The Belknap Press of Harvard University Press.

—— (2009 [1942]) *An Inquiry into the Meaning of Sin and Faith, with On My Religion*, ed. Thomas Nagel, Cambridge, MA: Harvard University Press.

Rayward, W. Boyd (1999) 'H. G. Wells's idea of a world brain: a critical reassessment', *Journal of the American Society for Information Science* 50(7): 557–73.

—— (ed.) (2008) *European Modernism and the Information Society: Informing the Present, Understanding the Past*. Aldershot: Ashgate.

Reisman, David (ed.) (1996) *Democratic Socialism in Britain: Classic Texts in Economic and Political Thought 1825–1952, vol. 2: The Christian Socialists*, London: Pickering & Chatto.

Reith, John (1924) *Broadcast Over Britain*, London: Hodder & Stoughton.

Ricci, Andrea (2003) 'The political internet: between dogma and reality', in Jan Servaes (ed.), *The European Information Society: A Reality Check*, Bristol: Intellect Books, pp. 177–204.

Richardson, Brian (2004) 'The public's right to know: a dangerous notion', *Journal of Mass Media Ethics* 19(1): 46–55.

Richardson, Henry S. and Weithman, Paul J. (eds) (1999) *The Philosophy of Rawls: A Collection of Essays, 5 vols*, New York: Garland.

Ronfeldt, David (1992) 'Cyberocracy is coming', *The Information Society* 8(4): 243–96.

Roszak, Theodore (1994) *The Cult of Information: A Neo-Luddite Treatise on High Tech, Artificial Intelligence, and the True Art of Thinking*, 2nd ed., Berkeley, CA: University of California Press.

Rothbard, Murray N. (1982) *The Ethics of Liberty*, Atlantic Highlands, NJ: Humanities Press.

Rowlands, Ian (1996) 'Understanding information policy: concepts, frameworks and research tools', *Journal of Information Science* 22(1): 13–25.

Royal Academy of Engineering (2007) *Dilemmas of Privacy and Surveillance: Challenges of Technological Change*, London: The Royal Academy of Engineering.

Runciman, W. G. (1989) *A Treatise on Social Theory, vol. 2: Substantive Social Theory*, Cambridge: Cambridge University Press.

—— (1997) *A Treatise on Social Theory, vol. 3: Applied Social Theory*, Cambridge: Cambridge University Press.

Russell, Bertrand (1896) *German Social Democracy*, London: Longmans.

—— (1920) *The Practice and Theory of Bolshevism*, London: George Allen & Unwin.

Sandel, Michael J. (1996) *Democracy's Discontent: America in Search of a Public Philosophy*, Cambridge, MA: The Belknap Press of Harvard University Press.

—— (2005) *Public Philosophy: Essays on Morality in Politics*, Cambridge, MA: Harvard University Press.

Saulauskas, Marius P. (2005) 'On the concept of "information society": counterfactuality, ideology and public discourse', in Jurate Baranova (ed.), *Contemporary Philosophical Discourse in Lithuania*, Washington, DC: Council for Research in Values and Philosophy, pp. 313–31.

Sawhney, Harmeet (2000) 'Universal service: separating the grain of truth from the proverbial chaff', *The Information Society* 16(2): 161–64.

—— and Jayakar, Krishna P. (2007) 'Universal access', *Annual Review of Information Science and Technology* 41: 159–221.

Schaefer, Richard J. (1995) 'National information infrastructure policy: a theoretical and normative approach', *Internet Research: Electronic Networking Applications and Policy* 5(2): 4–13.

Schement, Jorge R. (2001) 'Of gaps by which democracy we measure', in Benjamin M. Compaine (ed.), *The Digital Divide: Facing a Crisis or Creating a Myth?*, Cambridge, MA: The MIT Press, pp. 303–7.

—— and Curtis, Terry (1995) *Tendencies and Tensions of the Information Age: The Production and Distribution of Information in the United States*, New Brunswick, NJ: Transaction.

—— and Forbes, Scott C. (2000) 'Identifying temporary and permanent gaps in universal service', *The Information Society* 16(2): 117–26.

Schiller, Dan (2007) *How to Think about Information*, Urbana, IL: University of Illinois Press.

Schiller, Herbert I. (1996) *Information Inequality: The Deepening Social Crisis in America*, New York: Routledge.

Schroyer, Trent (1974) Review of the Coming of Post-Industrial Society, *Telos* 19(Spring): 164.

Schudson, Michael (1981) *Discovering the News: A Social History of American Newspapers*, New York: Basic Books.

Schuler, Doug (2001) 'Cultivating society's civic intelligence: patterns for a new "world brain"', *Information, Communication & Society* 4(2): 157–81.

Scruton, Roger (1983) *A Dictionary of Political Thought*, London: Pan Books in association with Macmillan Press.

Selwyn, Neil and Facer, Keri (2007) *Beyond the Digital Divide: Rethinking Digital Inclusion for the 21st Century*, Bristol: Futurelab.

Servaes, Jan (2003) 'By way of introduction', in Jan Servaes (ed.), *The European Information Society: A Reality Check*, Bristol: Intellect Books, pp. 5–10.

Servon, Lisa J (2002) *Bridging the Digital Divide: Technology, Community and Public Policy*, Oxford: Blackwell.

Shane, Peter M. (2006) 'Social theory meets social policy: culture, identity and public information policy after September 11', *I/S: A Journal of Law and Policy for the Information Society* 2(1) [23 pp.] Available at http://www.is-journal.org/V02I01/2ISJLPTOC.pdf (accessed June 30 2011).

Shannon, Claude E. and Weaver, Warren (1949) *The Mathematical Theory of Communication*, Urbana, IL: University of Illinois Press.

Shaw, G. Bernard (1982 [1928]) *The Intelligent Woman's Guide to Socialism, Capitalism, Sovietism and Fascism*, intro. Margaret Walters, Harmondsworth: Penguin.

—— (ed.) (1889) *The Fabian Essays in Socialism*, London: W. Scott.

Shuler, John A (2004) 'A postelection perspective: whither information policy? Part 1', *Journal of Academic Librarianship* 30(6): 499–501.

Skinner, Quentin, Dasgupta, Partha, Geuss, Raymond, Lane, Melissa, Laslett, Peter, O'Neill, Onora, Runciman, W. G. and Kuper, Andrew (2002) 'Political philosophy: the view from Cambridge', *Journal of Political Philosophy* 10(1): 1–19.

Sleeman, Bill (2004) 'Recent literature on government information', *Journal of Government Information* 30(4): 490–93.

Slevin, James (2000) *The Internet and Society*, Cambridge: Polity Press.

Smart, Barry (ed.) (2010) *Post-Industrial Society, 4 vols*, London: Sage.

Smith, Adam (1977 [1776]) *An Inquiry into the Nature and Causes of the Wealth of Nations*, Chicago, IL: University of Chicago Press.

—— (1976 [1759]) *The Theory of Moral Sentiments*, Oxford: Clarendon Press.

Smith, Martha (2001) 'Information ethics', *Advances in Librarianship* 25: 29–66.

Snow, Nancy (2003) *Information War: American Propaganda, Free Speech and Opinion Control Since 9/11*, New York: Seven Stories Press.

Stanley, Arthur P. (1844) *Life and Correspondence of Thomas Arnold, D.D.*, London: Ward, Lock & Co.

Steele, Jane (1998) 'Information and citizenship in Europe', in Brian D. Loader (ed.), *Cyberspace Divide: Equality, Agency and Policy in the Information Society*, London: Routledge, pp. 161–82.

Stehr, Nico (1994) *Knowledge Societies*, London: Sage.

—— (2005) 'Knowledge societies', in Nico Stehr and Volker Meja (eds), *Society and Knowledge: Contemporary Perspectives in the Sociology of Knowledge and Science*, 2nd ed., New Brunswick, NJ: Transaction, pp. 299–322.

Stein, Laura and Sinha, Nikhil (2002) 'New global media and communication policy: the role of the state in the twenty-first century', in Leah A. Lievrouw and Sonia Livingstone (eds), *Handbook of New Media: Social Shaping and Consequences of ICTs*, London: Sage, pp. 410–31.

Bibliography

Steinfels, Peter (1979) *The Neo-Conservatives: The Men who are Changing America's Politics*, New York: Simon & Schuster.

Stern, C. (2001) 'FCC's Powell discusses discusses TV, "digital divide"', *The Washington Post*, February 6.

Stevenson, Siobhan (2009) 'Digital divide: a discursive move away from the real inequities', *The Information Society* 25(1): 1–22.

Stewart, Concetta M., Gil-Egui, Gisela, Tian, Yan and Pileggi, Mairi I. (2006) 'Framing the digital divide: a comparison of US and EU policy approaches', *New Media & Society* 8(5): 731–51.

Stiglitz, Joseph E. (1994) *Whither Socialism?*, Cambridge, MA: The MIT Press.

—— (2003) 'Information and the change in the paradigm in economics, part 1', *American Economist* 47(2): 6–26.

Strickland, Lee S (2005) 'The information gulag: rethinking openness in times of national danger', *Government Information Quarterly* 22(4): 546–72.

Swift, Adam (2001) *Political Philosophy: A Beginners' Guide for Students and Politicians*, Cambridge: Polity Press.

Tawney, R. H. (1920) *The Sickness of an Acquisitive Society*, London: The Fabian Society.

—— (1923) *Secondary Education for All: A Policy for Labour*, London: The Labour Party (Education Advisory Committee); George Allen & Unwin.

—— (1943) 'The problem of the public schools', *Political Quarterly* 14(2): 117–49.

—— (1949) 'Social democracy in Britain', in William Scarlett (ed.), *The Christian Demand for Social Justice*, New York: Signet Books, pp. 96–126.

—— (1952) *The Philosophy of Socialism*. Unpublished Talk for the London University Fabian Society, 9 April, London: British Library of Political and Economic Science, Tawney Papers, Tss and Mss Box 20, Section 19/2. [29 pp.]

—— (1964a [1952]) 'British socialism today', in *The Radical Tradition: Twelve Essays on Politics, Education and Literature*, ed. Rita Hinden, London: George Allen & Unwin, pp. 168–80.

—— (1964b [1931]) *Equality*, 4th edn, London: George Allen & Unwin.

—— (1972 [1912–1914]) *R. H. Tawney's Commonplace Book*, ed. J. M. Winter and D. M. Joslin, Cambridge: Cambridge University Press.

—— (1979 [1942]) *The American Labour Movement and Other Essays*, Brighton: The Harvester Press.

—— (1981a [1935]) 'Christianity and the social revolution', in *The Attack and Other Papers*. Nottingham: Spokesman, pp. 157–66.

—— (1981b [1945]) 'We mean freedom', in *The Attack and Other Papers*, Nottingham: Spokesman, pp. 82–100.

—— (1982) [1921]) *The Acquisitive Society*, Brighton: Wheatsheaf Books.

Terrill, Ross (1973) *R. H. Tawney and His Times: Socialism as Fellowship*, Cambridge, MA: Harvard University Press.

Thompson, John B. (1995) *The Media and Modernity: A Social Theory of the Media*, Cambridge: Polity Press.

Toffler, Alvin (1981) *The Third Wave*, London: Pan Books in association with Collins.

Trotsky, Leon (1937a) *The Revolution Betrayed: What is the Soviet Union and Where is it Going?*, New York: Doubleday, Duran & Co.

—— (1937b) *The Stalin School of Falsification*, New York: Pioneer.

Tsay, Ming-yueh (1995) 'The impact of the concept of post-industrial society and information society: a citation analysis study', *Scientometrics* 33(3): 329–50.

Ulam, Adam B. (1951) *Philosophical Foundations of English Socialism*, Cambridge, MA: Harvard University Press.

United States Bureau of Labor (2008) *Percent Distribution of Civilian Employment approximating U.S. Concepts by Economic Sector, 1960–2007.* Available at http://www.bls.gov (accessed June 30 2011).

———— Department of Commerce, National Telecommunications and Information Administration (1999) *Falling Through the Net: Defining the Digital Divide,* Washington, DC: NTIA.

University of California at Berkeley School of Information Management and Systems (2003) *How Much Information? 2003* [100 pp.] Available at http://www.ischool.berkeley.edu/research/projects/how-much-info-2003 (accessed June 30 2011)

van den Hoven, Jeroen and Rooksby, Emma (2008) 'Distributive justice and the value of information: a (broadly) Rawlsian approach', in Jeroen van den Hoven and John Weckert (eds), *Information Technology and Moral Philosophy,* New York: Cambridge University Press, pp. 376–396.

van Dijk, Jan A. G. M. (2005) *The Deepening Divide: Inequality in the Information Society,* Thousand Oaks, CA: Sage.

———— and Hacker, Kenneth (2003) 'The digital divide as a complex and dynamic phenomenon', *The Information Society* 19(4): 315–26.

van Parijs, Philippe (2003) 'Difference principles', in Samuel Freeman (ed.), *The Cambridge Companion to Rawls,* Cambridge: Cambridge University Press, pp. 200–240.

Veblen, Thorstein (1953 [1899]) *The Theory of the Leisure Class,* New York: Mentor Books.

Vehovar, Vasja, Sicherl, Pavle, Husing, Tobias, and Dolnicar, Vesna (2006) 'Methodological challenges of digital divide measurements', *The Information Society* 22(5): 279–90.

Venturelli, Shalini (1998) *Liberalizing the European Media: Politics, Regulation, and the Public Sphere,* Oxford: Clarendon Press.

Von Hayek, Friedrich A. (1960) *The Constitution of Liberty,* London: Routledge & Kegan Paul.

Walzer, Michael (1981) 'From R.H. Tawney's Commonplace Book', *Dissent* (Winter): 487–90.

———— (1985) *Spheres of Justice: A Defence of Pluralism and Equality,* Oxford: Blackwell.

———— (2004a [1990]) 'The communitarian critique of liberalism', in *Politics and Passion: Toward a More Egalitarian Liberalism,* New Haven, CT: Yale University Press, pp. 141–63.

———— (2004b) 'What is a "good" life?', *Religious Socialism* 28(3): 1, 3, 12–14.

Warren, Samuel and Brandeis, Louis D. (1890) 'The right to privacy', *Harvard Law Review* 4(5): 193–220.

Warschauer, Mark (2003) *Technology and Social Inclusion: Rethinking the Digital Divide,* Cambridge, MA: The MIT Press.

Waters, Malcolm (1996) *Daniel Bell,* London: Routledge.

Webb, Sidney and Webb, Beatrice (1920) *A Constitution for the Socialist Commonwealth of Great Britain,* London: Longmans, Green & Co.

———— (1944) *Soviet Communism: A New Civilisation,* 3rd ed., London: Longmans, Green & Co.

Webster, Frank (2002) *Theories of the Information Society,* 2nd ed., London: Routledge.

———— (2004) 'Introduction: information society studies', in Frank Webster (ed.), *The Information Society Reader,* London: Routledge, pp. 1–7.

———— and Robins, Kevin (1986) *Information Technology: A Luddite Analysis,* Norwood, NJ: Ablex.

Weinberg, Alvin M (2003 [1966]) 'Can technology replace social engineering?', in Eric Katz, Andrew Light and William Thompson (eds), *Controlling Technology: Contemporary Issues*, 2nd ed., Amherst, NY: Prometheus Books, pp. 109–16.

Wells, H. G. (1901) *Anticipations of the Reaction of Mechanical and Scientific Progress upon Human Life and Thought*, London: Chapman & Hall.

——— (1927) 'The dreamer in the Kremlin', in *A Volume of Journalism, The Works of H. G. Wells, Atlantic Edition vol. 26*, London: T. Fisher Unwin, pp. 571–83.

——— (1935) *The Shape of Things to Come: The Ultimate Revolution*, London: Hutchinson & Co.

——— (1964) *Journalism and Prophecy 1893–1946*, ed. W. Warren Wagar, London: The Bodley Head.

——— (2005 [1904]) *A Modern Utopia*, London: Penguin.

Wiener, Norbert (1989 [1950]) *The Human Use of Human Beings: Cybernetics and Society*, London: Free Association Books.

Wilhelm, Anthony G. (2004) *Digital Nation: Toward an Inclusive Information Society*, Cambridge, MA: The MIT Press.

Winch, Peter (1972) 'Authority and rationality', *The Human World* 8: 11–21.

Wittgenstein, Ludwig (1974 [1922]) *Tractatus Logico-Philosophicus*, London: Routledge & Kegan Paul.

World Public Opinion.org (2011) 'Misperceptions, the media and the Iraq war.' Available at http://www.worldpublicopinion.org/pipa/articles/international_security_bt/102.php (accessed June 30 2011).

Wresch, William (1996) *Disconnected: Haves and Have-Nots in the Information Age*, New Brunswick, NJ: Rutgers University Press.

Wright, Anthony (1987) *R. H. Tawney*, Manchester: Manchester University Press.

Wyatt, Sally, Henwood, Flis, Miller, Nod and Senker, Peter (eds) (2000) *Technology and In/equality: Questioning the Information Society*, London: Routledge.

Young, T. R. (1987) 'Information, ideology, and political reality: against Toffler', in Jennifer D. Slack and Fred Fejes (eds), *The Ideology of the Information Age*, Norwood, NJ: Ablex, pp. 118–32.

Zelizer, Barbie (2004) *Taking Journalism Seriously: News and the Academy*, London: Sage.

Index